## DATE DUE

| | | |
|---|---|---|
| | | |
| | | |
| | | |
| | | |
| | | |
| | | |
| | | |
| | | |
| | | |
| | | |
| | | |
| | | |
| | | |
| | | |

GAYLORD        #3522PI        Printed in USA

ALSO BY RON ROSENBAUM

*The Shakespeare Wars*

*Explaining Hitler*

*The Secret Parts of Fortune*

*Those Who Forget the Past* (editor)

# HOW THE END
# BEGINS

## The Road to a Nuclear World War III

## RON ROSENBAUM

*Simon & Schuster*
NEW YORK · LONDON · TORONTO · SYDNEY

Simon & Schuster
1230 Avenue of the Americas
New York, NY 10020

First Simon & Schuster hardcover edition March 2011

SIMON & SCHUSTER and colophon are registered trademarks
of Simon & Schuster, Inc.

For information about special discounts for bulk purchases,
please contact Simon & Schuster Special Sales at
1-866-506-1949 or business@simonandschuster.com.

The Simon & Schuster Speakers Bureau can bring authors
to your live event. For more information or to book an event,
contact the Simon & Schuster Speakers Bureau at
1-866-248-3049 or visit our website at www.simonspeakers.com.

Text designed by Paul Dippolito

Manufactured in the United States of America

1   3   5   7   9   10   8   6   4   2

Library of Congress Cataloging-in-Publication Data

Rosenbaum, Ron.
How the end begins : the road to a nuclear World War III / Ron Rosenbaum.—
1st Simon & Schuster hardcover ed.
p.   cm.
Includes bibliographical references and index.
1. Nuclear warfare.   2. World War III.   3. Nuclear weapons—
History.   4. Deterrence (Strategy)—History.   I. Title.
U263.R67 2011
355.02'15—dc22
2010022474

ISBN 978-1-4165-9421-5
ISBN 978-1-4391-9007-4 (ebook)

*To Major Harold I. Hering (ret.)*
*For the courage to question*

"Please don't let it happen. But let me see it all the same, as it's happening and from every angle, and let me be among the first to know."

—FROM IAN MCEWAN'S *SATURDAY*


KENT: Is this the promised end?
EDGAR: Or image of that horror?

—*KING LEAR*


"It is an act of evil to accept the state of evil as either inevitable or final."

—RABBI ABRAHAM JOSHUA HESCHEL

# CONTENTS

1  "We Came So Close"                                                1

2  Major Hering's Forbidden Question                                31

3  The Forbidden Question at the Qwest Center                       44

4  The Number                                                       71

5  Bruce Blair: The Doomsday Discovery and the
     Real Danger                                                    88

6  Colonel Yarynich's "100 Nuclear Wars," and the
     Apocalypse Equation                                           111

7  "The Ashes Are Still Warm": The Second Holocaust,
     Israel, and the Morality of Nuclear Retaliation               132

8  Iran: The "Enigmatic Box" and the NIE                           166

9  Endgame                                                         209


   Notes                                                           261

   Index                                                           287

   Acknowledgments                                                 301

# HOW THE END
# BEGINS

# CHAPTER ONE

# "WE CAME SO CLOSE"

The London-based *Spectator* is the oldest continuously published periodical in the English language, dating back to
eighteenth-century London coffeehouse literary culture.
It has survived as a respected general interest weekly, politically
eclectic, culturally snobbish in a louche Old Etonian way, with
highly regarded sources from within the old boy network in the
leading British ministries.

But it rarely discloses anything as sensational and chilling as it
did in the opening paragraphs of an article in the October 6, 2007,
issue. It stopped me dead. It was not just the invocation of the jolt-
ing phrase "World War Three." It was the deadly serious way in
which it was invoked.

In most of the post–Cold War period, the so-called "holiday
from history" when many succumbed to a historical amnesia about
the dailiness of nuclear dread, the term "World War Three" has had
a ring of unreality. It usually sounded or read like an antiquated
paranoid fear from a half-remembered past, the way we feel when
we read of the "Black Plague," a relic of the bad old days that still
nonetheless conveys a ghostly chill. We were worried about nuclear
*terrorism* in 2007, but not nuclear *war*. Nuclear war: so retro.

But here, in these *Spectator* paragraphs anyway, nuclear war,
"World War Three," was something that had almost just happened:

# "SO CLOSE TO WAR"

*We Came So Close to World War Three That Day*

**James Forsyth and Douglas Davis**

6 OCTOBER 2007

On 6 September, when Israel struck a nuclear facility in Syria . . .

The article described what it called a "meticulously planned, brilliantly executed surgical strike by Israeli jets on a nuclear installation in Syria." It claimed the raid "may have saved the world from a devastating threat. The only problem is that no one outside a tight-lipped knot of top Israeli and American officials knows precisely what that threat involved." The article went on to say that this report has been confirmed by a "very senior British ministerial source," who'd said: "If people had known how close we came to world war three that day there'd have been mass panic. Never mind the [seasonal] floods or foot-and-mouth [disease]—[Prime Minister] Gordon [Brown] really would have been dealing with the bloody Book of Revelation and Armageddon."

There is no doubt, as was later confirmed, the raid happened. But how close did it bring us to World War Three? The question was a wake-up call, the return of the repressed—"the bloody Book of Revelation and Armageddon." We thought we had left that all behind.

But one could not read the story without war-gaming concatenations of regional nuclear wars that might cascade, through miscalculation or misperception, into global conflagration from such a close call.

It was not inconceivable.

Consider: the raid began with Israeli jets taking off after dark and proceeding north toward the northeast corner of Syria, toward a bleak barely habited stretch of land near the Euphrates. Subsequent reports indicated that electronic countermeasures (ECMs) were used by the Israelis to blind Syrian radar and antiaircraft installations as the planes crossed the border and approached their target.

Their target, later identified as a not yet operational nuclear reactor modeled on the Yongbyon reactor in North Korea—a uranium-fueled reactor that is capable of producing weapons-grade plutonium as a by-product—was destroyed. But the action could have triggered dangerous consequences. For one thing, the former Soviet Union, as well as the United States, is known to have satellite look-down capacity focused on trouble spots. There is little doubt the Russians would have picked up the Israeli jets' takeoff and—in the context of threats and counterthreats exchanged between Iran and Israel over the Iranian nuclear weapons program—they may well have warned the Iranians, with whom they have murky military and nuclear ties, that a potential Israeli attack on their nuclear facilities was under way. The Russians could easily have fired off an electronic warning to the Israelis not to attack Iran—and/or Syria—and implicitly or explicitly threatened "severe consequences" or some other euphemism for putting nukes on the table.

The Soviets, for instance, are reported to have sent an indirect nuclear warning to the Israelis at least once before—at the close of the 1973 war when the Israeli army was threatening to crush the Egyptian Third Army, the last barrier before Cairo. They dispatched an aggressive note to the United States warning of intervention if Israel persisted, which led the U.S. to raise its nuclear alert status to DEFCON-3 before Israel backed off. In other words, the Russians may have invoked that night what is known as a "nuclear umbrella"—or as U.S. nuclear savants more euphemistically call it, "extended deterrence"—in which a nuclear power uses nuclear threats to deter attacks against a nonnuclear ally.

Israel of course, though it has still not acknowledged it officially, is a substantial nuclear power with as many as two hundred warheads at its disposal, according to some estimates. Shortly after the Cold War, journalist Seymour Hersh reported that it had targeting contingency plans, which included sites in the Soviet

Union in preparation for a retaliation should such a Soviet threat have been carried out.

Complicating matters, if the Russians had issued an implicit ultimatum to the Israelis to back off, the Israelis would likely have instantly relayed that threat to the U.S., once again involving two nuclear superpowers in a potential nuclear showdown.

While the United States and Israel deny any formal nuclear umbrella arrangement, there is widespread speculation that the U.S. has warned nations contemplating a nuclear strike on Israel of severe consequences, which implies anything up to and including nuclear reprisal by the U.S. The possible existence of this putative assurance was brought out into the open by presidential candidate, now secretary of state, Hillary Clinton, who declared during the 2008 primary campaign that the U.S. would "obliterate" Iran if it attacked Israel with nukes.

And so by the time the Israeli jets reached the northeast corner of Syria and turned toward the Syrian reactor on the Euphrates, threats and counterthreats may well have been zapping through the ether and suddenly both nuclear superpowers with approximately five thousand land-based nuclear missiles on "hair-trigger" alert were on the verge of—only one misperception or hasty overreaction, one degree of separation away—being drawn into a potential regional nuclear war.

Then there's the wild card, Pakistan, with its "Islamic bomb," which is shorthand for some sixty to one hundred warheads under the kind of loose, decentralized control that could allow a regional commander with ties to Islamic nations such as Iran and Syria to step in and set off another variety of regional nuclear war with equal potential for escalation.

All those signals, threats, and counterthreats flashing through the night could easily have been known to the "very senior" British minister quoted in *The Spectator*, assuming he had access to GCHQ, Government Communications Headquarters, the legendary British signals interception facility, which, in tandem with the U.S. government's NSA (National Security Agency and its spy satellite system), can listen in to just about everything, even to secret military encryptions, in near real time.

What the very senior minister was describing was perhaps the most perilous—and emblematic—crisis of the second nuclear age thus far: it is a new world in which the bipolar "stability" of the "balance of terror" has degenerated into a chaotic state of multipolar nuclear powers with less control and less restraint and a greater chance of touching off a regional nuclear war that could escalate to global scale.

Nuclear proliferation scholar Benjamin Frankel tells us the "inherent complexity" of the new nuclear age "dooms multipolar systems to instability making them susceptible to crisis and war."

"The world has arrived at a nuclear tipping point," a Carnegie Endowment for International Peace study warned. "We are at the tipping point," former Senator Sam Nunn, co-founder of the Nuclear Threat Initiative, has said, "and we are headed in the wrong direction."

"The current global nuclear order," declared Harvard's Graham Allison, "is extremely fragile."

Already India and Pakistan nearly used their nuclear arsenals against each other in 1999 and 2002. That was still bipolar. The Syria raid, however, was the most dramatic embodiment of the difference between the bipolar Cold War type of nuclear war close calls, and the new type of multipolar chain reactions that could reach critical mass in our new nuclear age.

## THE COLD WAR CLOSE CALLS EMERGE

How should we gauge the seriousness, the closeness of close calls? How close are we from the beginning of the end? One disturbing result of recent nuclear historiography—and Freedom of Information Act (FOIA) declassifications—has been the revelation that even the purportedly more stable nuclear deterrence system of the Cold War produced a far greater number of close calls during the first nuclear era than we imagined. It turns out we weren't scared enough, or as much as we should have been. The more historians excavate the history of the Cold War, the more close calls they discover. We're only now learning the truth about how much closer we came—and how often—to nuclear war than we knew at the time. One of the great debates about nuclear deterrence—threatening genocide to prevent genocide—is whether we got through the Cold War because of the ingenious design of deterrence—the finely calibrated threats of annihilation—or because of sheer luck in close call moments. These new revelations tend to substantiate the luck rather than design theory of why we survived.

There was the revelation by Michael Dobbs in *One Minute to Midnight*, his 2009 book on the Cuban Missile Crisis, that Soviet nuclear missiles in Cuba were both armed and ready, contrary to U.S. intelligence, and that command over their launch had been turned over by the Russians to Fidel Castro. Castro swore that in the event of any kind of attack—of the sort the Joint Chiefs pressed on President Kennedy, confident the Soviet nukes were not yet assembled—he would have fired them at the U.S. mainland even if the move touched off a global nuclear war, as it likely would have. There was also the revelation by Dobbs that the captain of the Soviet submarine, which was escorting the Russian cargo ship testing the U.S. blockade of Cuba, said that on October 27, 1962, he had armed and aimed a nuclear-tipped torpedo at a U.S. blockade vessel at the height of the crisis, and was about to fire when the Russian sub fleet commander, who happened to be on board, overrode his decision.

Historians of the Cold War have also unearthed "false positive" nuclear alerts that could have led to mistaken launches: in the 1950s it was a flock of geese mistaken for incoming nukes on the U.S. side; in 1997 it was a Norwegian weather satellite launch taken for an incoming missile on the Russian side.

President Jimmy Carter's national security adviser told his CIA director, Stansfield Turner, a chilling story of his own. On June 3, 1980, at 2:26 A.M., Zbigniew Brzezinski was awakened by the NORAD (North American Aerospace Defense Command) warning center in Colorado, and was told he must notify the president that their screens showed an incoming nuclear strike. According to Brzezinski the error was detected only "one minute" before Brzezinski had planned to tell the president of a NORAD warning that 2,200 Soviet missiles had been launched against the United States. Brzezinski hesitated long enough for NORAD to call back and say a mistake had been made: the call had been triggered by nuclear warning training tapes being fed into the warning room screens and mistaken for the real thing.

And then there was Colonel Petrov; the midlevel Russian officer in the Strategic Rocket Force who was manning the Kremlin's underground warning center on September 26, 1983, when radar signaled a massive nuclear strike coming over the pole from the U.S. He had minutes to decide to awaken Soviet premier Yuri Andropov for a decision about whether to launch the Russian arsenal. He decided not to and it turned out to be a technical error.

There were other close calls on the Soviet side. A British mole in the KGB, Oleg Gordievsky, was able to convince his British intelligence contacts that the Kremlin believed an upcoming NATO exercise (in the fall of 1983, known as Operation Able Archer) was some kind of cover for a surprise attack against the U.S.S.R.—and that the Kremlin was making preparations for a preemptive nuclear attack to get the jump on the West. Gordievsky's warning led to some key decisions to diminish Soviet suspicion, such as President Reagan not leaving the White House for his "undisclosed location" command bunker that October as he would have if a real attack had been planned. No one can know how things might have turned out if a well-placed mole had not stopped the mutual ratcheting up of suspicion.

Luck: who knows what would have happened if Brzezinski had not hesitated, if it had been someone other than Petrov on duty, or if Gordievsky had not spoken up. Nuclear triumphalists look at this history and maintain that "the system worked." Nuclear deterrence worked. But did it work because it was so well designed, or only because we were extraordinarily lucky its failures and close calls did not result in nuclear holocaust?

Does that mean the system, such as it is, will continue to work under very different twenty-first-century circumstances with wild-card nuclear powers now in the picture?

The conviction that the system worked has allowed us to avoid the haunting questions of the morality of the system's mutual sui-cide pact. It allowed us to avoid serious consideration of the most profound moral question: is there an alternative to the system—to our continued dependence on the Cold War–generated genocidal threat of nuclear deterrence?

And then there was the question about that question: was it dangerous, perhaps immoral, even to ask the question, because such discussion undermined the credibility of the deterrent threat by depicting the possibility that a nuclear power would dither and moralize—and perhaps *not* retaliate? Would asking the question have the effect of making more likely the attack we were trying to deter, with its inevitable millions of casualties? What place does moralizing have when it comes to nuclear war? Because nuclear bombs may be exponentially more powerful than conventional ones, does the quantity of lives make the quality of moral analysis different? Why exactly should we feel worse about Hiroshima than the firebombing of Tokyo, which killed five times more innocents at least initially? We never settled these questions before the end of the Cold War. Now the threat of nuclear war is back and we have to face them again.

## THE YEAR OF LIVING DANGEROUSLY AGAIN

The Israeli raid on the Syrian reactor was, for this more than casual observer, the culmination of a number of disturbing developments in 2007, that year of living dangerously again, the year in which it was no longer possible to ignore the return of the repressed: the reality of the danger of nuclear *war*, as opposed to nuclear *terror*, a mere suitcase bomb. (Although nuclear war could be *set off* by nuclear terror.)

Looking back, the concatenation of nuclear events may have begun with the misbegotten announcement in April 2007 by the Bush administration that it was going to install interceptor rockets in Poland, purportedly to shoot down Iranian missiles that might put Europe at risk. The furious reaction of the Russians to the installation of any kind of Western missiles on their border may have soured relations for long after the decision by the Obama administration two years later, to abandon the Polish plan and shift to a sea-based interceptor system. But even that concession has not satisfied Russian opposition to any missile defense system near its borders.

The most dramatic reaction to the April decision was the August 17, 2007, announcement by Vladimir Putin that Russian long-range bombers would be resuming regular "strategic flights." "Strategic" is a widely used euphemism in nuclear affairs for "nuclear-capable."

While there were unofficial reassurances that the flights were "exercises" and that the bombers wouldn't be armed with nukes, it soon became apparent that this was more than a symbolic announcement, and had more than symbolic consequences.

Putin's decision to resume strategic flights meant he was putting his nuclear bombers in the air on a regular basis. It was a Cold War heightened-alert procedure, designed by both sides to prevent nuclear bombers from being caught on the runway by a surprise attack—as well as making possible a devastating first strike. Before the resumption of its "strategic flights," Russia's nuclear-capable bomber fleet had been virtually grounded by inaction, defunding, and disrepair for some years.

This is what Putin said that August of 2007: "I have made a decision to resume regular flights of Russia's strategic aviation. Starting today such tours of duty will be conducted regularly and on a strategic scale. Our pilots have been grounded for too long; they are happy to start a new life."

Do you think he mentioned "strategic" enough times? And "happy" is a curious note to strike about that particular "new life," especially since Putin left unanswered the question of whether these strategic flights would in fact be bearing nuclear bombs then or in the future.

Although that announcement drew a moderate amount of international media attention, the troubling consequences were less widely noted. Indeed it was only six months later that I happened to read in a small-circulation military magazine *AirForces Monthly* published in the U.K. that the U.S. and NATO were sending fighter jets to intercept Putin's Russian bombers on these strategic flights.

Dogfights with nuclear-capable bombers! I found it so hard to believe this hadn't been bigger news, or that the source was reliable, that I picked up the phone, called the Pentagon, and after a few connections was put in touch with a Canadian Air Force major named Bryan Martin, the designated spokesperson at NORAD's nuclear warning center in the hollowed-out interior of Cheyenne Mountain in Colorado. (NORAD is a joint U.S.-Canadian air defense command.)

I'd been there before—in 1977 on my Cold War–era tour of nuclear war nodes—inside Cheyenne Mountain, the place where the theater-size warning screens tracked every trace of a moving object heading for U.S. and Canadian airspace and determined whether it might be hostile. If two technical sensors—one radar, one satellite—were triggered, and this "dual phenomenology" as STRATCOM, the U.S. Strategic Command (formerly SAC, the Strategic Air Command), likes to call it—registered something incoming, then an "assessment conference" would be called and a decision would be made as to whether to notify STRATCOM's underground nuclear command center in Omaha, and brief its commanders about whether to call the White House so it could fire up the president's "nuclear football" for action.

Yes, the NORAD major confirmed to me, they'd been watching the Russian strategic flights and occasionally scrambling U.S. fighter jets to intercept them. In the six months since Putin's strategic flights program began, there had been no fewer than seventeen U.S. fighter jet interceptions of Russian bombers as they approached NORAD-patrolled U.S. and Canadian West Coast and Arctic airspace. There was an even greater number of such engagements over NATO airspace in Europe, he informed me.

Cheyenne Mountain's Major Martin informed me that the Russians sometimes announced vague exercises that would include such flights, so as to avoid misinterpretations of the strategic flights' intent. But anyone familiar with Cold War war-gaming knew that the best way to disguise a surprise attack was to have it develop out of what was announced as an exercise. The NORAD major said most of the intercepts were the result of Russian bombers "departing from the flight plan of the exercise they filed and approaching NORAD airspace."

The major described the typical outlines of the seventeen episodes: U.S. fighter jets buzzing the Russian bombers and causing them to turn back from the course that would bring them closer to U.S. coastal airspace.

But those seventeen episodes only involved U.S. pilots—they did not include all the intercepts of Russian bombers performed by every NATO and Japanese fighter in non-NORAD airspace. The major placed that total number at about seventy-five, substantiating the report in *AirForces Monthly*.

I'll mention just one of those interactions reported by the monthly between Russian strategic bombers and NATO jet interceptors. "On September 6, the biggest build-up of Russian airpower in NATO airspace saw as many as eight Tu-95s [nuclear-capable bombers] track their way from the Barents Sea and into the Atlantic . . . shadowed by 20 NATO fighters," it said. Was it a coincidence that the Israeli raid on the Syrian reactor, the one that allegedly brought us so close to World War III, took place on September 6? The monthly also quoted a Russian source that "the NATO jets approached at what he considered potentially dangerous distances—within 16–25 feet wingtip to wingtip." The story went on to say that "the fact that no emergency situation resulted . . . was a testament to the flying skills on both sides." Very reassuring! Let's applaud those flying skills.

Secretary of State Condoleezza Rice eventually condemned these strategic flights buzzing our airspace, but not before the most provocative development in the strategic flights program: in July 2008, shortly before Putin sent troops into Georgia purportedly to support pro-Russian independent enclaves, the Russian Defense Ministry announced some strategic flights would be landing in Cuba and, shortly thereafter, in Venezuela. This brought a remarkably sharp reply from U.S. Air Force general who said any such action—landing nuclear bombers ninety miles from U.S. shores—would "cross a red line."

Suddenly all the elements for a new Cuban Missile Crisis were there. All but one: the two superpowers were no longer declared enemies, locked in a balance of terror, zero-sum death struggle. They were no longer friends, it's true, more geopolitical rivals, but the rivalry was beginning to take a military turn. The strategic background, the context of these flights and intercepts and Cuban landings, was different from that of 1962, but it was getting progressively worse. The situation raised the possibility of what the nuclear strategists call "inadvertence"—an accidental nuclear exchange. To this day, Russia's strategic flights program goes on, as do the dangerous intercepts.

Meanwhile, the effort to limit the buildup of nuclear weapons between the two original superpowers had stalled. The Strategic Arms Reduction Treaty, or START, expired on December 5, 2009. For months, beginning in July 2009 when Russian President Dmitri Medvedev seemed to sign on to U.S. President Obama's goal of "a world without nuclear weapons," there were assurances from both sides that a new START treaty for further reductions in nuclear arsenals would be signed by that expiration day, or that if it didn't happen, the old treaty would simply be extended until the final, more bold ambitious one, was signed.

But December 5 came and went without any formal stopgap extension. The Russians instead expelled a U.S. verification team at a Russian missile factory, which had been part of START's verification infrastructure. Suddenly verification issues—as well as BMD (Ballistic Missile Defense) issues seemed to be a stalling point, with the Russians demanding less surveillance of them and more of us, specifically the right to be able to inspect the new sea-based missile defense system the Obama administration had decided to adopt after abandoning the Polish interceptors that the Russians so strenuously objected to.

The treaty was signed in April 2010 with much ceremony but only modest reductions in warheads, from 2,200 to 1,550 on each side. As of October 2010, it had not been ratified. There is opposition to its missile defense provisions in both ratifying bodies—Congress and the Russian duma—for opposite reasons: the Russians say they have the right to withdraw from the treaty if the U.S. takes any missile defense steps not to its liking, and anti-treaty forces on the U.S. side have argued against ratification because they believe it will hamper ballistic missile defense. A formidable stumbling block.

In addition, the Russian government has kept itself busy by announcing ambitious plans to build a trillion-dollar new generation of nuclear weapons and delivery vehicles. The program got the world's attention when one missile test went spectacularly awry in the skies over Norway on November 5 and put on an *Avatar*-blue tinted whirligig sky show just as world leaders were gathering nearby in Copenhagen to discuss global warning.

It is fascinating to hear the apprehension in a voice from deep inside Russia itself about this new bellicosity. Victor Mizin, the director of one of the few remaining independent think tanks in that country, the Institute for International Security Affairs, has written recently about a number of explicit, unilateral acts the Putin regime had taken that show a disturbing change in the superpowers' nuclear postures. In an article called "Russia's Nuclear Renaissance" he cited Russia's withdrawal from the Conventional Armed Forces Treaty in Europe along with its threats to withdraw from the Intermediate-Range Nuclear Forces Treaty, which limits the number of nuclear weapons based in Europe and Russia, along with an alarming buildup and modernization of its existing nuclear arsenal. And here's a stunning development not widely reported but that Mizin emphasized: Moscow has threatened, in response to U.S. and European plans for a limited ballistic missile defense, "to retarget nuclear missiles on Europe." Obama's cancellation of the Polish interceptor plan temporarily suspended this highly aggressive threat, but the new Pentagon plan to install BMD interceptors on Romanian soil does not bode well considering the short-fused Russian reaction to missiles on its borders.

Finally, in case anyone needs convincing, Mizin asserts that all of this suggests "that the Russian generals still view a nuclear war with either the U.S. or NATO as theoretically possible. . . . On a very basic level nothing has changed since Soviet times."

## THE MINOT MISTAKE

On the American side of things, in a sign that nukes seemed to be breaking out all over in the summer of 2007, there was the infamous Minot mistake. It took place in that same August in which Putin resumed the strategic flights. On August 31, an American nuclear-capable B-52 bomber took to the air from the Minot, North Dakota, Air Force Base with six—for some time the number was in dispute—nuclear-tipped cruise missiles suspended from one wing.

The bomber flew south to Barksdale Air Force Base in Louisiana where it was discovered that the cruise missiles were nuclear-armed—the first time nuclear weapons had been flown over American territory in forty years.

It was all a big mistake according to several levels of investigation, which eventually played a part in the firing of the chief of staff of the air force. Nuclear weapons were supposed to be stored in special areas, painted different colors—not stacked next to the conventionally armed cruise missile as these had been. Some said there was a "management problem" and that certainly seems to be true. (The widening investigation by the Pentagon of the management of nuclear weapons disclosed that, in addition, four crucial nuclear fuses had been shipped mistakenly to Taiwan that year, no laughing matter to nuclear-armed China.)

But on another level it was almost as if the loss of dread that once surrounded nuclear weapons seemed to have been exposed. Once there had been a bright line between the nuclear and nonnuclear realm, as there had been between the nuclear and the nonnuclear storage stacks. It reflects the cultural and political view that no matter how small, a nuclear weapon occupies a different military, political, metaphysical category from other weapons.

The Obama administration announced it will pursue its version of the Bush Pentagon's "Prompt Global Strike" plan to produce ICBMs tipped with highly lethal conventional explosives that would be capable of slamming powerful but nonnuclear warheads any place on earth within an hour (that "prompt"). The plan has raised both practical and philosophical questions. Won't those nations who see an American ICBM heading for their capital (or wherever) assume it's got a nuclear warhead despite all the "assurances" they may have received? And won't that assumption make them more likely to use whatever nuclear weapons they have in their stockpile before finding out for sure? Even if the ICBM is equipped with a conventional warhead, if its lethality approaches nuclear strength—if this conventional missile is more lethal than a small nuke, say—should its use raise the same moral questions as a nuke?

Are nuclear weapons just very powerful and efficient explosive devices, exponentially more powerful, but when it comes to war just the most explosive, and capable of being used in the same way as conventional weapons of mass destruction? Or was there something particularly demonic, Faustian, insidiously evil—"exceptionalist"—about them? Was it the invisible long-lasting half-life of radiation that made nukes not just different in degree but in *kind*? The way nuclear weapons didn't merely split the atom but somehow cracked the core of Newtonian being—the mechanistic, determinist way of explicating all events by iron rules of causality? Was it that they revealed the demon of unpredictability that reigns on the subatomic level. The ineradicable evil of ionizing radiation?

There was another aspect of the Minot mistake I found fascinating. Either inadvertently or not, coming two weeks after Putin's strategic flights took off into the air, a U.S. strategic bomber "mistakenly" takes off, metaphorically flaunting U.S. nuclear weapons. ("We got 'em too, Vlad.")

I don't actually believe there was a deliberate decision to deploy this mistake to send a message to the Russians. But a message was sent. Nor did I buy into the frenzied biogospheric speculations that began by making a connection between the Minot mistake and all the talk of a possible U.S. or Israeli attack on the Iranian nuclear enrichment centrifuges and the raid just one week later on the Syrian installation that purportedly brought us close to World War III. Barksdale, the conspiracists said, was a jumping-off place for U.S.

flights to the Middle East. Ergo the nuclear missiles on the plane were meant for launch at Iran; the Syrian mission was merely a rehearsal for the bigger plan. The blogospheric conspiracy theorists—worth studying as the nightmare id of the second nuclear age—proceeded to conjure up out of thin air an "alternate nuclear chain of command" secretly created by Dick Cheney. (Not that there are no real chain of command issues, as we will see.)

But one didn't need conspiracy theories to see the potential nuclear flashpoints approaching in 2007.

## THE IMPOSSIBLE PROBLEM

Pakistan has long been a regional nuclear war ready to happen. According to veteran *New York Times* foreign correspondent Raymond Bonner, "When Bill Clinton briefed President-elect George Bush at the White House in December 2000, he enumerated six major security threats facing the United States. Three were: Al Qaeda, nuclear tensions between Pakistan and India, and Pakistan's links to the Taliban and Al Qaeda." In other words: Pakistan, Pakistan, Pakistan.

Pakistan developed what it came to call the Islamic bomb in secret, using stolen and freely available Western technology assembled by the notorious Pakistani bomb maker A. Q. Khan, who has been called a "nuclear jihadist" (by Douglas Frantz and Catherine Collins in a book by that name). Kahn's "nuclear bazaar" delivered nuclear technology, fuel, and possibly assembled weapons to states like Libya, North Korea, Saudi Arabia, and an unknown number of "nonstate actors," i.e., terrorists.

The Pakistani bomb was ostensibly designed as a deterrent to the Indian nuclear bomb, which had first been tested in 1974. Once the two bitter enemy states went nuclear, every troop movement or terrorist incident in disputed Kashmir—the vast northern province ruled by India despite its Pakistan-leaning Muslim majority—became the potential cause of a regional war. So was every terrorist incident, from the bomb that blew up the Indian Parliament in 2005 to the attack on Mumbai by Pakistan-linked terrorists in November 2008.

It doesn't take very sophisticated war gaming to see how that regional war could turn into a global one:

Hindu and Muslim terrorism in Kashmir or elsewhere on the subcontinent escalates into preemptive nuclear exchanges between India and Pakistan. China comes to the aid of its traditional ally, Pakistan, against its traditional enemy, India. A rogue Indian general decides to strike China with a nuke, triggering reprisal. Muslim regional nuclear commanders in southern Russia (long a concern of both the U.S. and Russian military) enter the fray, perhaps seizing the radioactive fog of war to strike Israel, which retaliates against Russia, which strikes back, raising the possibility of drawing the U.S. into the conflagration. Once the nuclear genie is unleashed there may be no part of the globe that remains immune.

If not Pakistan and India, Pakistan and Israel. The more Pakistan has referred to its bomb as an "Islamic bomb" the more the Israelis have felt it as "an existential threat," a threat to its very existence. Israel, for its part, has been described by a nuclear strategist as "a one-bomb state" because one single-megaton-size bomb would be enough to render it an uninhabitable land of the dead and dying.

Thus the margin between existential threat to Israel and Israeli preemptive launch to prevent it is thin and getting thinner. Seconds. Minutes, maybe. Any serious threat, in other words, could be used to justify preemption. (See chapter 7.)

And should the Israelis get involved in a conflict with another Islamic state, Iran or Syria, say, what role would the Pakistani Islamic bomb play? Potentially an intervention on behalf of other Islamic states? Retaliation for Israeli use of nukes? Or could the Pakistani nukes just as likely become the target of a preemptive Israeli strike to ensure they could not be an instrument of any Islamic retaliation against an Israeli air strike against Iran, for example?

The problem with Pakistan is not just that it has a nuclear arsenal and is constantly threatening to use it against India. The problem is also that its government is unstable (in just the last three years, Pervez Musharraf was forced out, Benazir Bhutto came back and was assassinated), and the current prime minister, her husband, is regarded as slowly losing his grip on power and in particular on the nuclear arsenal to Pakistan's Inter-Services Intelligence agency, the ISI, which is widely believed to be infiltrated by Al Qaeda and the Taliban. The agency is deeply involved both in Islamist and terrorist plots against India, Israel, and the West. Some Al Qaeda experts argue that Osama bin Laden's search for some crude self-made nuke, or a suitcase nuke, from a rotting relic of the former Soviet Union hasn't been successful because he wasn't trying very hard. His real goal was simply taking over the Pakistani government and its sixty new nukes ready to fire by the "authorized" command. All he had to do was bide his time, let the trends play out, and ultimately they would fall into his hands.

And then what? Needless to say the war-gaming for this eventuality had been going on in the Pentagon for years. But no one seems to know—no one in the unclassified literature had even proposed—a game-winning strategy should the worst happen and bin Laden or an ally ends up heading a nuclear-armed Pakistani government.

If an ISI/Taliban/Al Qaeda–friendly coup was successful, the U.S. would have some hard decisions to make in a terribly short period of time. Take out, as in destroy, the Pakistani nukes, as many, as fast as we could? "Take custody" of them, as one expert put it? Of course there is the little problem that we don't know where all of them are. We could send in special ops teams to secure the ones we can locate, but even assuming that goes well (preemptive detention of another nation's nuclear arsenal), there is the risk of some remaining out of our reach.

On the other hand allowing an Al Qaeda–friendly government possession of sixty nukes? Hardly tenable. Which of course makes for some hard choices on the part of the putative Al Qaeda–friendly new Pakistani rulers as well. Expecting American intervention, they might well feel they would be in a "use it or lose it" position the moment they took control. We must use them before they're seized or destroyed. Or at least hide them before the Americans can seize them.

The Pakistani government has recurrently reassured the world that only "authorized" arms of the government have control over their nukes. But nearly simultaneous reports in the *New York Times* and the *Wall Street Journal* in late 2007 made clear that the U.S. had not given the Pakistanis a key bit of centralized weapons control technology called PALs (Permissive Action Links) that were meant to ensure that some local commander wouldn't decide to start a holy war on his own without the authorization codes from the central government. The obvious problem is that even if the nukes are ensured against *unauthorized* launches, the fragile central Pakistani government can fall into the hands of extremists, who will then have the power to make authorized launches.

A nightmare. And yet such a situation is not unimaginable. More than one nuclear strategist, including Israelis concerned about Iran, have told me that Pakistan is the most immediate, unstable, insoluble, potential nuclear flashpoint we face. Unless you count . . .

## THE UNFATHOMABLE AMBITIONS OF NORTH KOREA

North Korea is estimated to have eighty-two pounds of bomb-grade plutonium. That's what they've officially admitted to in the ever-breaking-down Six-Party talks with the North Koreans that are repeatedly announcing gains that are then reversed. This is about enough to make six powerful (one-megaton-plus) nuclear weapons, and some experts think they have enough to make twelve or more. They also have the No-dong missile, whose tests in the Pacific have indicated a range long enough to hit our West Coast. But that probably would not be a madman dictator like Kim Jong-il's primary target. More likely it would be war breaking out, either on purpose or accidentally, between North and South Korea, which is under our nuclear umbrella should it be threatened or come under nuclear attack from its northern enemy. "The bad news about North Korea," Jonathan Pollack, a North Korea expert at the Naval War College, told the *New York Times*, "is that we don't know much about their nuclear control system. Or even if they have much of one."

That's the bad news. He didn't mention any good news. Just

another rogue state flashpoint that could at any moment go from potential nuclear nightmare to horrific reality.

## IRAN, ISRAEL, AND THE NIE SCANDAL

It is not uncommon for Israel politicians to use two emotionally loaded phrases, often in the same sentence: "existential threat" and "second Holocaust." They are, needless to say, inextricably linked. An "existential threat" to the state of Israel, a threat to the very existence of the nearly six million Jews there, means, in effect, a "second Holocaust." And to many, there is something exponentially more horrific about the secondness of a Holocaust happening to the same people—something that virtually guarantees a third, retaliatory one, in response.

Yes there is dispute over how imminent the threat really is, especially from Iran. At the heart of the dispute is the 2007 National Intelligence Estimate (NIE) on Iran's nuclear program. The NIE is meant to synthesize the judgments of the entire spectrum of U.S. military and civilian intelligence. Control over NIE conclusions can mean control over policy. The 2007 NIE, if read closely, reported that Iran had suspended work on only one aspect of its nuclear program—warhead design. But according to unequivocal remarks by the high-ranking intelligence officials who signed off on the report—and according to later independently discovered facts by the U.N.'s International Atomic Energy Agency inspectors—the press and a world eager to believe that there was no problem anymore *misunderstood* the NIE and incorrectly headlined it as proof that Iran had ceased seeking nuclear weapons. While the warhead design program may have been suspended, work is racing forward on the other two aspects of nuclear weapon making: uranium fuel enrichment and nuclear-capable missile building.

And work on the warhead itself may have been halted because there was little left to do (the blueprints were available from A. Q. Khan, the rogue Pakistani nuclear scientist) but the uranium enrichment process and the missile testing process were bringing Iran inexorably closer to both weapons-grade fuel and bomb delivery systems—the two more difficult aspects of nuclear weapon making. Maybe not as soon as some said, but soon enough, and in all likelihood, inevitably.

Few in the field seriously believes that the Iranians will suspend their drive for a nuclear weapons capacity because of talks and sanctions and talks about sanctions. Sooner or later they will have enough nuclear weapons for an existential threat if the Israelis (or the Americans) don't act first. And because the Israelis cannot dismiss the ideology of suicidal martyrdom embraced on a national level by some Iranian leaders, they will act. Things will be terrible enough if they do. Perhaps even more terrible if they don't. The Israeli historian Benny Morris has argued that the only thing that would save us from an Israeli nuclear attack on Iran would be a successful Israeli conventional attack.

Let's assume the Iranians get the bomb, a bomb big enough to destroy a "one-bomb state"—and the Israelis for one reason or another don't take preemptive action before Iran weaponizes the uranium it is enriching and builds more than one bomb. On November 19, 2007, the Center for Strategic and International Studies, a widely respected middle-of-the-road Washington think tank headed by former Defense Department nuke specialist Anthony Cordesman, published a seventy-seven-page war game simulation of a nuclear war between Iran and Israel. It assumes Iran will have gone nuclear by 2020 at the latest.

Even on the conservative assumption that this will remain a "regional nuclear war" that might escalate to Syria and Egypt but not beyond, the CSIS study predicts a minimum of some 20 million deaths in Iran, close to a million in Israel, and some 18 million in Syria, if they should join in support of Iran, or if Israel preempts Damascus.

And then there is another route from regional to global nuclear conflagration, the Samson Option, a term first popularized in a 1991 Seymour Hersh book by that name. That's the scenario under which, in the aftermath of a second Holocaust, Israel's surviving submarines (reportedly five German-made Dolphin-class submarines) would use their nuclear-armed missiles to do more than retaliate against Israel's specific attackers but would use their nuclear missiles to bring down the pillars of the world (attack Moscow and European capitals for instance) on the grounds that their enabling—or toleration of—eliminationist anti-Semitism made both the first and second Holocausts possible. Indiscriminate vengeance that might even extend to the holy places of Islam (a nightmarish scenario feverishly discussed on the internet for some time) in retaliation for the hatred that brought about a second Holocaust. Have the Israelis already let the Iranians know that they would be responsible for the targeting of Islam's holiest sites if they struck Israel? Is that "the deterrent that dare not speak its name"?

But wait, we haven't finished enumerating the potential nuclear flashpoints, we haven't considered . . .

## THE NEGLECTED FLASHPOINT: CHINA AND TAIWAN

Threatening China with nukes has a history that dates back to John Foster Dulles, the secretary of state under President Dwight Eisenhower, who let it be known to Mao Zedong's mainland regime in 1954 that its threat to take the tiny Taiwanese-controlled islands of Quemoy and Matsu off the Chinese coast might be met with that kind of force.

Similar implicit threats emerged in the late 1990s and early aughts when the U.S. promulgated a doctrine of "nuclear ambiguity"—the refusal to rule out nukes—regarding any mainland attempt at military takeover of Taiwan. It was a threat that spiked every few years when Chinese exercises or coastal invasion fleets built up across the straits from Taiwan. The purposeful vagueness of nuclear ambiguity was meant to discourage Taiwan as well: it couldn't count on U.S. nuclear support if it behaved provocatively.

China is one of the few flashpoints that seem to have dimmed in recent years. But it's still there in America's master targeting plan known as the SIOP, the Single Integrated Operational Plan, now renamed OPLAN, for Operations Plan, 8022. China is still considered a "peer power," as major nuclear powers are called. Estimates of the number of Chinese nuclear weapons are highly secret. One Defense Intelligence Agency (DIA) report in the 1990s projected about 360 warheads; another, later, study would only say "more than 100." The Chinese are known to favor a "minimal deterrence policy," enough-warheads to inflict devastating damage on the U.S. with missiles whose range can reach the West Coast. One Chinese general, apparently going off message, in 2005 spoke of their ability to leave Los Angeles "a smoking ruin."

And just when you think a potential World War III flashpoint is diminishing in intensity comes the growing evidence of China's cyber-warfare capability. Since 2006 there have been recurrent reports of the growing sophistication of the Chinese People's Liberation Army's cyber-warfare capability, including hundreds of probes made daily on the Pentagon command and control cyber-infrastructure. And a 2008 report in the *National Journal* cited Tim Bennett, a leading civilian cyber-terrorism expert, who claims on the basis of conversations with government cyber-security experts that Chinese cyber-attacks were responsible for the 2003 Northeast power grid blackout. Bennett called this far-fetched scenario "the first act of World War III."

Two years later a front-page report on Chinese militarizing of cyber-space in *The Washington Post* dramatized the unceasing peacetime digital war being waged, making Bennett's World War III seem more than a metaphor. "They think they can deter us through cyber warfare," one source told the paper. Other scenarios had hackers inserting false warnings of attack into our warning and targeting software to provoke us to nuke others—or ourselves.

## THE END OF MAD

It was little noted and mostly classified but the administration of George W. Bush sought from its inception, in its 2001 Nuclear Posture Review to break the taboo against normalizing nuclear weapons use: to articulate the idea that nuclear weapons could be deployed in war fighting, in battlefield situations rather than as primarily deterrent threats of revenge. It was an idea that had been making progress up to the moment the Cold War ended, one that went into limbo until the Bush administration and 9/11, and then began to be embedded in our new nuclear policy as adumbrated by a little noticed but terribly important change in U.S. nuclear doctrine. That change was revealed when someone leaked portions of the top secret Nuclear Policy Review in 2002.

That review abandoned adherence to the Balance of Terror, the defensive standoff of genocidal threats also known as "Mutually Assured Destruction" (MAD), that had characterized Cold War deterrence. Instead the new doctrine was based on seeking and maintaining "nuclear primacy." In other words, the U.S. would no longer seek to deter a superpower opponent with nukes but to use nukes to intimidate it into submission, or "denial" of its goals, and if war came to defeat them decisively. In addition the new doctrine lowered the bar to use nuclear weapons on nonnuclear powers—on "rogue states" and "proliferators" such as North Korea and Pakistan, as well as on what are known in the trade as the peer powers of China and Russia.

This new thinking involved everything from a range of new weapons to new strategies. It was obsessed with developing and deploying still unproven ballistic missile defense weapons and with the creation and use of smaller tactical nuclear weapons, even mini-nukes that would purportedly be ideal to deploy against hard and deeply buried targets or HDBTs. The mini-nukes were given the suggestive nuke porn name Robust Nuclear Earth Penetrators.

Few facts have been gleaned about the new master nuclear targeting plan, once called "the most secret document in the world." But one part of it has been declassified in response to a FOIA request by Hans M. Kristensen of the Federation of American Scientists. Almost all the pages are marked top secret and are blacked out. But two blacked-out pages include titles that make clear that "regional states" (that is, nations in troubled regions who are close to going nuclear) have been included in the master nuclear target base list. According to Kristensen this means American doctrine now contemplates nuclear first strikes against them, where nuclear strikes were once restricted to nuclear powers. Could it be that this partial declassification was designed to draw attention to this new policy development? Was it our intention to let these regional states know we have first-strike targeting plans against them, buried somewhere in the software of the president's nuclear football?

The U.S. had long resisted the pressure by the anti-nuke elements of the international community, and some arms control specialists, to renounce the first use of nuclear weapons. We had adopted a policy of deliberate ambiguity, which in effect was an affirmation of the willingness to be the first to use nuclear weapons in an escalating conflict. During the Cold War we refused to refuse first use largely because of the desire by our NATO allies in Western Europe to feel they had a U.S. nuclear umbrella as protection against the Soviet Union and its Warsaw Pact allies. To the question of whether we'd be prepared to use nukes to stop an East Bloc advance and risk an almost certain nuclear attack on the U.S. in response—to fight the resulting global nuclear war to protect Alsace-Lorraine, in effect—we wouldn't say "no first use." (We wouldn't say whether we would use nukes to deter North Korea from attacking South Korea either.) Our policy was ambiguity.

Most Cold War historians regard our nuclear ambiguity over first use as especially important in preventing a conventional war from breaking out in Europe during the Cold War. Soviet conventional forces outweighed NATO's and the U.S. refusal to discount the option of going nuclear first—to stop the Soviets if they seemed to be breaking through Western lines—may well have checkmated that possibility, again at the risk of incinerating Europe to save it.

Still the concept of first use is different from first strike. The former is usually used in the context of defense and deterrence—a threat to deter a conventional war. The latter—first strike—is purely an offensive context, a preemptive nuclear strike, a surprise attack.

But first use, first strike preemptive nuclear war has developed a second life among the new Strangeloves, and some of the foremost old Cold Warriors.

On January 22, 2008, the U.K. *Guardian* shook readers with a report on a manifesto issued by former NATO commanders including General John Shalikashvili from the U.S., Lord Inge from the U.K., and Klaus Naumann from Germany. Under the headline "PRE-EMPTIVE NUCLEAR STRIKE A KEY OPTION, NATO TOLD," defense reporter Ian Traynor wrote: "The west must be ready to resort to a pre-emptive nuclear attack to try to halt the 'imminent' spread of nuclear and other weapons of mass destruction, according to a radical manifesto for a new NATO by five of the west's most senior military officers and strategists."

They were trying to shock complacent NATO governments into realizing that we had entered a new age of nuclear war and the rules needed to be changed. They argued that nukes must be brought to the fore again, contrary to NATO's trend toward de-emphasizing nuclear weapons. The only possibility of peace is rule by an iron hand, enforced by plutonium.

MAD is dead or no longer the certain deterrent it was in the bipolar Cold War. The rise of the ideology of suicidal martyrdom—even *national* suicidal martyrdom (say, Iran sacrificing itself to destroy Israel)—means deterrence can no longer actually deter "rogue states" and "nonstate actors" who are too fanatic to be concerned with retaliatory consequences or who can detonate a deadly "bomb with no return address" that cannot be traced to its origin and so makes MAD's threat of retaliation an empty one. According to these first strike manifesto generals, we should retain the ability to preempt a nuclear or near-nuclear power: Shoot first and ask questions later.

First on their list of threats that must be countered by nukes was proliferation by rogue states. The "risk of further nuclear proliferation is imminent and, with it, the danger that nuclear war fighting limited in scope might become possible," the manifesto said. For that reason, they said, "The first use of nuclear weapons must remain in the quiver of escalation as the ultimate instrument to prevent the use of weapons of mass destruction."

These are men, the first-use manifesto signers, who spent years with their fingers on the trigger. Their perception of what they called "an increasingly brutal world" is hard to argue with. And yet it's not a world that is as close—a shot away—from global nuclear war at any moment as it was during the Cold War, is it? Wasn't the prevention of global nuclear war an achievement—no small one—of no-first-strike MAD deterrence? Or—the recurrent question—was it just blind luck?

Whichever it was, the implications of the first strike manifesto were not lost on those paying attention. Suddenly, as Elbridge Colby, who served recently in the Office of the Director of National Intelligence, and has recently been engaged in the renegotiation of the START treaty, told me, it looks as if deterrence is under attack by critics "from left and right." Both groups are arguing that things are no longer simple the way they were during the bipolar balance of terror. The risks are multiple, asymmetrical, not susceptible to the binary logic of deterrence.

Why suddenly the first strike leap in the former NATO chiefs' manifesto? For one thing it's not as sudden as it seems. It represents the tip of the iceberg of a decade of think tank and military strategic revaluation of the post–Cold War, post–balance of terror use of our nuclear arsenal. And that attack on deterrence or passive defense has led to the rise of the movement for active Ballistic Missile Defense of the sort that led the Bush administration to pledge in 2007 to install ballistic missile interceptors in Poland and which may have been the real source of the spike in tensions between the U.S. and Russia that began with the strategic flights and broke out over the invasion of Georgia. Despite its name, Ballistic Missile Defense is considered a first strike *offensive*, not primarily a defensive, capability. It permits an offensive first strike to be carried out with less fear of a successful retaliation (assuming the so far unproven BMD technology actually works).

The Year of Living Dangerously Again may have been as much the product of the shortsighted, think tank, new-Strangelove nuclear strategy reflected in the first strike manifesto, as much as the result of Putin's empire building. But such manifestos are responding to something real and new in this second nuclear age: the loss in confidence in nuclear deterrence, in the stability that MAD once offered. To some, MAD is dead and we are the worse for it in the unstable situation it leaves behind.

## THE NEW UNTHINKABLE

When I began writing this book in that watershed year of dawning nuclear war danger, 2007, not many people seemed to share my alarm. Like me, till my wake-up call, most people thought we'd said "goodbye to all that" after the Cold War ended in 1991. We had other things to worry about.

"Nuclear holocaust"—that dreadful compression of the twentieth century's two worst inventions—seemed to be fading into the shadows with the other dread verbal formulations that accompanied it, such as the fate in which "the survivors envy the dead."

And then there is the phrase from that era that may be the ne plus ultra encapsulation of the ultimate end of nuclear war: "the death of consciousness." No one around to notice that there was no one else around.

I hate to be the bearer of bad news but we will have to think about the unthinkable again. But there's a new unthinkable in town: nuclear disarmament. Not a brand-new unthinkable concept, but newly thinkable because it's being pushed by the new president. The controversy over why Barack Obama got the Nobel prize so early in his presidency obscured something that was hiding in plain sight: the very first sentence of the citation he received for his Nobel Prize, which gave "special importance to Obama's vision and work for a world without nuclear weapons."

The Oslo committee members seemed to be reflecting the growing worldwide alarm over the return of nuclear war fear. In other words the prize may have been a hasty gesture because they were scared and knew time was running out on us again and it was a way of sending up a signal flare that the struggle for nuclear disarmament was relevant, urgent again.

Until recently, nuclear disarmament had been relegated to the scrap heap of Cold War–nuclear freeze–Jackson Browne–tie-died-hippie–no nukes nostalgia. It took the president of a nuclear superpower to rescue it for serious consideration. No small accomplishment.

So far whatever you think of him or the idea, Obama has been dogged about it. He declared in Prague on April 5, 2009, he wanted to see a world "without nuclear weapons," and that even if it didn't happen in his lifetime, the time to start was now. He made the same no nukes declaration in July, in London with Russian president Dmitri Medvedev joining him. It was a feature of his speech in the U.N. General Assembly on September 23, then the very next day he chaired a Security Council meeting on nuclear disarmament. On October 9 they gave him the Nobel, making it clear in the citation that it was not when he was nominated (February) but what he'd done since then was responsible for the prize.

Yes, it was an "aspirational" goal, an aspirational award some might say, gestural and all that . . . but it's hard to disagree with Joseph Cirincione, an arms control specialist in the Clinton administration, that it was a targeted gesture. "This is not about Obama. It is not about Bush. It should not be about domestic partisan politics, nor about who has the sharpest sound bite. This is about Iran being a few years away from a nuclear bomb. This is about Al Qaeda being a few kilometers away from Pakistan's nuclear bombs. This is about 23,000 hydrogen bombs in the world ready to use, thousands in U.S. and Russian arsenals still ready to launch in 15 minutes. Understand this: These threats have grown over the past 10 years. Our policies are not working. They are making the problems worse. We have to change course."

But Obama is up against an entrenched nuclear establishment that has its own self-preservationist agenda. Recent reports suggest he may be opposed by his own defense secretary, Robert Gates, and Gates's Pentagon allies, many of them holdovers from the Bush administration. If Obama's serious about disarmament, he needs a Zero czar.

His dream of Zero quickly turned into the beginning of what may be a full-fledged battle. Indeed I witnessed firsthand the first counterstrike in Omaha. (See chapter 3.) Obama's Prague speech in April 2009 led the Pentagon and the nuclear industrial complex to amass its phalanxes of forces in a supersized conference hastily called by the U.S. Strategic Command, STRATCOM, which has charge of all our nuclear forces. In July 2009 I attended the

STRATCOM push-back conference in which they summoned the nuclear elite not just of this nation but of every major nuclear power, including India and Pakistan, to Omaha, site of the nuclear command post beneath adjacent Offutt Air Force Base, the super-hardened megaton-resistant underground labyrinth that is one of the shrines of the nuclear priesthood.

The conference—held in the aircraft carrier-size Omaha Qwest Center Convention Hall—was called the First Annual Strategic Deterrence Symposium. The fact that it was conspicuously named "First Annual" implicitly suggested there would be many "annuals" to come in an unceasing attempt to rescue nuclear deterrence and nuclear weapons policy from Obama's abolitionist designs. These nuclear commanders were not going to be zeroed out by Obama's Zero campaign. Is MAD dead? No, said the four-star brass and the defense intellectuals. Cold War MAD may be on life support but the vogue term was "tailored deterrence." We're going to modernize and refine and tailor nuclear deterrence, the STRATCOM panelists declared at the Omaha conference.

It was only when coming home from that Omaha conference that I realized a historic struggle was developing, possibly the last chance, as they say, to put the nuclear genie back in the bottle, or as I prefer it, to save the nuclear Faust—us—from the flames of hell. The future is being decided now. Urgent debates unresolved by the "holiday from history" are being reinvigorated by the challenges of the second nuclear age. It may well be now or never. There is never likely to be another confluence of superpower president and an arms race on the brink of, but not quite, out of control. One or both factors may change for the worse at any moment. Later is likely to be too late.

Do you recall the end of the great nuke porn movie *On the Beach*? The last living human has died and in the empty streets of a radiation-poisoned Australian city the only human voice heard is the tinny static from the expiring battery of an abandoned revivalist truck loudspeaker. It is a tape stuck on the phrase "There's Still Time Brother," which echoes to the emptiness.

There may still be time. But not much.

CHAPTER TWO

# MAJOR HERING'S FORBIDDEN QUESTION

I n late 1973 a Minuteman missile crewman in training, Major Harold I. Hering, asked a Forbidden Question. He was swiftly yanked out of missile crewman class and consigned to a desk job on the way to being cashiered out of the service after two years of failed appeals. Major Hering's career-ending question, one that should earn him a previously unrecognized and heroic place in nuclear history, was this: "How can I know that an order I receive to launch my missiles came from a sane president?"

I first came across the affair of Major Hering's question when its denouement surfaced in a brief wire service story on an inside page of the *New York Times* on January 13, 1975. The story announced the results of Major Hering's appeal: AIR FORCE PANEL RECOMMENDS DISCHARGE OF MAJOR WHO CHALLENGED "FAILSAFE" SYSTEM.

It wasn't actually the working of the fail-safe system that the major had challenged—it was its very foundation. The fail-safe system was designed to ensure two things: that no unauthorized person would ever be able to order a nuclear strike of any kind and, its often forgotten corollary, that a strike ordered by the president (or his successor, in case the top of the chain of command had been "decapitated") would unfailingly be carried out at his command. No questions asked.

The president, the commander-in-chief, is the ultimate "authorizer." In the aftermath or imminence of nuclear attack his word means launch, his word is law, he has the Gold Codes in the nuclear football that identify him and only him as the ultimate authorizer of Armageddon. But what if his mind is deranged, disordered, even damagingly intoxicated? Should there be a breathalyzer lock on the nuclear football? A brain scan? Can he launch despite displaying symptoms of imbalance? Is there anything to stop him?

Major Hering's question was troublesome because it made explicit a question that has occurred to others contemplating the Rube Goldbergian architecture of our nuclear command and control system. It challenged the comfortable assumption that if we launched a nuclear weapon, it would be, backed by a serious military rationale, not because anyone in charge might be possessed by a private demon. But few have spoken aloud about this deeply troubling issue or put their doubts into print. The question had its origin in the Cold War, but hasn't gone away after it ended. To this day, there is no language about the president's sanity, his state of mind, in the fail-safe protocols, just his identity. It is assumed that in giving such an order, he is serving the interests of the government and people he was elected to lead and protect. You might think such a question—the sanity of a president who gives a nuclear launch order—would require some extra scrutiny, but Major Hering's inconvenient query put a spotlight on the fact that the most horrific decision in history could be executed in less than fifteen minutes by one person with no time for second-guessing.

And the major's impertinent query didn't end there. He also wanted to know, according to his lawyer, "what checks and balances exist to verify that an unlawful order does not get in to the missile men . . . and he was concerned with such things as Presidential imbalance or an unauthorized person infiltrating the system." An impostor command getting inside the system? The possibility, which may have seemed abstract thirty-five years ago, is now real: we know that hacker attacks, many believed to have originated from China's military, have regularly targeted the Pentagon and our nuclear command and control system. Major Hering's concern about an unlawful order getting "in to the missile men" is even more troubling when an infiltrator does not have to be a person, just a burst of digital code.

Major Hering was eloquent in defense of his question. "What are the checks and balances?" he wanted to know. "I have to say I feel I do have a need to know because I am a human being." Invoking his humanity—the words were so nakedly true. And he went further: "It is inherent in an officer's commission that he has to do what is right in the terms of the needs of the nation despite any orders to the contrary. You really don't know at the time of key turning, whether you are complying with your oath of office."

At the time of key turning. Holding the launch keys can have a transformative effect on human beings. They are the final link between the mind of the sane or insane president who gave the order and the missiles that will carry them out. They are the objective correlative of Armageddon. They make their holders lords of the nuclear Ring. Holding them leaves some scarred, few unchanged. And when he spoke of his officer's commission and the potential conflict between "the needs of the nation" and "orders to the contrary," he was, knowingly or unknowingly, invoking the Nuremberg trial precedent: just "following orders" isn't a defense for complicity in genocide. An officer has a duty to resist an illegal, immoral order. What he was asserting was the military tradition that officers take their oaths to the Constitution, not the president.

"I have always stated that I would perform the duties required of a missile launch officer with or without this information," Major Hering said, "but I would be unable to do so without a feeling of concern on my part as far as constitutional guidelines are concerned as I understand them." One is tempted to say that the "feeling of concern" would not mean much to the tens of millions dead as it would to the major, but one does not wish to diminish his honor and nerve in just raising the question. And then, at the heart of the sanity question, there's the problem the major raised of "constitutional guidelines." Could the president order a nuclear launch on his own without—or despite—consultation? Did he require more than his own will to destroy the world? Did he require evidence for his decision? If so, to whom did he have to show it? George W. Bush's vice president had a clear answer to these questions. In late 2008, Dick Cheney made the following claim about a president's ability to launch a strike: "The President of the United States now for 50 years is followed at all times, 24 hours a day, by a military aide carrying a football that contains the nuclear codes that he would use and be authorized to use in the event of a nuclear attack on the United States. He could launch a kind of devastating attack the world's never seen. He doesn't have to check with anybody. He doesn't have to call the Congress. He doesn't have to check with the courts. He has that authority because of the nature of the world we live in." In other words: nuclear weapons require instantaneous decisions, and in that fifteen-minute hair-trigger posture we retain from the Cold War, the president doesn't have to consult anybody. For Cheney, going nuclear means never having to say you're sorry. (Unless, as with Bill Clinton, you lose the codes for months as was revealed in October 2010 by former Joint Chiefs General Hugh Shelton.)

This set off a frenzy among constitutional scholars, who could not reach a consensus about whether Cheney was right, in part because of the ambiguity of the Constitution on the president's role. He is at once commander-in-chief who may be called upon to make immediate decisions about military responses to protect the nation, and as such his power is unlimited. On the other hand, the Constitution requires that he ask Congress for a declaration of war and Congress can defund any military activity he is engaged in. Looked at that way, he does have to check with others. But when there's no time? When delay or inaction is in effect action, self-destructive action perhaps? It's too late to defund a nuke once it's launched on orders of the commander-in-chief.

Defenders of Cheney argued the Supreme Court was on his side. In 1862, they said, it had affirmed Lincoln's unitary executive capacity to order military action against privateers that were trying to break the blockade of the Confederacy, without a declaration of war, since, as with terrorists today, there was no known return address or name to send the declaration to. It was also pointed out that those defending Pearl Harbor on December 7, 1941, the antiaircraft gunners firing back at the attacking aircraft, were taking military action before a declaration of war. They were acting, in effect, as agents of the executive branch. But ordering a nuclear strike, which requires record speed and carries civilization-ending consequences, does not fit neatly into those precedents.

So the question comes back to Major Hering's: If the president doesn't have to check with anybody, can he be trusted to do the right thing? If not, what system is in place to stop him? Back when he raised the issue, there was special reason for concern because the guy with the nuclear keys at his command, Richard Nixon, seemed to be losing control over his own mind as the Watergate scandal began engulfing his presidency. The concern was so acute that one cabinet member, Defense Secretary James Schlesinger, had in fact set up a secret system to monitor any orders that would result in turning those keys. According to newspaper reports at the time, Schlesinger had issued hush-hush orders to those below him in the nuclear chain of command that anyone receiving "unusual orders" from President Nixon was to immediately report back to him, Schlesinger. According to one report, Nixon had told a group of Congressmen during the time of his impeachment hearings that "I could leave this room and in 25 minutes 70 million people would be dead." Schlesinger never denied the story about his nuclear precautions, which was scary on two levels: first that the fate of the world was in the hands of an unstable president, and second that the secretary of defense was nervous enough about the situation to take proactive measures to guard against the possibility of him nuking another country in a fit of rage. Think about that: 70 million dead in 25 minutes. It helps to cut through the numbness to have a number, even if it is the number inside the unbalanced mind of a president.

## THE LARGER SANITY QUESTION

What Schlesinger did—and what Major Hering's question implied—is more than raise the issue of the sanity of a single president. They raised a larger question: the sanity of the command and control system itself. Think about it: What could Schlesinger do? What could any future secretary of defense do in such a case? Race to the White House and grab the nuclear football out of the president's hands? (Remember the war room scene in *Dr. Strangelove*? "GENTLEMEN, you can't fight in here! This is the War Room!") Or would we have a situation when the secretary of defense would be on one line ordering the chief of the Strategic Air Command to disobey the orders of his commander-in-chief and not launch his missiles while the president on the other line was telling him to do exactly that? Or perhaps the reverse: the secretary of defense screaming for an immediate launch, the president hesitating.

In theory the president would win such a struggle. The president has the constitutional power to fire the secretary of defense and appoint a compliant subordinate, as Nixon reminded us all in 1973 when he ordered his attorney general to fire Special Prosecutor Archibald Cox and then when the attorney general and his successor both refused, fired them, until he appointed someone compliant, Robert Bork, to do the job. But the outcome of Schlesinger's jury-rigged solution to the Nixon problem cannot be predicted. Perhaps the SAC commander would side with the fired secretary of defense and they would both seek to have the president declared incapacitated under the 25th Amendment. By then we'd be in coup territory, or inside an episode of *24*. And what is sanity or insanity? What if the president refuses to carry out the deterrent threat of genocidal retaliation once it's failed to deter a strike on us? Can those around him force the president to give them the Gold Codes and in effect give the launch order? Who determines who is sane and who is insane?

After his dismissal from the Air Force, Major Hering took a job as a long haul trucker, so he was hard to find. When I finally reached him two years after he had been let go, he seemed eminently sane. He was soft-spoken and earnest, and not a pacifist or a shirker. He had won a Distinguished Flying Cross for missions over Vietnam. He was willing to twist his launch key—he just wanted to know it was the right thing to do, the right order to follow. My father, a wartime second lieutenant, used to cite the slogan "There's a right way, a wrong way, and the Army way," and you do things, right or wrong, the Army way. Major Hering just wanted to believe the Army way was the right way.

When I spoke to him he told me he still believed his question was valid, but he was not obsessed by it, the way I had become by then. He had done his job as an officer sworn to protect and uphold the Constitution. He took the task of asking the question seriously, as part of his duty to his country, and after he had exhausted his appeals, had accepted the consequences and become a trucker. He still is. Yes, he told me, he felt lonely being the only one to stand up and ask the question but he said he had not been alone: other crewmen felt the same doubt; they just kept silent.

Major Hering may have moved on, but the whole question of nuclear command authority, and of who takes control of that authority if the president is killed in a nuclear attack, has frustrated experts and politicians for decades. Yale Law School professor Akhil Reed Amar has called the confusing succession problem "a disaster waiting to happen." Even before Major Hering came along, Congress passed in 1947 the Presidential Succession Act. But it was full of absurdities. Do you know, for instance, about its "bumping" provision? If a decapitating strike leaves, say, the treasury secretary as the top surviving constitutional successor and he takes the oath of office and begins to act like the president, it is still possible for the secretary of state, who may have been away on a trip to Malaysia when the attack hit, to come back and "bump" that lower-ranking treasury secretary off his perch when she comes home and asserts her claim to the presidency. What if the treasury secretary—now president—objects? Who would decide it? A decimated Supreme Court or a Congress without a quorum? Madness!

As it turns out, Major Hering's question helped trigger an investigation by the International Security subcommittee of the House Committee on International Affairs in March 1976 into nuclear command and control procedures. The Ottinger Committee, as it was known after its chairman, New York State representative Richard Ottinger, featured University of Maryland professor George Quester as its main witness. Over several days of testimony he made the entire structure of command and control of nuclear weapons look like a house of cards whose orderliness on paper could not survive the first strike that disrupted communications between the president and SAC and between SAC and its bombers and missiles. The hearings were largely ignored and ten years later, the House Government Operations Committee held a subcommittee hearing, featuring the testimony of Bruce Blair, a former missile crewman who had gone on to Yale and the Brookings Institution and written a study of command and control flaws. Blair too had been moved by Major Hering's question and had started asking questions of his own. Blair told the committee that "American nuclear doctrine has been racing way ahead of" the command and control system, which he said was now "geared for launch on warning." He said that "because launch on warning is less likely to allow decision makers sufficient time to weigh options rationally, the control system itself has introduced volatility into crisis decision making." The key point here is that there will not be time to weigh options "rationally."

In an attempt to bring clarity to the situation, two of Washington's most venerable think tanks, the Brookings Institution and the American Enterprise Institute, in 2002 jointly formed a commission to consider continuity of government after a catastrophic attack. Suffice it to say that the final report issued in June 2009 doesn't answer who will be in charge in the aftermath of a decapitating attack.

The report begins with a dramatic section entitled "SCENARIO: CONFUSION." It posits a strike by a suicide plane on the Capitol during the State of the Union address when the heads of all three branches of government are "decapitated" and "the military informs the Secretary of Agriculture that there is no contact with anyone else in the line of presidential succession." (One cabinet officer is always stationed in a secure undisclosed location during such occasions.) But, it asks, what if the president is still alive but incapacitated? How exactly would power be transferred to the secretary of agriculture? "The lack of clarity would grow if another higher ranking cabinet member would be found alive after the Secretary of Agriculture took office. . . . Who would control the nuclear codes if they were needed? Who would be able to launch military action?"

After a hundred or so pages, the commission is raising still more questions and finding no answers. It concludes by saying, "It is the finding of this commission that the current system would be inadequate in the face of a catastrophic attack that would kill or incapacitate multiple individuals in the line of succession. The current system must be corrected to ensure continuity in the executive branch." This extensive study with its urgent warnings was largely ignored.

To compound the confusion; in April 2007, President Bush issued an executive order (National Security Presidential Directive-51) establishing an incredibly elaborate extra-constitutional "continuity of government commission" that was given authority to make decisions, including nuclear ones. That commission's authority seemed to trespass on the already disastrously conflicting and cross-wired statutory lines of succession, in that it seemed to allow a whole shadow government to emerge in the event of a crisis and announce, in effect, "No matter what else you've heard, we are in charge."

The nuclear command and control culture has tried to get around the problem of succession with a novel concept: pre-delegation. It means that if the government itself is incapable of issuing orders, the military will know what to do under a system of decisions that have been agreed to by everyone in advance. Pre-delegation is an attempt to strike the right balance between a centralized system with a single person authorized to make launch decisions (with the risk of an unbalanced president ordering one) and the risk that this system will be vulnerable because it is so easy to decapitate, leaving no one in charge.

But if you decentralize the system, and delegate in advance the authority to launch nuclear weapons, haven't you created another beast? Haven't you put the ability to start a nuclear war in the hands of regional commanders who might turn out to be lone madmen like Kubrick's Colonel Jack D. Ripper? This solution just multiplies Major Hering's sanity question. As it is, since it is assumed that it is possible to destroy communication with silent-running nuclear-armed submarines, their captains must have some way to launch on their own authority if they believe the chain of command has been decapitated and retaliation is necessary. But if true, the actual mechanism is one of the best-kept secrets of our deterrent system. Mel Halbach, who served on a nuclear-armed submarine between 1975 to 1980, told me that crewmen were always discussing this challenge and found no answers, but that the responsibility of a launch weighed heavily on his captain. Such delegation authority is a problem that cuts two ways: it ensures that a decapitating attack would be answered. But it also makes a mockery of centralized control of nuclear weapons and puts us at the mercy of a nuclear sub commander or a crew member who may want to make his own foreign policy.

## "LAST RESORT"

Two years ago, I learned of a new twist on the pre-delegation concept. It is the one used by the U.K., the one known as the Letter of Last Resort. In late 2008, the BBC's Radio 4 broadcast a documentary about a handwritten letter penned by every new prime minister as soon as he takes office. Four copies of it are dispatched to the U.K.'s nuclear submarine fleet (the U.K. has gone to an all-submarine nuclear force). The sealed letter is to be locked inside a safe, which itself is locked inside a safe on the sub's control room floor. Both safes and the letter were only to be opened during certain specified conditions that indicate a nuclear attack has cut the submarine off from home island guidance. The prime minister's letter—the last resort for his decision on retaliation to prevail—is to tell the sub commander what he thought he should do with his nuclear weapons and under what circumstance he should fire them.

There is something seductive about this sort of ultimate secret hidden within a safe, something primal, mythical Grimm's fairy tale about it. And a safe within a safe redoubles the grimnoire quality of it all. But think about the complications: if the letter orders him to retaliate, then retaliate against whom? How massively? The submarine commander and his second in command, who were both authorized to read the Letter of Last Resort, could disagree with the prime minister, or with each other. And would any prime minister, any human being, write a letter ordering the unnecessary deaths of tens of millions of people, knowing he and his government and nation were most likely obliterated and genocidal punishment would not bring them back to life.

There are other complications. If the Letter of Last Resort is written by the prime minister upon accession to office, how would the prime minister know who is a likely attacker and why? And if the letter is only to be opened when the prime minister and a designated second are killed, how would a submarine commander know for sure that silence equaled death? London's *Daily Mail* reported that "there is a complicated series of checks that the submarine commander must perform to establish the true situation, one of which, curiously, is to determine whether Radio Four is still broadcasting." Oh great. The radio goes off the air and it's time to launch. I'm oversimplifying, I know. But again, when we hear of "checks and balances" we should (metaphorically) check for our wallets.

I asked David Murtagh, a senior officer in Her Majesty's Navy whom I'd met at the National War College seminar on deterrence, for confirmation that the Letter of Last Resort existed. This is what he eventually wrote me after he'd returned to the U.K.: "The U.K. MOD [Ministry of Defence] acknowledges that these letters exist but will not discuss them. On the chain of command issue, the U.K. MOD line is: 'As a relatively small country, the U.K. has a different requirement for an assured second-strike capability compared to other nations with nuclear weapons. The U.K.'s minimum nuclear deterrent, as the ultimate guarantor of national security, must be able to function irrespective of any preemptive action that may be taken by a potential aggressor. Critically, this must include an overwhelming "strike out of the blue." Such a strike might conceivably disable the Government's immediate ability to use communications links to exercise normal command and control.'"

Beneath this bland nondenial, in the submarine-depth subtext, was the assumption that the letters are instruments of deterrence invariably ordering retaliation. They give credibility to the threat of retaliatory attack and act as the "ultimate guarantor of national security," as the MOD puts it. The assumption of the British government in this statement is that no captain or crew would ask Major Hering's questions about the sanity or morality of such an order. There was no room for the possibility that a prime minister might write a letter saying he personally opposed wreaking pointless vengeance on tens of millions of people, or even that he was leaving it up to you, commander, or to you and your crew.

The response from the Ministry of Defence left me with more questions than answers about the U.K.'s chain of command and its nuclear intentions. Why would a nation with the Official Secrets Act allow this to leak unless it wanted it to? Did it believe that it reinforced deterrence? It seemed to be a deliberate attempt to create ambiguity that would cause a potential foe to ask: "Do I feel lucky?" It further obscured in uncertainty—to its own citizens— what its government was going to do in the event of nuclear war. To cite another movie: "You can't handle the truth."

In any case, in addition to Major Hering's question about the president's sanity, we now have the question raised by the Letter of Last Resort about the sanity of two dozen submarine commanders in the U.K. and the U.S. Because although the Pentagon refused to comment when I asked whether we have our own version of the Letter of Last Resort, some workaround seemed likely to be the case if our own Ohio-class submarines, the ones carrying nuclear missiles, are to act as deterrents. Otherwise we are inviting a decapitating strike.

The 2008 leak of the Letter of Last Resort's existence was another reminder that Major Hering's questions were not left behind with the end of the Cold War. In fact, thirty-five years after he asked them, they invite the Larger Sanity Question: What does all this say about the nature not just of our sanity but of our species? Is Faust our fate? Was there a tragic rendezvous between the DNA molecule and the unstable interior of the uranium nucleus? Was our scientific curiosity radioactive? Are the seeds of our own self-destruction encrypted in the intellectual genome? Is there something encoded in the schizoid nature of our collective consciousness that was destined to sync up with the fissile nature of the uranium nucleus so we could go crazy together? Is there something embedded in our very inquisitiveness that was destined to drive us to find some infallible, ineradicable way of making self-destruction possible?

It's a Question of Last Resort. In *War in Human Civilization*, the historian and anthropologist Azar Gat argues that there is a dark self-destructive strain in human nature, perhaps a now-maladaptive residue of what originally was an evolutionary valuable aggressiveness.

Political scientist Peter Berkowitz argues that the answer to how we ended up here, so close to hell, comes less from evolutionary psychology than from philosophy: "I sometimes think it's Hobbes versus Rousseau," some brutish nastiness built into us in a Hobbseian way, he told me.

I have begun to wonder about the power of apocalyptic narratives contained in so many major religions. I don't believe that any holy books were written by God. I don't believe in a Freudian death instinct. But I do believe the fact that the hand of man finds itself recurrently, obsessively scripting fiery, self-immolating cataclysmic conclusions to the human saga may well be, at the very least, self-fulfilling prophecy. It may also say that deep down, we really are a species obsessed with its own self-destruction—one that knows it deserves to be cleansed from the world, by fire this time.

# CHAPTER THREE

# THE FORBIDDEN QUESTION AT THE QWEST CENTER

H appy Hour at the nuclear deterrence symposium at Oma-
ha's Qwest Center, July 2009. I'm having a drink with
Hans Kristensen of the Federation of American Scientists.
"They're scared," he was telling me.

They didn't look scared to me, this massive convergence of the
nuclear weapons elite. Not even nervous. Frankly I felt more than
a little nervous having just asked a forbidden question of the U.S.'s
chief nuclear commander, Kevin P. Chilton, four-star general and
head of the U.S. Strategic Command that rules our nuclear weapons forces. A question about the morality of genocidal retaliation.
He hadn't looked scared. Puzzled maybe. (Who let this guy in?)
But not scared.

But Kristensen—one of the foremost investigators of the secret
innards of our nuclear war policies and co-author of an important
new treatise on "minimal deterrence" that argues the world would
be safer if the U.S. and the Russians could get their nukes down to
less than a hundred—gazed at the heavily be-medaled crowd and
concluded they collectively felt threatened by the new commander
in chief's declared goal of Zero. Nukes and their minders who had

once reigned serene and untroubled had suddenly been put on the defensive and forced to justify themselves. This massive convocation—despite its superficial air of optimism about the bright future of nuclear weapons—might be the equivalent of a show of force, the first act in a dramatic showdown over the future of these weapons.

Something about the STRATCOM nuclear convocation at the Qwest Center in Omaha recalled to me the *Canterbury Tales* pilgrimage. It's true Chaucer's was a pilgrimage of the (mainly) humble; there's a knight but no four-star-general types among them. But in each case the goal of the pilgrimage was the veneration of numinously powerful shrines, cathedrals founded on faith whose spires soared to the heavens and whose power came from the invisible secrets of creation. The fact that these were all *nuclear* warriors in one capacity or another endowed them with a kind of transcendent purpose. They were the guardians.

And so it was that in the last days of July 2009, from all corners of the earth, the major players, the worldly powers of the nuclear weapons establishment, had made a pilgrimage, undertaken a mission, a quest to Omaha's Qwest Center, the nearest gathering place to the shrine to our nuclear-tipped spires, the underground nuclear command center at nearby Offutt Air Force Base, beneath which was the cathedral of the Church of Nuclear Deterrence, the war room of our entire nuclear arsenal. The shrine of the faith-based doctrine it was built on: nuclear deterrence. It was a shrine that felt under siege by heretics, unbelievers. Besieged by Zero.

And so when STRATCOM—the United States Strategic Command, master of all America's nuclear assets—summoned the nuclear elite to the First Annual Strategic Deterrence Symposium, to bolster the bunker against Zero, the nuclear priesthood booked their flights.

I did too. What impelled me to return to Omaha was a feeling of unfinished business.

## THE DOOR THE LAUNCH KEYS UNLOCK

I'd first been there at the height of the Cold War. I'd been driven out to Offutt Air Force Base, then taken down far beneath the blast-proof super-hardened surface to the underground war room of the Strategic Air Command, the key node of U.S. nuclear war fighting.

Through a series of radiation-proof, sealed, and double-locked chambers I'd been ushered out onto the "Command Balcony" of the SAC war room. It was there that the general then in charge of the Strategic Air Command, in charge of all our nuclear-armed bombers and land-based missiles, would receive, on the so-called Gold Phone, the order, direct from the president, to launch a nuclear attack. After that, the SAC commander would pick up the Red Phone to convey the coded orders to the bomber pilots who would take to the air, and to the missile crewmen who would twist the launch keys in their slots and thereby execute whatever their targeting plan was. Execute—within less than an hour—tens, perhaps hundreds of millions of unarmed human beings on the other side of the planet.

The Command Balcony in the Omaha war room was the first stop on a strange and memorable odyssey that would end with my holding launch keys in my hand and twisting them—hard right for two full seconds—in test console slots so I could see how it felt, physically at least, to send thermonuclear death by the millions rocketing toward its victims.

It all started with the Major Hering story. It disappeared from the press, but for nearly a year I couldn't get it out of my mind and I persuaded Lewis Lapham at *Harper's* to assign me a piece about the case, the Larger Sanity question it raised, and the questions about command and control of the nuclear trigger.

Back then, the first thing I'd done was travel down to Washington and spent weeks immersing myself in the voluminous and disturbing transcripts of the congressional hearings on the nuclear command and control system, with particular emphasis on Professor Quester's questions about the system's flaws. Then I crossed the Key Bridge from Washington to the Pentagon where I presented many pages of scrawled questions to a gung ho Air Force information officer who—to my surprise—took them seriously and decided that the best way to reassure me about the efficacy and safety of the nuclear command and control system was to authorize access for me to the key nodes of its operation.

They let me take a seat in the "battle chair" on the Command Balcony that overlooked the theater-size radar and satellite screens of the war room, darkened for security reasons while I was there. (Omaha's Command Balcony has been the primal scene of so many nuke porn movies. Larry Lasker, who co-wrote the movie *WarGames*, told me they had based their scene there on my account of my visit. Though it's been mainly off limits to the press since 9/11, it still has an iconic presence: a Hollywood simulacrum of the Command Balcony made an appearance—Red Phone and all—in the 2010 Angelina Jolie thriller *Salt* whose climax was the attempt to start a nuclear war.) They let me pick up the Gold Phone and the Red Phone on the console in front of the battle chair, miming the act of ordering nuclear war, though hearing only a blank hum on the lines. They took me up into the "Looking Glass Plane," the airborne emergency nuclear war command post for the (presumably) evacuated president, from which he would direct the remains of our arsenal at the remains of our nuke-struck foe. They let me go down into the hollowed-out core of Cheyenne Mountain in Colorado, the Early Warning Center that would be the first to alert Omaha of an incoming nuclear attack, an alert that would then light up the president's "nuclear football." And then I was permitted to descend deep beneath the frozen prairie of the Great Plains to a Minuteman missile launch control center where two crew members in charge of some fifty thermonuclear ICBMs awaited the Armageddon order. And, finally, at another missile base I got to hold and twist the launch keys, the objective correlatives of the apocalypse.

To say I felt distinctly out of place in these environments would be an understatement, particularly considering my youthful ban-the-bomb activities (actually little more than mailing in membership requests to an indiscriminate variety of peacenik groups such as the Quaker-sponsored Fellowship of Reconciliation, the War Resisters League, and undoubtedly some anti-nuke communist fronts.)

It's true that after exposure to the foreign policy "realists" at Yale, with their sophisticated game theory analyses of nuclear strategy I'd become uneasily "sophisticated" myself. Or maybe "conflicted and torn" would be a better way of putting it. I hadn't learned to "love the bomb" à la *Strangelove* but I'd learned to live with it. Yet I still felt the lingering thrill of the "nuke porn" films and novels I'd devoured as an adolescent and which turned me into a peacenik, the ones like *Failsafe,* where the trembling world was brought to the brink of a cataclysmic nuclear climax, and *On the Beach,* the tragic romantic account of humanity's last post-nuclear war survivors expiring in a haze of radioactive tristesse.

Before long I'd graduated to the more hardcore studies, the work of the "nuclear intellectuals," the "wizards of Armageddon," as Fred Kaplan memorably called them. I found myself mesmerized by nuclear strategy literature, the nuke porn of the intellectuals, such stuff as Herman Kahn's *On Escalation,* with its deliberately bad-boy erectile language of a "ladder of escalation," 44 exquisitely calibrated steps that led to "all out spasm war" or, as he sometimes called it, "wargasm." I knew it was absurd in a Strangelovian way, but I also learned how absolutely real it was, beginning with my first visit to Omaha and my subsequent travels in what *Harper's* would title "The Subterranean World of the Bomb."

And by the time I arrived in Omaha the first time, I was torn between my youthful no-nukes instincts and my awareness of the peril of moral relativism inherent in a unilateral disarmament stance, whereby in a democracy you got to shout "No Nukes" while in a murderous police state, if you did, you likely died in a gulag. I found myself in a netherworld of tragic absurdity and moral confusion, and focused on the scandalous flaws in the fail-system: if we were going to have nukes we should make sure we knew how to prevent their unintended use.

It was only with the missile crewmen, after I twisted the keys, that I had a frank discussion of the great Forbidden Question at the heart of nuclear deterrence that had obsessed me since adolescence: the morality of nuclear retaliation. Would it be justice, vengeance, or pure genocide to strike back once the threat of deterrence failed?

But if you raise that question, especially in a place like this, this

Omaha Deterrence Symposium I was attending, if you make it an issue, aren't you paradoxically making an initial genocidal strike *more* likely by reducing the certainty of retaliation a foe might feel? This was a question that originated in the Cold War but had never been answered.

Still, I think I wouldn't have gone back to Omaha if it hadn't been for my close encounter with the launch keys, the keys to kingdom come. The keys themselves didn't seem extraordinary except in their low-tech ordinariness: they seemed curiously old-fashioned brassy-looking implements. Bates Motel–type keys, I recall thinking. Big keys with an ovoid hollow at the top, the better to grasp on to and twist. Twisting those keys, feeling the tensile strength of them, unlocked a door that I could never close again.

Only one other experience has had the kind of lasting effect that twisting the keys did: going to Hiroshima. Going to a place that had been on the receiving end of a twisted key did not have the immediate effect I thought it might. Its effect on me was slow-acting— like radiation poisoning of the soul. But it was undeniable. Lucy Walker, the director of a recent documentary about nuclear peril, *Countdown to Zero*, used the metaphor of the strange—at the time— fates of the radiation-poisoned survivors of Hiroshima. No obvious damage to many of them but radiation was eating away their lives from within. They became known as "walking ghosts." The presence of nuclear holocaust haunting the planet still makes us all a species of "walking ghost" waiting for our time to be up.

I tried to leave behind the nuclear realm after *Harper's* published the story. It had some small influence. Jonathan Schell, who would go on to write the classic of no-nukes polemics, *The Fate of the Earth*, told me he'd been influenced by it. I know the Air Force read it because they fixed the flaw in the two-key fail-safe system I disclosed and they invited me down to speak at the Air War College at Maxwell AFB in Alabama, an invitation I declined but which indicated the mixed messages the story conveyed. More disturbingly, the man who published the diagrams for the manufacture of a hydrogen bomb, Erwin Knoll, the late editor of *The Progressive*, who did so in the hopes of showing how easy it was in order to scare us into banning the bomb, told me he had been inspired to do it—despite an initial federal injunction against it—after reading my story. Great. Somebody builds and sets off a homemade thermonuclear device from diagrams in old issues of *The Progressive* and I'm responsible.

So here's the unfinished business I had left behind in Omaha: while I'd had some utterly fascinating conversations with the missile crewmen who would turn the keys about the morality of nuclear retaliation when the threat of deterrence failed I lacked the access and perhaps the nerve to ask that question of the men who would give the orders in Omaha.

Now I had the chance. Would I have the nerve to ask the nuclear commanders gathered here the Forbidden Question this time? The question about our willingness to commit retaliatory genocide, a question that had been an almost lifelong obsession for me?

## HAIR TRIGGER: OBAMA VS. THE GENERAL

Before I made my first approach to a member of the Pentagon's nuclear high command I got a feeling for the strength of the opposition Obama was up against. I heard it in nuclear supremo General Chilton's introduction to the morning's first panel. Nuclear deterrence had been very, very good to General Chilton's career. He had most recently been the commander of Air Force Space Command in Colorado, master of the hollowed-out mountain in Colorado where the Space Command's array of orbiting satellites would relay warnings of incoming missiles. And he had soared into space himself on several shuttle missions before becoming STRATCOM's Joint Functional Commander for Space and Global Strike and then boss of the whole nuclear operation. Until 1992 land- and submarine-based nuclear weapons, had been under separate commands, the Air Force and Navy. But a decision by the George H. W. Bush–era Pentagon in 1992 placed all of them under the Air Force's STRATCOM command at Offutt. This had the effect of making General Chilton—a slender, genial, balding man who didn't quite look the part—perhaps the single most powerful commander in U.S. history.

The nation's supreme nuclear commander opened the proceedings with an encomium to nuclear deterrence, nuclear weapons, and the challenging but bright future they faced, regardless of the president's dream. In full sky-blue uniform with four stars gleaming, ribbons covering his chest, General Chilton made light work of his commander-in-chief's goal of Zero. He barely paid it lip service and when he did, it was with barely constrained disdain. He talked about how radically different the new nuclear age was, with its new enemies ("transnational entities," "nonstate actors, or terrorists") and its new battlefields ("space and cyber-space"). He credited nuclear weapons and deterrence with preventing a conventional World War III for sixty-four years. "Was it just a coincidence?" he asked, the absence of a Third World War? (Some think it was, or at least a lucky accident.) Then he pronounced the conference to be about "how we wage deterrence in this new environment."

Note the verb: *wage* deterrence. "Waging" usually suggests physical armed combat, rockets' red glare, bombs bursting in air, at the very least a finger pushing a button or twisting a key. But with this kind of waging, we're really not lifting a finger, so much as—metaphorically, *conceptually*, doctrinally—wagging a finger: don't you dare, or else. We're waging war conceptually every moment we wage deterrence. Is waging deterrence, threatening genocide, different from waging wars? In some ways yes, we're waging war with a future, notional enemy. To oversimplify: a man who puts a gun to your head but doesn't pull the trigger is still using the gun.

Oh and yes, that Zero thing. Here's what the nation's nuclear commander had to say about the commander-in-chief's vision of Zero: "Regardless of whether you believe the idea that a nuclear weapons–free world is a possibility," General Chilton said dismissively, clearly indicating he was not one of those tie-dyed dreamers, "the reality is that nuclear weapons will be with us in the foreseeable future."

Again, an interesting choice of words, "foreseeable." The commander-in-chief had explicitly said he wanted to make it our national goal to make a nuclear-free world foreseeable. But the president's top nuclear general does not foresee it in the foreseeable future, and had nothing good to say about the value of making it foreseeable. He was all about making nuclear deterrence even more useful. Preserving, modernizing, "tailoring," sophisticating, reshaping, extending, enhancing deterrence—deterrence 2.0. That's what this conference was about. Getting the most out of our nukes, not getting rid of them. A common theme of the conference was that it was time—despite what some might say—to stop being ashamed of nuclear weapons and nuclear deterrence. They saved lives. Say it loud: We got nukes and we're proud.

It couldn't have been, in a coded low-key way, a more dramatic repudiation of the president.

General Chilton had already clashed openly with the president over a nuclear issue earlier that year. During the campaign, Obama had pledged "to change a situation in which our nuclear missiles are on hair-trigger alert." In January 2009, shortly before Obama's inauguration, General Chilton made a point of taking aim at that idea in a speech in Orlando in which he denied any of our weapons were on hair-trigger alert. "It is misleading to use the term 'hair-trigger' when describing the U.S. arsenal," which he said remains safe from accidental or unauthorized launch. "It conjures a drawn weapon in the hands of somebody," said the general, speaking at a two-day conference on air warfare. "And their fingers on the trigger. And you're worried they might sneeze, because it is so sensitive." The reality of our alert posture today, he said, "is that the weapon is in the holster." He explained that "it takes two people to open those locks," and "they can't do it without authenticated orders from the President of the United States."

General Chilton was cleverly redefining the semantic argument over what was, and what wasn't, "hair-trigger." He was saying that the guns can't be fired instantly without deliberation and proper orders. But the issue over the wording for our alert posture ("hair-trigger," "launch on warning," "launch on alert") goes to the question of whether, in the twenty years since a Cold War–kind of deadly hostility ended, we and the former Soviets have ever realistically de-alerted the land-based missile forces that still face off against each other.

At her confirmation hearing, Secretary of State designate Hillary Clinton said the incoming administration wants to end the Cold War practice of keeping intercontinental ballistic missiles ready for launch "at a moment's notice," though she added the proviso that this de-alerting must be done "in a mutual and credible manner."

According to the *Washington Post* account of Clinton's testimony, calls for previous administrations to take weapons off the hair-trigger alert "have failed because the Air Force thought its missile launch officers would lose their edge if they no longer did alert duty."

Sometimes it's too easy to see the absurdity in such pronouncements. Duty officers need to put the world in peril, need to maintain hair-trigger alert postures, so they will keep their edge? In other words, we need to put the world in peril to do what a cup of black coffee could do. Maybe what the Pentagon needs for duty officers is better baristas—but that's one worthy of the Catch-22 file.

How about de-alerting nukes so duty officers won't have to be on edge, as if on edge is the main thing you want your officer to be, tremors and spasms of nervousness shaking his being as he tries to decide whether a blip on the radar screen requires an "assessment conference."

The fact is we have de-targeted our missiles, but in a way that's easy to re-target: we have just removed, say, the Moscow-specific GPS codes from the interior of the missile software. But the codes still exist on the missile base computers and just need a nanosecond burst of code to aim the missile again, according to Bruce Blair. So de-alerting is a sham, and so is de-operationalizing missiles. What that means is that a missile is separated from its warhead. But in practice, the warheads are often stored on the same base, where they can be reassembled fast.

Worse than sham de-targeting, and sham dismantling, though, is that we've never de-alerted. Our alert time is generally thought to be fifteen minutes or less because that is the window between the moment radars or satellites pick up the launch by an offshore nuclear submarine, and detonations on or above coastal cities like Washington and New York. We have fifteen minutes to decide whether—on the basis of radar and satellite traces—to pull the

trigger. If that's not hair-trigger, it doesn't exactly leave much time
for contemplation. In some cases it could even allow us to justify a
launch upon the simultaneous confirmation of what the Air Force
likes to call, probably because it sounds so super-scientific, "dual
phenomenology." Which just means two sources of signals: radar
and satellite. They are the two types of technology that are supposed to be able to tell us whether the "missiles" being tracked on
an attacking path toward us are real or not. Officially, our policy is
called "launch under attack." But, our de facto policy with only fifteen minutes warning time is "launch on warning," since the fifteen-minute warning window will put us in a "use it or lose it"
situation: we need to fire those missiles out of their silos before
they are destroyed while they are still in them. Thus we have a policy in which a launch can be triggered by pixels on a screen rather
than unmistakable real missiles.

This hair-trigger issue provokes hair-trigger tempers in the
Pentagon, as General Chilton's extraordinary decision to discuss
launch policy in public in order to rebuke the president demon-
strates. To sum up a long debate, it all depends on what you mean
by hair-trigger. If you think people using the phrase are attribut-
ing to us the ability for something like the instantaneous firing of a
gun that already has the safety off and the trigger cocked, then our
nuclear posture is not hair-trigger. But if you think the ability to
get our missiles off with less than fifteen minutes notice on potentially ambiguous or unconfirmed warning data in such a hectically
compressed interval that you might be justified in using the phrase
hair-trigger for it, I wouldn't disagree.

General Chilton's performance at the conference was one clue
that it was one giant pushback against Obama's Zero. But so was
the essay I found in *Strategic Quarterly*, the STRATCOM journal
handed out to everyone who registered in Omaha. It was written
by the first panel's moderator, Dr. Keith Payne.

Dr. Payne is officially the head of the double-plus bland-
sounding National Institute for Public Policy, a Beltway think tank
that focuses on national security. But in fact he belongs to the new
generation of sophisticated nuclear hawks who have not gotten the

attention of the showy Cold War "wizards of Armageddon" such as Herman Kahn.

The highly controversial 2001 Nuclear Posture Review, the first in the George W. Bush administration, reflected ideas Dr. Payne had been nurturing and promoting during the '90s when many nuclear strategists had abandoned the field. His ideas became Bush's nuclear policy.

Many of these ideas were criticized by the liberal arms control community for lowering the nuclear threshold, expanding the possibility of first use of nuclear strikes on nonnuclear powers and rogue states. Dr. Payne is also one of those who kept alive the sputtering flame for the space-based ballistic missile defense known as Star Wars, whose promise was that it could shoot down missiles aimed at our nation. He did so on ethical grounds, arguing it was immoral not to take active measures to protect your noncombatant citizens. He took the lead in advocating junking the antiballistic missile treaty (ABM), which is what happened in 2002, and became a tireless advocate of nuclear "bunker busters," those Robust Nuclear Earth Penetrators" designed to take out "hard and deeply buried targets."

You could think of him as a second-generation Dr. Strangelove, or a less flamboyant but more effective Herman Kahn, the man on whom Dr. Strangelove is partly based. In fact, I first heard his name in a conversation I had a year before the Deterrence Symposium with Max Singer, who was a founding partner of Herman Kahn's Hudson Institute. Singer himself was still in the game. He was working on a government contract involving ballistic missile defense that had run into the problem of balloon decoys. Ballistic missile defense advocates still had to contend with metal-covered balloon decoys that attacker missiles could release to make targeting a nightmare. Baloonacy, if you ask me. Singer said Dr. Payne was the nuclear intellectual of the moment. And as I discovered by reading his work, he was a razor-sharp polemicist—so good at articulating the value of nuclear weapons that I began to think of "the Payne effect."

His essays seemed so well argued that I would begin to forget that the whole system he was defending involved a logic that led one to accept the necessity of placing the entire population of the world, or the Northern Hemisphere anyway, in jeopardy of multiples of a hundred Hiroshimas. What fascinated me was how different an attitude he had toward nuclear weapons. They had feelings. Dr. Payne felt their pain. In the closing section of the essay handed out at that conference, he wrote: "Winston Churchill warned, 'Be careful above all things not to let go of the atomic weapon until you are sure and more than sure that other means of preserving peace are in your hands!' There is no known basis for concluding that those other means are at hand or that threats to peace will disappear. Until then embracing nuclear disarmament seriously as the priority U.S. goal should be recognized as entailing the serious risk of further vilifying those U.S. forces that may be important to deter future wars, assure allies, and help contain nuclear proliferation."

"Vilifying" nuclear forces! The *nerve*! Some would just look at their capacity to kill 10 or 20 million people at a time as a bit of an obstacle to celebrating them. But Dr. Payne nearly implied it was "the forces" themselves, meaning the bombs, that were being vilified. They had feelings too! By saying don't vilify nukes or those who command them, he's actually performing an act of intellectual daring: sympathy for the devil. He is opening up the possibility that they deserve more than a defensive crouch in polite company, a cringe away from the light, but the thanks of a grateful nation.

Being good to our nukes was a subtext of the conference. Virtually everyone there was pushing the development of a generation of more technically advanced nukes that went under the rubric of the RRW, the Reliable Replacement Warhead. Dr. Payne is big on this. The RRW people depict the current generation of warheads as aging, decrepit, and decaying despite the so-called Life Extension Program, the LEP, initiated in 2003 by the Energy Department, which is officially in charge of nuclear warhead production. The LEP was meant to prolong the utility of the current Cold War–era warheads rather than spend trillions on a whole new set of high-tech nukes. Dr. Payne and his cohorts love the RRW because if they were developed, they would need to be tested, and there would be no need to ratify the Comprehensive Nuclear Test Ban treaty, which the Senate initially rejected in 1999.

## THE FOG OF "FOGBANK"

The whole issue of what to do with our aging nuclear warheads is at the heart of of the mysterious FOGBANK Controversy. It arose from a 2008 leak in a nuclear industry magazine about difficulties being experienced in the Life Extension Program in the key nuke-making lab known as Pantex, in Amarillo, Texas. In February of that year, the Energy Department announced that it had accepted the first of the new life-extended nukes, but in late May, *Global Security Newswire,* a valuable source for collecting reports on nuclear weapons developments, reported that Pantex was having difficulty delivering the actual refurbished weapons. The claim was that those working on refurbishing old nukes under the LEP were running into trouble because they had lost the know-how, skill, secret formula—it wasn't clear—to make an ingredient necessary to hydrogen bombs, an ingredient evocatively code-named FOG-BANK. "I don't know how it developed that we forgot how to make FOGBANK," said an Energy Department spokesman without irony.

There has been a fog of war surrounding what FOGBANK is, and whether the problem about producing it had been solved. But the hawks used the development as an alarming example of the loss of "intellectual infrastructure" we had suffered from not giving enough TLC to our nukes. In November 2009 a Pentagon-sponsored panel, having reviewed the aging warhead Life Extension Program, announced that the program was working and would until the foreseeable future, FOGBANK or no FOGBANK.

The hawks may have experienced a minor setback, having failed to kill Life Extension, so to speak. But they were girding for the real showdown with Obama in Omaha. And I was girding myself to ask the generals there the Forbidden Question I'd put to the missile crewmen, the ones who showed me their launch keys at the Minuteman silo launch control center during the Cold War. Their answer had haunted me ever since.

## THE MUTANT BUNNY RABBIT MOMENT

That encounter had occurred shortly after Easter 1977 in the ready room, the plywood paneled concrete rec room with the soda and candy machines where missileers got ready to be shuttled out to their underground command silo, deep beneath the earth amid the silo farm of missile-size shafts sunk in the prairie that housed, beneath hardened domes, the actual one-megaton thermonuclear warhead–bearing missiles.

A handful of missile crewmen was awaiting the shift change. They showed me the test console that had been set up to prepare for some competitive missile crew Olympics (seriously) that would be held at Vandenberg Air Force Base the following month. They let me handle the launch keys, they showed me how to twist them in their slots "hard to the right and hold for two seconds." Two seconds and there they go.

I've always wondered about that two-second hold. Evidence of deliberate action; yes, they really meant it. That was the original point one imagines: no accidental key turning. But two seconds: time for deliberation? For hesitation? For remorse? What does one think when one is about to kill 20 million people with the twist of a key. Are two seconds enough—or just not enough—time to think: what am I doing?

They were a good-natured bunch, kind of like nerdy frat boys, the missileers, in their dark blue jumpsuits and shiny military-style ascots, but I still felt ill at ease asking them an uncomfortable question: What's the point of carrying out the threat of retaliation, and committing genocide once the threat of deterrence has failed?

"One thing you have to assume," a lanky missileer answered, "is that when I get an authenticated launch order I have to figure my wife and kids would be dead already up above. The base is ground zero. Why shouldn't I launch? The only thing I'd have to look forward to if I ever got up to the surface would be romping around with huge mutant bunny rabbits."

We all laughed. I'm not sure how funny it is in retrospect. It was a metaphor, it was black humor, he didn't believe mutation occurred overnight. But it captured the absurdity of the horror they had learned somehow to be stoic about. My family is dead, there's going to be nothing for me up there, so why not slaughter tens of millions of families on the other side of the world for no useful purpose?

Every time I thought back to the mutant bunny rabbits I wondered whether I should have felt more censorious about him taking it so lightly, but I think now it was his way of dealing with—insulating himself from—what lay beneath. The bunny rabbits were a distraction from the dead family, his dead children. He did not say it with even a hint of vengeful rage at the murder of his family "up above." It came with the territory. It just didn't seem real. And if it didn't seem real to the man who would launch the missiles then, how real does it feel now?

I nervously persisted with questions of the missile crewmen: "Okay, if you assume that when you get the launch order everyone on our side has been devastated by a Soviet first strike, is there any purpose served by destroying what's left of humanity by retaliating purely for revenge?"

One of the crewmen took what seemed like a more serious approach than the mutant bunny rabbit.

"What it all comes down to," he said, "is the Judo-Christian ethic."

"You mean Judeo-Christian?" one of the other missile crewmen said.

To this day I'm not sure if "Judo-Christian" was a malapropism, a kind of martial arts interpretation of the scriptures, or an equally deliberate send-up of them. But he stuck to "Judo," perhaps conflating the martial art with the "eye-for-an eye" revenge dictum in the Old Testament.

"Right, like I said," he continued, "the Judo-Christian ethic teaches that you never strike first, but if someone hits you, you can strike back."

Looking back on it, "Judo-Christian" had a touch of the humor in Terry Southern's dialogue for Sterling Hayden's Colonel Jack D. Ripper to it.

I skipped over the Judo/Judeo matter and raised the question of Christianity, which, at least in the eye of those such as Hamlet, frowns upon revenge (as does Judaism with "vengeance is mine, sayeth the Lord" as the final word on the subject).

What about then President Jimmy Carter, I asked the crewmen, a self-professed born-again Christian, certainly well aware of the Bible's instructions to "turn the other cheek" and "love thy enemy" despite having served on a nuclear submarine. He was president at the time. I asked the crewmen to imagine they were Carter and "for some reason the Soviets are tempted to strike or preempt our strike. You see those missiles coming in on the radar screen and know mass murder is about to happen to your people and there's nothing you can do to stop it. Is there any point in committing another act of mass murder in return? You might succeed in exacting revenge, but you might not even succeed in killing those responsible for the attack while meanwhile you murdered tens of millions who had nothing to do with it."

Looking back on it I was implicitly accusing these crewmen of willing complicity in potential mass murder.

The response that ended the discussion was this: "You think he should surrender?" one of the crewmen asked me.

"I don't know," I said, taken aback by the abruptness of his question. That would be surrender, wouldn't it, however ethically, morally, and theologically correct?

Surrender. In 1958 Congress had actually passed a resolution forbidding the use of any defense appropriations to think tanks for the study of "surrender." It was a silly resolution prompted by the discovery that a RAND Corporation analyst had done a paper on "strategic surrender," a comparative historical examination of how nations that surrendered in war had nonetheless found ways to maximize their position. It argued, among other things, that the French in 1940, for instance, had done better than expected in their surrender negotiations while the Germans at Versailles turned a truce into a humiliating surrender, even though their military situation was far stronger than France's a generation later. The main result of the congressional move was the development of a euphemism for surrender in the nuclear strategy community: "war termination." It continued to be studied and generated a black-humored joke by Henry Kissinger in his 1960 book *On Nuclear War* where, in the index under "Surrender," the reader finds "See victory, Total."

But for another crewman in the group, twisting the keys was not a matter of genocide or surrender, but part of a routine in a day's work. "That's the thing you know," this other crewman said, "Once you start thinking about all that your head starts going in circles. You got to change the subject. There's a point where you gotta stop asking questions and go to work. You've got to have faith that you're doing the right thing. It all comes down to professionalism. We know our presence here helps deter war and . . ."

My source on Cold War nuclear submarine culture, Mel Halbach, who is making a documentary based on interviews with his fellow crewmen, says that they never stopped talking about the question of their inevitably genocidal retaliatory mission, and that the Navy never stopped worrying about whether they would actually follow a launch order because, he says, so many peaceniks joined the Navy to escape the draft. He recalls that every serious launch-related drill was executed with officers wearing guns and that a tommy gun was always present at the entrance to the engine room, for fear that crew would refuse to launch.

In that bunker on that day, the missile men disclosed to me something I thought at the time was subversive: it turns out, they said, that it is possible to get around the fail-safe system that requires two men at some distance from each other to turn two keys simultaneously in order to launch a nuclear attack. For years I misinterpreted their revelation of the workaround as an act of rebellion. But they saw it as an instance of professionalism of the highest order.

The way the system worked at the time of my visit was that down in each of the underground launch control centers was a crew of two men who mainly sat at consoles awaiting the possibility of an alert or a launch order. They spent days going through endless drills in which they had to perform every item in a checklist of readiness, up to twisting their keys in the launch slots.

Each of the two-man crew in the launch control capsule underground was assigned a key. Once they got the launch order they would feed the targeting codes into the missiles under their control, and then, when they'd been given the final go-ahead and made the final confirmation of the authenticity of the launch order, each of them would twist his key.

There was one condition. They had to twist them virtually simultaneously. And the two launch consoles with the key slots were built a distance apart, which kept one crewman from, say, twisting his own key with his left hand and reaching over to twist the other key with his right hand. In other words, he could not accomplish a launch alone.

But the missile crewmen told me they had come up with a way around this, which they called the "spoon-and-string" trick. Here is how it works: First shoot or immobilize the other crewman. Then tie a long string to the handle of a spoon. Insert your launch key in your slot and the other launch key into the other guy's slot, and tie the other end of the string to the other launch key's top. Go back to your launch console and then twist your key at the same time that you yank the spoon and string forcefully enough to twist the other key in sync with yours.

When I first heard about it, it seemed like a fairly serious flaw in the fail-safe system that would allow a lone genocidally homicidal maniac to launch missiles. I assumed that was what prompted them to warn me about the makeshift spoon-and-string maneuver. But in fact what motivated the crewmen to come up with the trick was not the risk that a madman would launch an attack alone, but that, as one of them said to me, "one of the guys turns peacenik and refuses to twist his key." One of the guys turns peacenik!

I later learned from Bruce Blair, who had been a congressional investigator on missile command and control issues, that nuclear engineers have reconfigured the launch control consoles so that it is no longer possible for the spoon-and-string trick to work.

The point of the story is professionalism. I had assumed the crewmen had told me about the spoon-and-string maneuver because they knew I was a reporter and would alert the outside world that the fail-safe system had a flaw. But they were telling me the story because it demonstrated how determined they were to find a way to make an authorized launch work even if one of the crewmen "turned peacenik." They were being professionals. To me, however, there was a larger, metaphorical point to the story too: that the entire sophisticated fail-safe system, designed to assure the smooth operation of the finely crafted delicate balance of terror, was really founded on the kind of tricky legerdemain that evoked a shakily improvised spoon-and-string trick.

## GENERAL ALSTON'S MORAL CALCULUS

And so thirty years later in Omaha, I found myself staring across the bagel- and muffin-heaped buffet table at an imposing figure whose ID badge identified him as Major General C. Donald Alston, a large, somewhat florid-faced man in full-dress Air Force uniform. I checked my program and discovered he was a high-level official in the Pentagon's "Strategic Deterrence and Nuclear Integration" division. A liaison between Pentagon war planners who select the targets and the Omaha executioners of our nuclear war plans. A perfect person to ask the Forbidden Question about retaliatory genocide.

I began the conversation by asking Alston about the Minot mistake in August 2007. Trying to begin on an anodyne note, I asked him about the discrepancy in reports of whether there were five or six nuclear cruise missiles involved. Six, he affirmed.

General Alston had been involved in the investigation and he made heads roll. The chief of staff of the Air Force was fired along with dozens on the chain of command below him. Disturbing flaws were found in the maintenance of our "backup and stored" nuclear warheads. Military chat rooms spoke of the way the Minot mistake resulted from the fact that nukes were no longer a great career path for an aspiring Air Force officer. Alston was promoted to the Pentagon's nuclear planning team right after shaking things up.

"Say deterrence fails," I finally asked the major general. "If we get attacked, a surprise attack. What in your view is the morality of retaliation at that point?"

"Well it's awfully hard for you to—I mean this is the first time I've heard the scenario laid out like that."

This was kind of shocking in itself. How could you not ask your-self that question? Or how could it not have come up in the course of a career like his?

He went into a somewhat puzzling digression on the buildup to a nuclear crisis. That we probably wouldn't be a victim of genu-inely surprising surprise attack. A red herring. So what if it's not a total surprise?

"I do find it hard to accept that we would be so incompetent on the intelligence side, reading the geopolitical elements. I think that this would be a moment that would build up in a crisis and that through that crisis we would be going for some way to achieve geo-political stability as you're escalating and escalating.

"I mean," he continued, "if we were attacked by a nuclear weapon is it launched from—I mean do we have the forensics"?

Ah yes, "the forensics." Nuclear forensics is a very sophisticated science that claims to be able to identify the "isotope signature" or "fingerprints" of trace metals and fissile material and thus fol-low the bomb back to the precise source of the bomb making. It is about finding the radioactive fingerprints of the weapon maker in the rubble of the blast.

The problem, in this new multipolar, chaos-prone, terrorist-haunted nuclear age, is that nuclear forensics is a kind of deceptive science. It can trace the origin of the bomb, but not whose hands it went through, who sold or stole it between its manufacture and its detonation. So whom do you retaliate against? Some say hold the source, the state of origin responsible, regardless of the end user, which will motivate the source to keep a tight rein on nuclear mate-rial. Others are not sure it's a reliable way of protecting against such an eventuality, that nuclear forensics are overrated.

General Alston changes the subject from nuclear forensics to nuclear public relations.

He wants to make sure any attack on us is well publicized. "I mean how exposed was the use of nuclear weapons," he asked, rhe-torically, "so that the world could see where this came from, so that now the world could see what it did and so that now the world is awaiting our response to it."

"Well let's assume all that is true, our choice still is to retaliate and maybe kill 20 million civilians or not. What's your opinion?"

"Well I guess in the position I'm in I'd say . . . I would say response in kind." Interesting that he doesn't suggest that it's necessarily what he believes is right himself. It's "the position I'm in." Something he seems to confirm when he speaks of the "pressure" to respond "in kind" as if it were not something he welcomed.

"I think there would be pressure for response in kind. I think the nation would have an expectation that had to be an option the president would seriously consider."

Without prompting he brings up the difficulty of deciding what "in kind" would mean.

"What would be—how would you do the calculus on what response in kind would be? So I think that [response in kind] would be one course of action but that he [the president] wouldn't be brought a singular course of action." In other words, he'd have options other than retaliation.

If I'm reading this right and I relistened to the tape, he's showing a reluctance to retaliate. He's positing that the difficulty of calculating what "in kind" means serves to discredit it as an option. Did I find a peacenik general?

It comes down to a moral calculus. Should it be purely numerical? Should it be based on the number of warheads times megatons per warhead that we're hit with? Or on the number of casualties? Or on the intention of the targeting: to attack military capabilities or population centers.

What does "in kind" really mean? Should it be qualitative and ethical as well as quantitatively appropriate: should the immorality of the initial attack require no mere tit for tat, or twice the tat, to punish the initiator—the way a jury awards actual and punitive damages? Here, punitive damages for initiating evil. A punishment that would deter further acts of evil. But would the punishment fit the crime or would the punishment itself be a crime? And would it all be too late?

The major general sought to minimize the possibility of a large-scale great power nuclear confrontation version of the problem in the post–Cold War era.

"What is the purpose, what is the advantage being sought in a great power attacking another great power?" he asked.

"It's totally illogical, I agree, but there are madmen and also we live in an age of suicidal martyrdom," I said.

"Sure, but then you've got to change the scenario," he said.

"Well let's go back to the suicidal madman," I said, thinking of Kim Jong-il of North Korea.

"Well that's too hard for me," he said, sounding a little hostile.

"You never war-gamed that?" I asked.

"Well we war-gamed it and then, unfortunately, I think we stopped the war game as soon as there was an exchange. And there's typically an exchange." Meaning a nuclear one.

"Simultaneous?"

"No," he said. "The big debate is, do you wait? Wait and shoot or do you shoot while they're en route? But we stopped the war games. Now we're starting to get more aggressive in war games. To really work through the geopolitical consequences."

I think what he meant by being "more aggressive in war games" was carrying them through to the bitter end, but I must admit thinking to myself: isn't it a little late in the game for all that?

General Alston is all about improving the war games, though: "Bring in real policymakers. Typically not the guy in the job but the guy who had the job. I think our thinking needs to be more fresh. It needs to be more integrated in how you try to get through this."

Wait a minute, I found myself thinking to myself. I'm talking to the Pentagon's assistant chief of staff, Strategic Deterrence and Nuclear Integration Headquarters, and he's telling me they stopped the war games before contemplating the calculus of retaliation? They have to make the war games more aggressive. What kind of effete, namby-pamby nuclear war games have been going on up until now?

Then he said: "In my job I have no propensity for response in kind."

He repeats: "In my experience I have no propensity for a knee-jerk response in kind. They achieved their objective, what would be our objective in our reply?"

I felt a little uncomfortable. My badge said "journalist." I had introduced myself as writing a book on nuclear questions. I was holding up my tape recorder. And yet here was one of the Pentagon's top nuclear people rather blithely telling me that if he had his druthers he wouldn't retaliate. At least "in kind."

Not with nukes, at least. He would retaliate with shame. He would show the world our injuries. Or was he saying we wouldn't retaliate immediately, we would first prepare the groundwork, establish the moral high ground—and unleash the dogs of cable TV?

"It could be in this day and age with cable TV with fantastic transmission and all this stuff, if there was a way, and there is a way, to collect every piece of information, if we could project out there that this attack was an unprovoked attack. So that there's such world attention on how the injured . . . the United States intends to respond, but there is a great deal of extraordinarily difficult decisions and there's got to be cases for alternative decisions other than just nukin' 'em back.

"With such world support, why would the United States take a course of action A, B, C? So I think that you just can't uncomplicate this."

True, you can't decide until you know the specifics. But I found it difficult to uncomplicate his answer. The cable TV offensive would substitute for "just nukin' 'em back"?

Right, sic Fox News on the attacker. That would show them! And Olberman: Worst Country in the World! That would hurt. So it would be part of the retaliatory strategy, a media offensive to lay the groundwork for the genocide to come? Or the stiff U.N. resolutions condemning the attack?

Things got a little testy between the general and me when I sought to lead up to the "ambiguities of warning" question and we started to discuss what I called the "ride-out doctrine." Do we have enough confidence in the hardening of our missile silos so that we can adopt a launch on attack alert posture? "Launch on attack" means we don't have to rely on dual phenomenology warnings with their risk of triggering a mistaken response. And we believe that enough of our missiles would survive attacks on our silos for us to retaliate "in kind." And so we ride out an attack and then assess its damage and our surviving assets and what to target for retaliation. We avoid a launch on warning with its risk of mistakenly starting a nuclear war based on false pixels. Our official policy had been the ride-out.

So I decided to ask the general: "Are we still on a ride-out doctrine, in other words we wait till we hit to return fire?" That seemed to be the implication of his cable TV offensive.

"I don't know what doctrine you're talking about," he said.

I was momentarily stunned. It's pretty common parlance in nuclear circles.

"By ride-out, I mean launch on attack," I said, not just on warning.

"I have never felt, I mean there is no doctrine that rides out or preempts or any of that. In fact I think there's ambiguity. That's the term."

"So you can't answer the question is what you're saying," meaning for security reasons. He seemed to take it the wrong way.

"Well I don't think you've asked a good question."

"What would be a good one?" I asked. "How about this: there's an assessment conference, dual phenomenology says we're in a use it or lose it situation . . ."

"Well we have a balanced triad, you know, to the point that what you'll do is certainly lose a part of your force but we have distributed that risk across these varied capabilities." What he means is that we are not necessarily in a use it or lose it situation because we have nukes attached to our submarines and bombers. He says, "But I understand your scenario."

I was glad to hear we were on the same page, at least in some respects. Frankly I think he knew exactly what ride-out was, but didn't want to erase the ambiguity about whether we would be reluctant to launch on warning.

I spent the rest of the day, indeed much of the rest of the conference, buttonholing leading nuclear figures of this and other nations with that same forbidden question: what happens if deterrence fails and you have to decide whether to kill millions of innocent civilians because you threatened to? None would foreswear genocidal retaliation.

My favorite answer came from the Chinese representative, Senior Colonel Yao Yunzhu, who was described in the program as having been "awarded the title of 'March 8th Red Banner' and in 2006 was nominated as a candidate for 'China's Sixth Annual Top Ten Excellent Women.'" When I asked Colonel Yao what would happen if deterrence failed her nation, she smiled sweetly and said, "Deterrence will not fail."

But the top U.S. nuclear commander was not as serene about it all as the excellent woman from China. It was just before the Happy Hour of the first day that I finally cornered General Chilton, the head of STRATCOM.

Actually I didn't corner him. He was standing in the long corridor of the Qwest Center that linked the ballroom where the panels had been held and the Happy Hour bar set up. Someone was bending his ear but at last I had my chance. At last I got to The Man. The Supreme Nuclear Commander. General Chilton.

I moved in, introduced myself and asked him The Question:

"What if deterrence fails, we are attacked deliberately by a peer power or a near–peer power. Is there any point in retaliation and killing 20, 40 million people once the threat of retaliation has failed?"

"That's a very interesting question," he said, "and if you contemplate the question you must face some vision of what the world order would look like after a nuclear attack. And whether it mattered."

Fascinating, ambiguity again.

"But the other thing you have to be cautious about when discussing a philosophical or, truly, hypothetical, question is that you don't send a mixed signal that would confuse anybody about your intention. Your will."

In other words to talk about whether we will, or should, retaliate is to invite a foe to think there's a chance we won't and thus make an attack more likely.

"So it's a terrible paradox," I said.

"It is. It is a paradox. You're exactly right. It's a moral one. I know that every president of the United States since we invented this massive retaliation capability, has lost sleep over this."

"Have you?"

"Um." He laughed. "Not till I got this job."

There was so much contained in his remarks: The use of "massive retaliation" is not a fashionable term anymore, but it tripped off his tongue. He conceded it was a moral question. He hinted retaliation might not be automatic. He warned about the paradox.

He said both he and the president lose sleep over this choice.

And that's not the only reason to lose sleep.

# CHAPTER FOUR

# THE NUMBER

D oes "the number" change things—the number of those who will die in a nuclear war? Does a greater magnitude of mortality entail a different mode of morality (or immorality)? It was sometime in 1961 that Daniel Ellsberg, then an attaché in John F. Kennedy's Defense Department, asked the Joint Chiefs of Staff a forbidden question: how many would die in a nuclear war under the current nuclear war plan?

The answer he got still haunts him nearly a half-century later; it was to be a focus of our breakfast meeting in New York in September 2009. Ellsberg had looked me up on a visit to New York. He had a question to ask me about the spoon-and-string maneuver. He wanted to talk about command and control issues. He was a command and control aficionado. He had been there on the ground floor of command and control of nukes planning. Now he had newly declassified documents about predelegation to discuss. As always he was obsessed.

Ellsberg is the man made famous, of course, for leaking the Pentagon Papers to the *New York Times* in order to expose the deceitful, secret behavior of two successive Democratic administrations that led us into Vietnam. He was in New York for the premiere of a documentary on his life called *The Most Dangerous Man in America*. The title "Most Dangerous Man" came from the words Henry Kissinger spoke to Richard Nixon in the White House shortly after Ellsberg had been exposed as the source of the Pentagon Papers. The documentary uses Kissinger's quote somewhat opportunistically since the film focuses mainly on the Pentagon Papers and elides over the likelihood that Kissinger did not call Ellsberg "the most dangerous man" because of the Pentagon Papers leak. The papers were already out and they mostly implicated the opposition party. He used the phrase for another kind of secret, a more dangerous one. The danger Kissinger was speaking of, the danger that led Nixon to risk and lose the presidency because he gave his blessing to a break-in at Ellsberg's psychiatrist's office and lied about it—was something else. Something that few knew about Ellsberg at the time: his nuclear past.

Few aside from Nixon and Kissinger knew, in fact, how close Ellsberg had been to the most secret of nuclear war secrets, and how easily he could have spilled them. Ellsberg knew or had known America's "above-top-secret," super-classified nuclear war plans— and he had been the first person to seek out the Number.

When I met Ellsberg for that breakfast in 2009, he was bearing his armload of declassified documents and he still seemed to be bearing, even more burdensomely, the guilt of a penitent.

He was spending a lot of time uploading hundreds of these documents to his Web site, all the while writing new installments of a memoir on the fly, running as if time were running out, for him and for us.

At seventy-eight, his metabolism was certainly in high gear. We met in the bleak and chilly concrete courtyard "garden" of the Wyndham Garden Hotel, a budget tour-group destination in a warehouse neighborhood near Penn Station where he was staying with his wife, Patricia. Ellsberg had piled his plate high from the breakfast buffet and was devouring a mountain of eggs, bacon, sausages, fried potatoes, waffles, the works, although he's thin as a wire and just as electrified. If no longer the Most Dangerous Man in America, he may be the hungriest.

Indeed hunger is the word. Ellsberg seems a haunted man, hungry for something more than food, with the burning eyes of a heretic priest, dark circles under them the only signs of exhaustion. He is hungry more than anything for penitence, to exorcise his guilt, his sense of complicity in plans for genocide. His conscience, anyway his feeling of guilt, is his shirt of Nessus, the mythical garment that was a gift to Hercules but which when donned burst into unquenchable flame and adhered to his back until the agony caused Hercules to immolate himself on a funeral pyre. I've often thought of the black briefcase nuclear football as the president's shirt of Nessus, the way it adheres to him every moment of his life in office. For Ellsberg his shirt of Nessus is his ineradicable nuclear past.

Ellsberg feels the fire. He's wired with intensity, from his gray curls to his spring-trap mind. I would call it electricity but it's more like radioactivity.

In fact, before he became an antiwar dissident Ellsberg had been the very model of a rising young Strangelove. He had studied nuclear strategy at Harvard under the Yoda of nuclear strategists, Thomas Schelling. This is no small matter. Ellsberg was—and still is—awed by Schelling's brilliance. He was seduced by the strategists, the so-called Wizards of Armageddon who introduced "scientific" game theory to nuclear war strategy and locked us into its logic. Schelling is credited with developing the use of "calculated irrationality" in nuclear war game theory. The History News Web site quotes Tyler Cowen, one of Schelling's former students at Harvard, who explained Schelling's irrational-behavior theory relative to nuclear deterrence this way: "Ever see *Dr. Strangelove*? Tom [Schelling] developed the idea that deterrence is never fully credible. (Why retaliate once you are wiped out?) The best deterrent might involve pre-commitment [e.g., the Doomsday Machine] some element of randomness, or a partly crazy leader [e.g., a madman such as General Ripper]. I recall Tom telling me he was briefly an advisor to Kubrick." Fascinating, the master strategist's parenthetical dismissal of retaliation!

After Harvard, and after serving in the Marines, Ellsberg put his war game training in the service of the RAND Corporation, the legendary Santa Monica–based nuclear war think tank, then a Pentagon-financed entity. He was the prototype of the civilian nuclear strategist, a "defense intellectual" who helped provide the flyboys of the Air Force with the intellectual heft they needed to muscle their way into control over most nukes in the early 1960s, and give the Air Force's nukes, intercontinental missiles based in underground silos, primacy in the American arsenal over the ones loaded on submarines. The Air Force victory in making land-based missiles the heart of our nuclear strike force was one of the worst, most dangerous decisions of the first nuclear age: it created a vast apparatus of highly vulnerable, hair-trigger lethality beneath the badlands of the U.S. and the steppes of the U.S.S.R.

Ellsberg was dangerous because he had been on the inside, all the way inside, before he stepped out of bounds with the Pentagon Papers. He would eventually sum up his studies in the art of nuclear blackmail in a RAND paper called "The Theory and Practice of Blackmail." He had specialized at RAND in the arcane but extremely vital growth area in nuclear war studies: command and control. He had begun to notice that, while our ability to precisely carry out nuclear war orders looked good on paper, chaos lay just beneath the surface.

He had been inside the Pentagon planning rooms where they had argued over how many megatons to deploy against Moscow and how many were needed to vaporize Murmansk. He had been a junior member of the Ex-comm, the Executive Committee that made the Cuban Missile Crisis decisions, and had seen at close, all too close at hand, a Third World War nearly begin. He was a nuclear elite initiate. He had seen the SIOP, the Single Integrated Operations Plan, our targeting plan for nuclear war. He had virtually written the template for it during the time he served in the Pentagon of Secretary of Defense Robert McNamara, and then briefly in Henry Kissinger's National Security Council apparatus.

Those who actually knew what the SIOP was—and what was in it—were like a high priesthood into whose custody was placed the unholy ark of our nuclear cult. They were the only ones allowed to gaze at its virtually radioactive glow.

The nuclear priesthood is one of those cults it is dangerous to betray. The Rosenbergs were, little doubt, spies. But it is likely the Rosenbergs were only given the death penalty because the secrets they passed on—primitive thirdhand versions of secrets—were atomic. Ellsberg's secrets were firsthand, created through his own work. He could have given them to the Russians as Nixon feared. Or, as with the Pentagon Papers, he could have given them to the whole world and, in doing so, shook the delicate balance of terror to its foundations by forcing us to face the Number.

Years before my breakfast with Ellsberg, I too had a close encounter with the SIOP of a different sort. At the height of the Cold War during my odyssey through the subterranean world of the bomb, my Air Force escort, Lieutenant Loki (yes, I know, Loki is the Norse god of mischief), had actually led me down to the computer room where the SIOP hummed away in daily digital battle with its eternal foe, RSIOP, the Russian Single Integrated Operations Plan, or at least the one we imagined the Soviets had devised.

The SIOP computer was a huge object, the size of a big oil heater. My escort was a little puzzled when I asked if I could put my hand on top of it. I felt a little foolish, but in some primal way I wanted to put myself in touch with nuclear war. I could have sworn I felt a subtle vibration and a faint warmth to the touch, a warmth I imagined from an array of vacuum tubes that glowed as its innards pitted the nuclear powers against each other in war games in which, I was told, variations of the "targeting menus" of the SIOP were fitted in various crisis configurations against variations in the targeting menus imagined for the RSIOP, the Red foe. It was nothing like the operational closeness, the planning of the World War IIIs within—that Ellsberg felt. But I found some kind of numinous high-tech dread communicated by the touch that perhaps bore some relation to his.

Initially there was only one targeting plan in the SIOP, according to Ellsberg. But by the time McNamara and his successors were through, by the time I got to the SIOP in 1977, there were many more options—more "flexible responses," more differential target menus for limited or escalated single or multi-site war plans.

So why didn't Ellsberg tell all he knew about the SIOP back then? That question still haunts him—and drives him—now.

I don't think it was fear of the Rosenbergs' fate that prevented

Ellsberg from revealing what he knew about the SIOP. When I spoke to him he referred regretfully to that period when he was transferred from nuclear war planning to National Security Council Vietnam policy duty in November 1964. It ultimately led to his revelation of the Pentagon Papers but forced him to lose access and leave contemplation of what he'd grown to believe was the insanity of our nuclear policy behind. He told me he'd thought of exposing our nuclear insanity, but "then got distracted by Vietnam and the papers." And it's true he had transferred from nuclear planning to a Vietnam advisory role. But by then he had already learned the Number. He saw it in the first SIOP he was shown at the Pentagon.

And he left the machinery of genocide in place, unshaken, even after learning of it. Sure, he was arrested in later years in antinuclear demonstrations—hundreds of times—but he is an extreme moralist of the John Brown absolutist abolitionist type, burdened with a sense of his own sin in participating in the SIOP system. There is no stricter judge of his own behavior than he. And so there's a bit of the wandering self-flagellant prophet of doom in him. He told me the story of learning the Number over and over again like a penitent telling one priest after another of a crime that he could never receive absolution for. The Number. Ellsberg knew the Number. He had found out the Number. There may not have *been* a number until he asked for it. Getting the Number made it—our capability—real.

Kennedy indirectly gave Ellsberg the assignment. Sometime in the first year of his administration, before the Cuban Missile Crisis, he had passed word through McNamara that he wanted to know the number of deaths a U.S. nuclear strike on the Soviet Union would cause according to our then current targeting plans, the ones that accompanied him everywhere in the black briefcase. Specifically, he wanted to know just how many people would die from an all-out U.S. attack alone, not counting the death toll from any retaliation or even from the first strike that might provoke U.S. retaliation. Ellsberg was detailed to get the Number from the Joint Chiefs of Staff. Kennedy had been frustrated by previous attempts to get the Number from the Joint Chiefs.

Ellsberg communicated the president's impatience through

Pentagon official Robert Komer, later to be known during Vietnam as "Blowtorch" Komer for his fiery temper. When Komer got an answer from the Joint Chiefs, it came in the form of a deaths over time chart: it plotted the number who would die in the initial blasts and how that number would rise over the next six weeks from radiation poisoning and radioactive fallout.

Ellsberg showed me the chart over breakfast. There were two lines: initial deaths, 275 million. Adding in deaths over a six-week period, 325 million total. When he asked whether the total would be different under another target plan, he was told there was only *one* targeting plan: all-out attack. Massive retaliation. Ellsberg says he asked Komer about the deaths in the nations bordering on the Soviet bloc, including China, who would be subject to major fallout, and Komer went back to the Pentagon. Make that 600 million, the Joint Chiefs said.

Or as Ellsberg translated it for me that morning, "one hundred Hitler Holocausts." Later he learned the Joint Chief's estimate didn't figure into their account the inevitable tens even hundreds of millions more deaths from the Hiroshima-like firestorms that follow nuclear detonations. That factor was almost never included in official and unofficial estimates until 2003, when a sobering study of nuclear detonation firestorm death estimates was published by Cornell University Press: *Whole World on Fire* by Lynn Eden. It demonstrated how previous Pentagon and other official estimates had failed to include these kinds of convulsive and uncontrollable conflagrations. Suddenly, almost without anyone taking notice, nuclear war got worse. Not in reality—it was always that bad—but certainly in the perception of anyone who cared enough to look closely. The whole picture of the magnitude of even a "small" nuclear war changed. We'd been shielded from the full awfulness of the truth, the real number.

Indeed a few months from the day of our meeting the Number grew larger. *Scientific American* published the projections of the atmospheric effects of a "small" nuclear war, an exchange between India and Pakistan, not an unlikely occurrence. The magazine said that the megatons of ash and particulate residue from explosions would dim out sunlight sufficiently to cause worldwide crop failure and, as a result, the magazine asserted, a billion more people would die of starvation alone.

It almost seems as if every time you look at the real number from another perspective it shifts upward by a billion. And it is another reminder that what we are talking about here is not nuclear *terrorism*, the legendary perhaps mythical "suitcase nuke," the radiological "dirty bomb" that the men in the HAZMAT suits can clean up eventually.

But should a mere number change things?

Ellsberg believes that had the Joint Chiefs included the firestorm figure in their original estimate it would have brought the number more realistically closer to one billion. But even that billion is optimistic. It counts only deaths from our attacks on a nuclear superpower, not our deaths from retaliation by a nuclear superpower and the exponential damage of a potentially species-destroying nuclear winter.

One billion. There are arguments about this number. But even among the minimalist faction of nuclear war death estimates, I think most will agree the upper limit they imagine is an order of magnitude above the 60 million people who died in World War II. Is there an order of magnitude in measuring sanity? A point one reaches when a system that started out marginally sane, and may—we will never know—have prevented tens of millions of deaths in conventional wars, becomes irrevocably and ineradicably suicidally insane? Can you measure that point on a chart, with a number, a percentage of humans left alive?

In other words beyond a certain, say, ten-figure number—a billion—are you dealing with a different phenomenon not merely in degree but in *kind* from the 60 million dead in World War II? Assuming the morality of that war and bracketing the question of whether it could have been avoided by a minor bit of French assertiveness in the Rhineland in 1936, is there any upper limit to the number of lives worth losing for moral reasons?

If 60 million is tragic but sane—worth the sacrifice to win—is 600 million? A billion? Extremism in the defense of liberty is no vice, Barry Goldwater famously said. What about total extinction in the defense of liberty? A virtue? If we reject that, then what number short of total extinction will we accept?

The Pentagon had made the actual digits of mass death elusive, but would the fact that a president, a nation, had been forced to imagine the death toll from Pentagon estimates have made a difference in the future we were preparing with our Soviet partners in crime?

It didn't make a difference back then, the Number, and the question is: in this second nuclear age, should it now?

Once Ellsberg got the Number, once that variable was assigned an actual value, so began the calculations of a number-based moral algebra. Suddenly, nuclear war's consequences could be based on something real, even if it was an estimate. That estimate could either be embraced as necessary or rejected as intolerable.

In this second nuclear age, the question of numbers has often come down to arguments over the moral status of lower death tolls. Consider, for instance, the problem of the "medium size" nuclear attack on Israel. Peter Berkowitz, a frequent essayist on national security matters for the last two decades, most recently for the Hoover Institution, returned from a conference in Israel with a question that few people in the nuclear elite are willing to speak about out loud.

"Most everyone [over there] is thinking about a massive wipe-out strike on Tel Aviv that kills a million or so instantly and essentially destroys the state of Israel, leaving only its nuclear-armed subs to retaliate, which we assume they do massively," he told me over coffee in New York. "But what about if someone offshore from Haifa lobs a watermelon-sized nuke that hits that city and kills 19,000 people. Does Israel retaliate massively, assuming they identify the perpetrator? Do they retaliate against Iran, even if they can't be sure? More importantly, how do you gauge what kind of retaliation you take after the medium-sized strike? With proportionality? Or are all nuclear strikes disproportionate?"

I'm glad I don't have to answer these questions. But it is not an unlikely scenario in this second nuclear age, and there is no moral algorithm that allows someone to find the appropriate number for retaliation for a given number of initial deaths. Do nuclear weapons occupy a separate ethical and moral realm of their own that requires us to rethink whether "just war" theology applies? When the number of deaths leaps by an exponential order of magnitude, does the moral nature of the system that produces that number turn into something more evil by an order of magnitude? This is the "exceptionalism" question, one asked by those who study iconic figures such as Hitler (is he on the continuum of other wrongdoers or in a category all his own) and Shakespeare (a very great writer or in some ways in a category that transcends other great writers?) When the National Conference of Catholic Bishops declared in 1983 that "no previously conceived moral position escapes the fundamental confrontation posed by contemporary nuclear strategy," they were making an exceptionalist argument.

"Just war" theorists of conventional war talk about "proportionality" and "distinction." The word "distinction" refers to the ability to distinguish between combatants and noncombatants, even if a strike on purely military facilities is not designed to kill civilians. Most just war thinkers argue that the military intent is not sufficient cause for an attack that is likely to cause large numbers of civilian casualties as collateral damage. But is it possible to make any distinctions with a nuclear attack? And here is another question: will a disproportionate response to deter future medium-size attacks be paradoxically proportional considering its future effect?

Since Ellsberg was assigned the job of retrieving the Number, the question of the death toll in our nuclear strike plans has become even more deeply shrouded in mystery. It is now virtually forbidden for the Pentagon to talk about civilian casualties from our nuclear strikes, whether preemptive or retaliatory, even in top secret heavily classified documents. This is something I noticed reading more recent declassified nuclear strategy and deterrence documents. In there you would never know that nuclear weapons kill any unarmed noncombatant civilians. Targets that are likely to lead to extensive civilian casualties are euphemized frequently as attacks on "economic infrastructure." That they happen to be coextensive in most cases with densely populated areas known as "cities" is not acknowledged.

In another one of its euphemisms, the Pentagon strategists frequently refer to a preemptive nuclear strike as "damage limitation." The phrase sounds so innocent, but it means launching a decapitating surprise attack, a first strike against a foe in order to take out leadership targets like Moscow and military targets, especially nuclear weapons. Collateral damage? You betcha. But since it's damage limitation, presumably we'd only do it when we thought a preemptive attack on us needed limiting. Or a response to our first strike needed minimizing. Thus it can be euphemized as a defensive response to save our civilian lives. Human damage limitation.

The Number becomes smaller and initiating a nuclear war becomes more "humane." That's the theory anyway.

It is disturbing to contemplate hypotheticals such as this, but when I hear them broached I often find myself surprised that they are rarely discussed beyond the narrow circle of nuclear war game initiates. Everyone has an opinion on global warming and detailed plans to respond to it. Few are willing to speak frankly about the continued threat of global incineration. Perhaps we only have room for one doomsday scenario, or perhaps the focus on global warming is a sublimation of the fear of global incineration. In any case, a kind of eclipse: Global warming, at least, offers paths to successful activism: science will solve the problem. Global incineration, on the other hand, seems a possibility beyond our rational control.

But one thing a U.S. president with dreams of Zero ought to do right now is what Ellsberg failed to do when he was on the inside, what he's trying to do now: make the Number real, open it up, talk about the magnitude of casualties in a nuclear war. Look how powerful the "3 A.M." ad was in almost derailing Obama's primary campaign. The one that depicted a president awakened by an urgent early phone call. Everyone who saw it knows that "3 A.M." was a kind of code for a nuclear terrorist crisis of some kind. We've all been watching *24*, which makes nuclear terrorism more real for some, less for others, but marginalizes nuclear *war*. We've seen how powerfully a book and film like *The Road* by Cormac McCarthy can bring home the horror of a nuclear winter–like aftermath.

But we've never seen the mechanics of how a nuclear war begins. And a U.S. president could bring it to us. He could go a long way toward waking us from our holiday from history and changing a culture that normalizes genocidal deterrence threats just by giving all of us a demonstration of what it would be like to launch a nuclear strike. Televise his next black briefcase drill! Let the nation see the nuclear football up close! Challenge the Russians to do the same, simultaneously! Split the screen for all the world to see. Then take us inside the missile crewman underground launch control capsule and watch them go through a launch drill. Open it up! Punch in some code. Let's leave nothing to the imagination. Bring the world in on the mechanics of the choice so they can see why it is worth focusing on the morals.

I'm not suggesting we download and share the SIOP (or OPLAN or CONPLAN as it's now known). But on the other hand, why not? We should be aware of what's been too long hidden or half-forgotten: the president's power to destroy the world. We should be aware that when he's pulling the trigger by punching in a code to the keyboard inside the black briefcase, it's our hand that gave him the power to do it. We're pulling the trigger, punching in the codes, turning the keys, filling out the checklist. Finishing the job. If the world can be rallied to the cause of earthquake or hurricane or tsunami victims in the moments after they happened, what about the prospective victims of nuclear war in the moment—speaking metaphorically—before it happens?

The last time I'd seen Ellsberg before our breakfast meeting— some three decades ago—he had been giving a talk at the old Catholic Worker storefront headquarters on the Lower East Side of Manhattan then still maintained as a refuge for the homeless by Dorothy Day. There among the tubercular coughers she ministered to, he spoke to a small group of attendees, still seeking forgiveness for his SIOP role. This time around he was just as driven to atone by shaking up the complacency of this second, even more dangerous, nuclear age.

Ellsberg told me he had looked me up because he recalled reading the story I had written after Major Hering's case. He too had been inspired by the major, he said—both by the nature of the question he asked, which went to Ellsberg's specialty, nuclear command and control, and Hering's willingness to sacrifice his career to ask it. And—this tells you everything you need to know about Ellsberg—he had saved for more than three decades the original newspaper clippings about the major's case, which he had scanned and emailed to me. He also remembered the flaw in the "simultaneous two-key twist" fail-safe provision I had disclosed, the spoon-and-string maneuver. He too had been struck by how salient Major Hering's question was, how many implications it entailed. After all, he had been at the top of the chain of command programming what would be vaporized when Major Hering, down at the bottom of his silo, would twist his key and send his missiles to their—to Ellsberg's—target objectives.

One of Ellsberg's specialties at RAND had been "ambiguities of warning." Ellsberg knew that the major's question disclosed the absence of any real, effectual checks and balances once the first ambiguous warning of nuclear war appeared on radar screens. He had done the math on the likelihood of launching an accidental nuclear war based on an ambiguous warning that turned out to be a false positive. And he knew that those ambiguities made it likely we would be in a de facto launch on warning posture, because we would have only fifteen minutes or less to react to radar and satellite signals before the detonations began.

Ellsberg also knew that the system of predelegation had never been thought through. Early on in his work for McNamara he had been assigned to make a tour of the Pacific admirals who had nuclear weapons under their command to determine whether they believed they had authority to launch nukes on their own if they felt cut off from the chain of command in wartime. He found out that they did. He also found out that they believed there was a letter from President Eisenhower that had granted it. When I met him in September 2009 he was bearing among other recently declassified documents a set of papers on predelegation that had been obtained by the National Security Archive at George Washington

University and that revealed the existence of the rumored Eisenhower letter.

Should Ellsberg have seized the opportunity to give the world
a Major Hering moment when he was in the Pentagon? There are
those who say no, that it all worked out for the best because we
never had to use the weapons of genocide. But intending to do evil
is the moral equivalent of doing it, some would say. Surely doing
evil to noncombatants, on the scale of the Number, is. And the
fact we had the "moral luck," as the ethicists say, not to have to do
what we convinced ourselves we might have to do for moral reasons, just raises another question: can there be a moral reason to
commit genocide?

Some would argue we had no choice considering the rapacity
and oppressiveness of our foe. We were confronting an evil empire
(I won't argue with that). We thought we had to threaten genocide
to stem their expansion, or, eventually through sustained pressure
and threat, to cause the dissolution of the regime that created the
gulags in which Hitler-like numbers had died. How do you compare evils? I'm not sure there's a good answer.

Ellsberg wants to return to us our capacity to be shocked and
alarmed by the immoral persistent presence of genocidal nuclear
weapons. We spent some time speaking of the relationship between
the morality and the legality of nuclear weapons. The International
Court of Justice in The Hague, the one known as the World Court,
which puts war criminals on trial, issued an advisory opinion in
1996 that the entire system of nuclear deterrence was a war crime.

For centuries military planners have made the moral high
ground a strategic tool, given morality a grudging respect by rec-
ognizing the morality codified in international law, or in the just
war moral ethical and theological principles that lie behind it. During the Cold War some theologians such as Paul Ramsey sought to
defend the threat to use of nuclear weapons in some cases. But the
theological debates go back even further, to the time the flaming
catapult became a siege weapon, which could not be guaranteed to
strike only military defenders behind a beseiged city's walls. Still,
as the Conference of Catholic Bishops put it in 1983, "no previ-

ously conceived moral position escapes the fundamental confrontation posed by contemporary nuclear strategy."

In other words, nuclear weapons are not just greatly magnified flaming catapults. They represent a new kind of entity from all previous weapons of war, and so just war theology dating back to the flaming catapult must be tossed aside when considering the flaming ember the world could be turned into by a global nuclear war.

And it is that exceptionalist bright line notion of nuclear weapons that is at the heart of the World Court's 1996 opinion: "Nuclear weapons have unique characteristics," including "their destructive capacity, their capacity to cause untold human suffering and their ability to cause damage to generations to come . . . their destructive power . . . cannot be contained in either space or time."

Not contained in either space or time! That language captures the uniqueness that make nuclear weapons an exceptionalist case morally. They don't, as the Catholic bishops suggested, fit into the old categories. They command time and space and poison not just the present but the indefinite future, which includes about everything in existence, doesn't it? It's rare to hear a court make a pronouncement that broad, almost mystical.

The court explicitly addressed the moral status of the threat to use nuclear weapons, the heart of deterrence, and found it no less a war crime. The words the court used in its opinion on July 8, 1996, were that "the threat or use of nuclear weapons is generally illegal and states are obligated to bring to a conclusion negotiations on nuclear disarmament in all its aspects." In other words nuclear weapons are not on the continuum of other weapons, not to be judged by the same rules as other weapons of war. They require special prohibitions. In effect the court was codifying, formalizing, incorporating into just war law what has come to be called "the nuclear taboo."

Does this apply to nukes of any size? To tactical nukes with less destructive power than some blockbuster conventional weapons, to nuclear artillery shells for instance? I think the court intended its opinion to cover them as well. It's not the size of the blast—it's the nature of the weapon. I would suggest that behind the court's radical opinion are two factors: the specter of nuclear escalation, which means that once the nuclear threshold has been crossed by use of the smallest of tactical nuclear weapons, it in effect legitimizes, encourages gradual or rapid escalation to larger and larger nukes and so even the smallest must be banned if we want to ensure the largest will not be used.

Second, the court also made clear it was setting up what Talmudists call "the fence around the fence." As the court saw it, the maintenance of a nuclear threshold—preserving the bright line from blur—requires not only non-use, but non-threat of use.

Toward the end of my conversation with Ellsberg, in the chilly cement garden of the Wyndham Garden Hotel, I asked him the larger sanity question.

"When you saw the Number, when it registered, was that the moment that you began to question the sanity of the entire system?"

"No," said Ellsberg. "The [sanity of the] species."

"The *species?*

"Yes, the species. Just the fact that the Chiefs could be so matter-of-fact about the number."

Darwin explained the biological origin of the species. No one has yet explained its moral nature: the paradox of the ability to recognize great evil and yet still tolerate and commit or be complicit in it. Ellsberg's comment made me think of a conversation I had with George Steiner when I was writing about Hitler. The Holocaust "breaks the reinsurance on human hope" is the way he put it, meaning the safety net beneath which our estimation of the depths of human nature could go. It was a lesson in the true nature of human nature, the human potential for evil. The Number removes the safety net under the moral justifications for deterrence. It tears through it, the way 70 million did when Nixon said he could leave the room and in twenty-five minutes 70 million would die. Ellsberg was raising a question that was larger than the larger sanity question. How did we get ourselves into a state where having escaped the dailiness of dread of the Cold War, we are still content to live with the possibility of annihilation? That we profess the same doc-

trine, deterrence, genocidal nuclear retaliation? The same willingness to threaten evil to prevent evil on a multiple genocidal scale?
The same apparatus to accomplish it?

Was there a doomsday machine encrypted in the code within
our chromosomes—within human nature—more dangerous than
the one embodied in the nucleus of the unstable uranium isotope?

Whatever the answer to that question, there is a real doomsday
machine buried beneath the Ural Mountains in the former Soviet
Union and I decided to seek out the first Westerner who learned
about it.

# CHAPTER FIVE

# BRUCE BLAIR: THE DOOMSDAY DISCOVERY AND THE REAL DANGER

I first came across the name Bruce Blair in connection with the so-called doomsday device—not the mythical one featured in the movie *Dr. Strangelove*, but the real one, the one the Soviets, and now the Russians, have installed as the heart of their nuclear command and control system. The one they have code-named the PERIMETR system.

This semi-automated doomsday device can be switched on at a moment's notice, at any moment now. It is one of those Cold War horrors that have been hiding in plain sight and shock you—at least at first—when your attention is drawn to them.

Bruce Blair had been the first Westerner to disclose its existence, as P. D. Smith, a British Cold War historian, reported in a book *Doomsday Men* in 2007, which is where I first learned of it.

Blair had first made reference to PERIMETR in a 1993 piece in the *New York Times*, and had written about it elsewhere. In addition to appearing in Smith's book, it showed up in my 2007 *Slate* essay based on Smith's book. But little notice had been taken of it until it presented itself again in the David Hoffman's scrupulous 2009 chronicle of the Cold War legacy, *The Dead Hand*.

Before Blair made his revelation, we only knew of the movie version of a doomsday machine. In *Strangelove,* the doomsday device is a fully automated guaranteed-retaliation-worldwide-human-species-extermination system installed by the Soviets. It is a form of ultimate dead hand deterrence carried out by a machine involving a linked network of cobalt-jacketed hydrogen bombs. In Peter George's novelization of the film, the deadly cobalt bombs have been secretly implanted by the Russians all over the globe and they are "connected to a giant complex of computers. In order for the [computers'] memory banks to decide when . . . a triggering circumstance [a hostile nuclear attack] has occurred, they are linked to a vast interlocking network of data inputs, sensors . . . stationed throughout the country and orbited in satellites. These sensors monitor heat, ground shock, sound, atmospheric pressure and radioactivity."

This is how it works: "When the sensors decide *on their own* that nuclear attack has occured, they automatically signal the previously embedded cobalt bombs to explode, causing the death of life on earth." (Italics mine.) A total extinction due to the especially long-lasting "half-life" of radioactive cobalt fallout.

In his book, Smith focuses on Leo Szilard, the Nobel Prize–winning nuclear physicist who conjured up the idea of a nuclear chain reaction weapon in 1933. He began his career in the U.S. by urging his friend Albert Einstein to push FDR for a crash program (the Manhattan Project) to prevent the Germans from getting it first, then became a key figure at Los Alamos in devising the first atomic bombs, and then in the 1950s became an antinuclear activist, another penitent trying to shut the gates of hell he had opened. (I think it was Szilard's collection of antinuclear science fiction short stories, *The Voice of the Dolphins,* that helped turn me into a prepubescent ban-the-bomber.)

In a dreadful kind of irony Szilard came up with the notion of the doomsday machine in 1950 as a way of trying to shock the world into the real possibility of self-extinction. He shocked fellow scientists when he actually broadcast a description of his fallout-intensive cobalt-jacketed arsenal of multiple hydrogen bomb devices on a University of Chicago radio program in February 1950 in which he said, according to a transcript obtained by P. D. Smith, "how many neu-trons or how much heavy hydrogen do we have to detonate to kill everybody on earth? . . . I come up with about 50 tons of neutrons which is plenty."

Szilard managed to shock fellow scientists, but few in the public at large paid attention to his notion until Kubrick's movie; Smith, a professor at University College, London, believes that Szilard was the "real" Strangelove in this respect. And few gave credit to the pos-sibility that this was more than just a cinematic device until Bruce Blair went public in 1993 with the assertion that the PERIMETR system was already operational. By that time we were all on that holiday from history and didn't much want to look into it.

Smith never disclosed how Blair came to know about the real one built for the Soviets. So I went to see Blair myself.

I had become fascinated by him because he had a unique career arc that—like Ellsberg—allowed him to speak from inside and then outside the infrastructure of nuclear war. But unlike Ellsberg, he had seen it from ground level, from below ground level. That tra-jectory had taken him from his post as underground missile crew-man in charge of a wing of two hundred Minuteman missiles, to a Yale Ph.D. when he left the Air Force, to the Brookings Institution, to the job of congressional investigator specializing in command and control of nuclear weapons, to working with Russians on their own command and control system after the Cold War, to founder of his own nuclear arms control think tank—and ultimately to becom-ing the leader of the worldwide nuclear abolitionist Global Zero Initiative. I traveled to D.C. to talk to Blair at his office in the Carn-egie Endowment for International Peace building near DuPont Cir-cle, where he heads up two think tanks, the Center for Defense Information and the World Security Institute.

What I knew about the Russians' PERIMETR system at the time was what Blair had told Smith about it for his book. "It was designed to circumvent the possibility that a 'decapitating' surprise nuclear attack on Russia (something that was a persistent preoccupation of Soviet paranoia) would prevent the chain of command from

ordering retaliation from the worldwide array of missiles, bombers and submarines equipped to strike back, but requiring [top-
down] authorization to do so." The way PERIMETR was designed
to work, he explained, is that "In a real nuclear crisis, [in which
the top has been decapitated or incapacitated from issuing retaliatory launch orders] communication rockets, launched automatically by radio command, would relay fire orders to nuclear combat
missiles in Russia, Belarus, Kazakhstan and Ukraine. The doomsday machine provides for a massive salvo of these forces. Weapons commanders in the field may be completely bypassed. Even
the mobile missiles on trucks could fire automatically, triggered by
command from the communications rockets."

In other words, it was the Soviet version of the Letter of Last
Resort, only it was a Machine of Last Resort—one that would make
judgments about the reality of an attack without human input, one
that would carry out orders even after the human order givers had
been obliterated. When I met Blair, he confirmed the details of the
PERIMETR system, and the fact that it was still in place and operational, although he qualified this assertion somewhat by saying
there may be at least one human in the decision chain with the job
of verifying whether the decapitation signal is real or a signals error.

One human link.

PERIMETR was the centerpiece of the Soviet, and now the Russian, command and control system. In his 1993 *New York Times*
piece, Blair described one of PERIMETR's command centers, in
the heart of the Ural Mountains. "The Yamantau command center
is inside a rock quartz mountain, about 3,000 feet straight down
from the summit. It is a wartime relocation facility for the top Russian political leadership. It is more a shelter than a command post,
because the facility's communications links are relatively fragile.
As it turned out, the quartz interferes with radio signals broadcast
from inside the mountain."

A quartz nuclear war mountain! Something phantasmal about
it, a satanic big rock candy mountain. A super-weapons Fortress of
Solitude! But the quartz mountain melts in comparison with the

PERIMETR dead hand system at Kosvinsky, in the heart of another mountain in the Urals.

"Kosvinsky," Blair tells us, "is regarded by U.S. targeters as the crown jewel of the Russian wartime nuclear command system, because it can communicate through the granite mountain to far-flung Russian strategic forces using very-low-frequency (VLF) radio signals that can burn through a nuclear war environment. The facility is the critical link to Russia's 'dead hand' communications network [i.e., PERIMETR], designed to ensure semi-automatic retaliation to a decapitating strike."

Of course, there's a world of difference between a semi-automatic doomsday device and the totally automatic—beyond human control—doomsday device in *Strangelove*, something that Blair is careful to note. Well, maybe not a world of difference—one or two human being's worth of difference. The Soviet-built facility does require a human hand for the final fatal push of the button. But Blair believes that the human brain behind that hand has not been programmed to turn peacenik. And the details of the device are still far from reassuring.

"This doomsday apparatus, which became operational in 1984, during the height of the Reagan-era nuclear tensions, is an amazing feat of creative engineering," P. D. Smith writes. "According to Blair, if PERIMETR senses a nuclear explosion in Russian territory and then receives no communication from Moscow, it will assume the incapacity of human leadership in Moscow or elsewhere, and will then grant a single human being deep within the Kosvinsky mountains the authority and capability to launch the entire Soviet nuclear arsenal."

Since the U.S. and the former Soviet Union have formally de-targeted each other, when PERIMETR is activated against whomever it is activated, Blair believes it will only take "a short burst of code" into its software to transmit launch orders to the warheads PERIMETR commands. (No one has ever disclosed any of the target menus in the Russian equivalent of our SIOP/OPLAN.)

There has been some confusion in the reporting about the PERIMETR system, particularly in its description as a "dead hand" doomsday machine, totally automated. In fact the system remains operational now, but it is not always in operation. It can be switched on or off during periods of crisis and retargeted according to the circumstances of the crisis. But even now, it is misleading to call it a dead hand system, if by dead hand the implication is that it can operate utterly automatically without that one living human link, that one living hand turning a key.

Blair is a soft-spoken sixtyish fellow who retains the military bearing of his Air Force career. He turns out to be one of the few people who know both the U.S. and the Russian nuclear command and control system intimately. He helped troubleshoot both, in fact. He too had once held the keys in his hands, the operational keys to a Minuteman missile launch, the keys to the kingdom. He had held the Russian keys as well, and it had changed his life.

This is how it happened. After studying and critiquing the flaws in the U.S. system as an investigator for the Congressional Office of Technology Assessment, where he'd been given above-top-secret security clearance to the apparatus of the sacred SIOP, and writing highly technical books on the subject, he had gone over to consult with Russian specialists in command and control and had discussed ways in which both nations could design systems better equipped to prevent accidental or inadvertent nuclear war. In the short-lived era of good feelings that followed the collapse of communism, when the two nuclear superpowers were feeling their way toward working together to reduce the possibility of an accidental nuclear exchange, he had even received funding from nongovernmental services to keep Russian "nuclear design studios" working on safer launch control systems seeking a more rational mutual relationship between the nuclear superpowers. I later confirmed his account of his Moscow work with Blair's Russian co-designer, Valery Yarynich.

"I had a design bureau [in Moscow] virtually working for me in the 1990s," Blair told me. "It was because they were broke."

Blair described a strange interregnum when there was considerable interchange between American and Russian nuclear designers, almost all of whom were looking forward to a future of mutual cooperation and reassurance so that we could slowly climb down together from the twin peaks of nuclear hostility.

"It was a design bureau responsible for missile attack, early warning, using ground radars. They weren't being paid, they were broke. I was taking money over to them."

"To whom?" I said, the implications only dawning on me.

"To the Russians—in belts, when I was at Brookings—and I kept this design bureau afloat. It was hundreds of people for months— for six months. They were using their computers and calculating all sorts of things, and I made a lot of great friends. The chief scientists of this design bureau and I were really close."

But this window of goodwill quickly closed. The Russians went from being a superpower to a Third World economy with a super-power's nuclear arsenal. When the Russians discovered oil and gas and felt powerful again, they unleashed their resentment at what they felt was their post–Cold War humiliation by resurrecting their nuclear ambitions. Blair had felt a disturbing change in the atmo-sphere in Moscow in the last few years. He told me his Russian colleague in command and control theory, Valery Yarynich, was scheduled to come over to the U.S. in 2008 under the auspices of Blair's think tank to discuss further efforts at preventing accidental nuclear war, but that he'd been having "visa problems." I told Blair I'd go to Moscow if necessary.

But Blair said there was "an atmosphere of fear" over there, one he had not seen since the end of the Cold War. If I wanted a chance to talk freely to Yarynich, I should wait for him to come here because "nobody talks in Moscow anymore. Everyone's completely puckered about these things now, they really are."

Puckered?

"Military slang for fear," he said. "It's a completely different world," Blair said. "People are going to jail." He's referring to the many politicized purges of Putin enemies on trumped-up charges, the domination of the Russian government by former KGB com-rades of Putin, who often use KGB methods of enforcing his author-ity, the murder of journalists such as Anna Politkovskaya, whose book *Putin's Russia* exposed the regime's Soviet style of jailing those who were threats to state security. Then the blatant poisoning of a dissident using a lethal dose of radioactive polonium in his tea at a London meeting. That sort of thing, which had gone on somewhat in the shadows, was now the virtual daily subject for anyone following the news out of Russia.

## THROUGH THE LOOKING GLASS

Blair has changed radically since he held the keys. Back then in the early 1970s his desire was not to abolish nuclear weapons—like the other crewmen I spoke to, he was ready to twist his key under the appropriate authorized circumstances. He started at the top. His initial assignment in the Air Force was supervising the missions, the frequent drills engaged in by the Looking Glass plane, the 747 crammed with electronics, radar, and communications gear that was designed to pick up the president (or his successor) at the onset of an attack and loft him above the mushroom clouds during a nuclear war so he could decide what to target with what was left of our nuclear arsenal or when to engage in "war termination" talks with the enemy. I'd been given a tour of the Looking Glass plane on my deluxe tour of nuclear installations in 1977—yes, the duty officer escorting me said the name "Looking glass" came from Lewis Carroll.

The Looking Glass plane operated out of Offutt Air Force Base in Omaha, the site of our nuclear war command post. After serving there, Blair transferred to a missile base in Montana where he became a wing commander in charge not only of his own crew's ten Minuteman missiles but also of twenty other crews. He thus had some two hundred missiles under his command, enough to kill a hundred million people depending on what part the missiles would play in the targeting strategy. Down there in the deeply buried, hardened command module of the Minuteman missile silo fields, Blair began to develop some concerns. Some troubling flaws in the nuclear warning, command and control system surfaced that led him to think about the danger of accidental nuclear war, or the chance that a deliberate madman could get around the safeguards.

After Blair left the Air Force and got a doctorate in organization science, he began writing a book on nuclear command and control that was published by the Brookings Institution. It was called *Strategic Command and Control: Redefining the Nuclear Threat*. The real threat, he argued in that book and in congressional testimony back in 1985 at the height of the Cold War, is not to our ability to attack, but to our ability to launch a retaliatory strike under nuclear attack when, for all we knew, our nodes of communication between the chain of command and the men with the launch keys had been cut off.

Nodes of the command, control and communications system, known as C3, including relay stations that transmitted launch orders from the National Command Authority, officially the president and the secretary of defense, to nuclear submarines running silent miles beneath distant seas, were precariously protected. They were dependent on ground-based relay stations to reach nuclear sub-dedicated satellites or to send VLF and ELF (Very Low Frequency, Extremely Low Frequency) radio signals through the earth, and not invulnerable to being disabled on the ground or in orbit. Both ground stations and satellites are locatable and trackable, unlike the undetectable deep water subs.

Unless we fixed the system, we were vulnerable to having our megatons of weaponry neutralized.

"The main problem with command and control is the threat of decapitation," he told the Government Operations subcommittee in their 1986 hearings on behalf of the Office of Technology Assessment. "Missiles fired by submarines off the coast can have flight times as short as 5, 6, 7 minutes to Washington and that is simply in my judgment insufficient time really to be able to perform the function necessary to launch forces on warning. One simply cannot assure the survival of the national command authorities or at least the president and his legal successors. Nothing is going to alter that far short of altering our form of government."

Blair blamed the nuclear strategists who changed the nuclear mission from one focused on deterrence to one focused on war fighting, drawing on concepts like "flexible response" and "controlled escalation."

These were the grails of the hawkish strategists and generals during the Cold War. They believed—and they believed the Soviets believed—that nuclear weapons should be treated just like other weapons, not merely for threat and deterrence but for use. They believed that a flexible response allowed us to calibrate their use in a way that would be more efficient militarily and more humane to civilians by focusing not on massive retaliation on whole cities, but on precise military-related targets.

Blair was arguing in public that controlling or calibrating nuclear war once it broke out was impossible, and that it was a delusion to think that communications links could allow command and control to be executed with war-fighting precision. His testimony caused a furor, not merely because of the substance of his words but because he had been allowed to say them at all. His critics included the Joint Chiefs of Staff, who, when they were given a copy of Blair's report, immediately ordered that it be classified as "extremely sensitive information," according to the *New York Times*.

Blair clearly was a Man Who Knew Too Much. A committee spokesman said "Blair was able to produce a report that is more sensitive than what it is based on because of his knowledge of the field and ability to synthesize information."

The Pentagon said it was scandalous that he had been given security clearance to glimpse the SIOP. According to a March 25, 1985, report in *Defense Week*, "the security problem . . . arose because Blair's synthesis of diverse secret pieces of the command and control puzzle allowed him to discuss the capabilities and vulnerabilities of the communications networks, warning systems and operating procedures that would dictate the course of a general nuclear war."

There ensued a mad scramble to retrieve Blair's report from the congressmen who commissioned it. Congress and the Pentagon went to war: the former said it had the right to know why it should spend billions fixing the command and control system; the latter was offended that its secrets had been aired in the first place. "Congress," as *Defense Week* pointed out, "is being asked to allow billions of dollars to be spent in the next few years as the Pentagon improves its strategic command and control system in an effort to persuade the Soviet Union that a nuclear war could not be won simply by cutting off American decision makers from their retalia-tory forces—a war strategy known as 'decapitation.'" And yet Con-gress was being refused access to a report on the system's defects.

"The report I wrote was reviewed by the Joint Chiefs of Staff and declared so sensitive that all the copies had to be recalled from Congress to the Pentagon," Blair told me, "and they took it away from all the civilians including the assistant secretary of defense for command and control."

"The guy in charge wasn't allowed to read a report on his own operation?" I asked him.

"He didn't have access."

"Did they get it all back?"

"Well they did, but then some congressman found this out and got really pissed off and tried to get them back again and had hear-ings about that."

The comic tug-of-war ended up obscuring the fact that Blair had put the pieces together and discovered the system's funda-mental defects. Actually it would be more comic if the system's same defects were not inherent to the system we use now, as Blair maintains.

## FINDING THE GAPS

Blair never set out to become a nuclear missileer and later prophet of Zero. "I got a low draft number," he told me. As a result he decided to enlist in the Air Force rather than get shipped off as a draftee to Vietnam and after a quick trip through Officer Candidate School he wound up in Omaha. He soon found himself in the thick of nuclear strategy intrigue. "I was assigned to a reconnaissance unit and was actually an aide to the wing commander of the unit that flew these secret missions mainly around the Soviet Union."

These reconnaissance missions went under the code name Rivet Joint and involved RC-135 jets probing the electronic, radar, and satellite defenses of Russian airspace.

These were delicate, dangerous, provocative, and sometimes disastrous missions. "Our unit had lost a big plane in like 1960 or 1961, something like that. Got shot down in the Baltic or the Bering Sea. And these were very secret missions. A lot of them were directed by the National Security Agency right here and others were being run at the direction of the Strategic Air Command. But my unit flew those reconnaissance missions about China and the Soviet Union. Because China was also in SIOP."

Blair says the risky reconnaissance flights of the type that his unit made at the height of the Cold War still go on for the purpose of feeding data on the location and range of Russian coastal radar. "I periodically go out to Omaha and talk to crews of the Rivet Joint project, the RC-135 reconnaissance flights, and I'm always surprised that we still do that. If you go out there you may just bump into a crew that's just come back from a mission to the northern border of Russia to try to identify holes in the radar through which we could fly our strategic bombers to drop nuclear bombs in the event of war with Russia."

This is the post–Cold War twenty-first century. "We're still looking for—?"

"The gaps, the corridors to fly the bombers in so they won't get shot down with cruise missiles."

He cites the Chinese interception of one of these recon planes, which was forced down and the crew held captive. Things like that happened to these missions back when he was on duty. "We had the occasional incident. If you go back far enough there are a lot of serious problems in the 1950s and 1960s with planes literally being shot down in these interactions."

"Is that true?"

"Oh yeah. There were lots of planes that were shot down. Loss of life. We didn't shoot their bombers down, but they shot our reconnaissance aircraft down. I'm always surprised that we still do that," he said of the RC-135 flights.

"In other words we're still looking for an edge in a nuclear war with Russia?"

"We never brought our bombers right up to their coasts. Our bombers usually went to their fail-safe points, which is the point at which Soviet radar would pick them up. And so just before they got to that point they would turn back. We didn't want to light up the Soviet Union's air defense system and have them see a lot of bombers headed their way."

Except we did, at least once. Jeremi Suri reported in *Wired* the declassified records of 1969's Operation Giant Lance, which Nixon and Kissinger sent large numbers of nuclear-equipped B-52 bombers flying toward Soviet airspace past the fail-safe points. The mission was purportedly meant to validate Kissinger's "Madman" theory of nuclear strategy: in order to make the strategy of deterrence more credible—intimidate the Soviets over Vietnam—they needed to convince them the commander-in-chief is crazy enough to start a nuclear war.

"So our bombers kept their distance," Blair continues, "but our reconnaissance aircraft got really close, and that's where you get a lot of these encounters. And there were major U.S. reconnaissance planes shot down with loss of life back in the 1950s and early 1960s. And then the norms evolved and basically it became a kind of cat-and-mouse game for everybody, except during a few periods of tension like in 1983 when the Soviets shot down the KAL [Korean Air Lines civilian] airliner. They thought it was our RC-135, just a sort of Rivet Joint plane." I found myself thinking about the seventy or more NORAD and NATO jet intercepts of Putin's strategic bomber flights in that past year. How many more would it take before a similar incident blew up?

What alarms Blair now is that this whole Cold War apparatus remains, for the most part, intact, except for parts of the Russian system that have deteriorated into uselessness. "We're just kind of caught in this time warp," he told me. The time warp: both superpowers, all dressed up and ready to go for so long, had no way to climb down from their Cold War ledges and brinks.

Eventually, Blair told me, resuming the narrative of his nuclear career, he found himself bored by the Looking Glass plane and RC-135 duties at SAC headquarters.

"So I wanted to hightail it out of Omaha as fast as I could and the only way to get out of Omaha at the time was to be accepted into some sort of critical job for which there was some acute personnel shortage because no one wanted the job. And there's only like two of those jobs, one was a nuclear weapons control officer stationed north of Thule, Greenland, in some sort of Eskimo hut, and the other was to be a launch control officer for Minuteman or Titan missiles—which was a great assignment, as it turned out."

He remembers every detail from forty years ago because it was a life-changing period.

"So they told me I could catch the next [missile crew] class if I was willing to pack up in twenty-four hours and get out to Vandenberg Air Force Base and start training the following Monday. So I threw some stuff in the car and I drove for like twenty-eight hours nonstop. I stopped in Salt Lake City to throw up from coffee and cigarettes. And I wound up doing a three-year stint in Montana at Malmstrom Air Force Base.

"And I wound up being assigned—because I was so on top of the war plan and all that—to the alternate wing command post, which is one of the underground centers that had the responsibility not for just ten primary and secondary missiles but for the whole base of two hundred missiles."

"And when you say 'responsibility,'" I asked him, "in case of crisis what exactly would you be doing?"

"Beyond launching—?"

"Would you be turning a key yourself?"

"Yes," Blair said. "Turning a key. You interviewed these guys [the missileers]. You cited the spoon-and-string."

We spent some time discussing the shift in console alignment and design inside the launch control capsule that made the spoon-and-string ploy no longer possible.

But as I've suggested the spoon-and-string flaw in the two-key system can serve as a metaphor for the rickety architecture of the entire nuclear command and control system. And according to Blair, he discovered, in his capacity as wing commander, that the reality was worse. Because not only was the two-key system vulnerable, so was the "two launch votes" backup requirement, which requires two two-man launch crews to consent, "vote," that a launch order is authenticated. One of the things Blair learned as a missile crewman was that he could have launched all two hundred of his missiles on his own.

"I had the duty of launching—participating in the mass launch of my wing of fifty Minuteman missiles," Blair recalls. "And then additional responsibility for making sure that the rest of the wing—the other 150 missiles—got launched."

And what would that entail, I asked.

"Making sure everyone received the launch orders and repeating the message if need be. You need two votes normally. But if the other votes don't come and you've sent in your vote and the other votes don't come [presumably] because they've been blown away, then one vote will launch the force after a short delay." He could launch two hundred missiles with just one vote—his own—but that was not the half of it.

"As it turned out, later in my work I discovered there was widespread delegation of launch authority throughout the military chain of command. And there were some scenarios in which low-level officers could have created the launch command."

How?

"Well people like me breaking into the safe [the glass-fronted box located above each console that contained the launch-enabling codes], getting out the codes, and putting those authorization codes into a launch order and then disseminating, communicating the launch order to my 'friends.' And that meant that people like me—our standing rule was if you receive a valid and authenticated launch command from any source you're to carry it out . . . You're supposed to fire without hesitation. That rule was long standing. It finally was changed when it was discovered that there were deficiencies in the system that would allow unauthorized people to do exactly what I said, which is to communicate launch orders that were not intended to be communicated that would be received and interpreted as valid and authenticated."

In other words, not only could someone disseminate a nonauthorized order to launch a nuclear weapon, but the system itself had no way to make certain that the order came—ultimately—from the president. Alas, Blair insists—with a kind of desperate hopelessness—nothing has changed. Blair brought to my attention a draft of a letter he had written in 2008 to the *Bulletin of the Atomic Scientists* in response to an excerpt it had published of a book called *A Nuclear Family Vacation*, an account of a husband-and-wife report-ers' tour of nuclear sites. The excerpt detailed the then current silo command and control safeguards.

Blair's letter expresses not so much a wish to quarrel with the authors, as with the Pentagon PR people who were deliberately or inadvertantly passing along misinformation to journalists. It was a lifetime of frustration trying to get across a few basic facts about the flaws in the command and control system and the Pentagon's misplaced confidence in it.

### Letter to the Editor

I thoroughly enjoyed and admire the nostalgia-inducing arti-cle on nuclear missileers by [Nathan] Hodge and [Sharon] Weinberger. . . .

It illuminates the core unresolved issue of their post–Cold War mission—what is the meaning of nuclear deterrence in the absence of enemies other than terrorist groups? It is gen-erally accurate and quite insightful on many levels. The arti-cle fumbled some key details, however, some of which are important to get straight.

The assertion that missileers can only launch their missiles after receiving codes that come directly from the president is not correct. The codes in question are not held by the presi-dent, but rather by various command elements of the U.S. mil-itary. All of the codes used to authenticate launch orders and unlock missiles for firing are strictly held in military hands. They are widely dispersed among commanders to ensure that attacks on high-level command centers could not "decapitate" the authorization process. Such decapitation fears in the past led the Strategic Command to secretly circumvent the coding system mentioned in the article, unbeknownst to the Pentagon and White House.

Let's pause here to digest this not well understood point: according to Blair, the president does not have the launch codes. He only has the Gold Code to identify himself and he has the targeting menu's choice designations (plan g4: "take out all Russian leadership targets," say). But he can't personally translate this plan into launching a missile because the computer codes to feed into a missile's GPS guidance system are in the hands of widely scattered military commanders. How many and who? Blair says he doesn't know. But even if these codes need to be Gold Code–enabled, so to speak, it suggests the real possibility of workarounds by regional commanders that would allow them to effect launches on their own, especially in the event of a decapitating strike.

Blair's letter continues:

> The president possesses codes that are neither necessary nor sufficient to physically enable strategic missiles for launch. All this together with a long history of presidential pre-delegation of launch authority down the military chain of command raises some vexing questions about the true origin and lawfulness of a launch command. Although as the article intimates the issue rarely haunts the minds of firing crews, at least one courageous and conscientious missileer has ended his career by raising this issue.

He was referring, he told me, to Major Hering and his still unanswered question about how a missileer in his capsule beneath the prairie can know a launch order is legitimate or at least comes from a nominally sane person.

> Throughout and after the Cold War STRATCOM managed to keep the issue well hidden under the radar and to suppress the inconvenient truth that in many wartime scenarios a military commander instead of the President or his/her legal successors might have been the source of a lawful-appearing launch order.

So for all the billions the Pentagon has spent promising to upgrade command and control, Blair is saying, we still can't have complete confidence that a "lawful-appearing" launch order is actually lawful. Now he comes to his most sensational assertion.

> The article's discussion of launch "voting" in which four people in two separate capsules are allegedly required to initiate a missile launch omits the exceptions to this rule. Everything in the nuclear world does not go in pairs, contrary to the article's characterization. In reality, a single "vote" issued by a single two-person launch crew in a single capsule will do the trick in some circumstances. As many as all fifty missiles in the squadron's field can be launched this way if one capsule is the sole survivor of an attack, or if other factors cause launch crews in other capsules to take no action to inhibit a single-vote launch. Without straining credulity too much, suffice it to say that a variety of these factors exists, ranging from human error to confusion to negligence to terrorist sabotage. Uncertainty over the validity of a launch order may generate such unusual voting results. "Napping" crew members with alarm circuit breakers pulled to enhance their rest could also generate such strange voting scenarios. By the way, it's not rare for the missileer keeping watch while the other naps to fall asleep too. The prudence of allowing napping at all escapes me, since it technically violates the fundamental safety canon of nuclear weapons operations—the 2-person rule that normally requires two competent and watchful individuals working in tandem in sensitive positions. Tolerating an exception for duty launch crews for economic reasons is dubious judgment.

Who knew that napping had the potential to be so apocalyptically significant?

But Blair's urgent point was that a single canny missileer could, for whatever mad reason, launch fifty missiles on his own given the right circumstances. Unlikely yes. Low probability, but apocalyptic impact.

As it turns out, the flaw in the two-man capsule crew was not the only command and control problem left unresolved at the end of the Cold War. The system's entire architecture was vulnerable. Blair was the first former Pentagon employee to point out publicly in his 1985 testimony to the Government Operations Subcommittee that EMPs—or electromagnetic pulses—made the whole nuclear command and control system vulnerable: he was aware of top secret studies that modeled the effect of high-altitude nuclear blasts, or super-powerful laserlike pulses of electromagnetic radiation on the electronics that linked the nation's entire command and control system together. The gloomy conclusion of these studies was that while certainty was impossible until the horrific moment, it looked like a suborbital nuclear air blast could zap our system into uselessness. We wouldn't know what was about to hit us, nor would we be able to hit back. The enemy would not have to bother to cut off the head of our top leaders with a nuclear strike; it would just have to, in effect, cut off their *hands so* they could not push the button. Or cut off the button from the rest of the system.

"I was there in 1971 when Omaha had just discovered the devastating effects of electromagnetic pulse, EMP," he said. He described the drama of the realization that an EMP from an airborne nuclear blast could fry ground-based electronic systems, making them unworkable.

The Air Force sought to devise workarounds once the magnitude of the EMP threat to controlling nukes pre- and post-attack began to emerge. "They did a quick-and-dirty assessment of our last gasp at command and control, with the Looking Glass [plane that could relay signals to missiles underground] at the heart of it, "Blair told me." And the conclusion basically is that the whole command and control system could be neutralized. We could be unable to retaliate. That our deterrent threat was hollow. And a hollow deterrent threat virtually invited a surprise nuclear attack."

"This was 1971 when it was discovered?"

"Nineteen seventy-one when it was discovered. This was highly secret at the time because we were trying to figure out workarounds for the planes, ways to protect it on an emergency basis."

"Workarounds for the Looking Glass plane?"

"That plane and all the other planes in this fleet," Blair said. "There were planes that connected all the way from the East Coast, which was where the president's plane—Kneecap—the Doomsday Plane, was—"

"Kneecap?"

"Spelled NEACP, for the National Emergency Airborne Command Post, and it was to be connected to other planes in this chain, the system is called PACCS, Post-Attack Command and Control System."

The workaround system seemed remarkably primitive: "A series of the planes were tied together electronically, line of sight. Strung together they would relay messages from the president who might be orbiting somewhere over the East Coast in his plane, all the way out to Looking Glass, beyond Looking Glass then to these planes that can fire these missiles from the air—the ALCC, the Airborne Launch Control Centers. So we were sort of in a panic at the time because they could all be rendered mute by an EMP."

"Did we know if the Russians knew they could do this?"

"I wasn't privy to the intelligence of what the Russians knew; I only knew what we believed our vulnerabilities were. And we had to assume there'd be at least a random good luck shot by the Russians, a cheap shot, just in case. Because they [the Russians] knew about electromagnetic pulse. They wouldn't know about our specific vulnerabilities, more generic kind of vulnerabilities. They would know that EMP would create huge electronic current on the skin of an aircraft and that it would sort of flip fuses and burn out circuits and all that, but they couldn't know precisely the degree of damage."

And now?

"We still don't know because it took decades for us to begin to really learn scientifically what the dangers were. We had to create this huge trestle EMP simulator to put things in and zap them and sort of measure the outputs."

He is describing a test system that subjects potentially vulnerable electronic elements of our C3 system to simulated electromagnetic pulse radiation to see whether they still function.

"So we lived in the 1970s in a state of acute uncertainty about the viability of our nuclear deterrent force if it's used in a second strike mode," Blair says.

Acute uncertainty? Not what we were told. We were told that Mutually Assured Destruction made us safe; it was stable. If we believed our deterrent was sketchy—and we believed that they believed we believed it was—then we were all in trouble.

We still are in trouble. Listening to Blair is like having gone through the Looking-Glass and coming back—although not all the way back. He is still deeply enmeshed in the world he left behind and the ways in which he believes it has become even more dangerous.

In fact, I came to see that Blair thought my concern about the existence of the dead hand PERIMETR system in Russia was misplaced. It was something to be thankful for.

Why? By giving the Russian chain of command confidence that they could execute retaliation even after a decapitating strike. If we are aware that they can carry out a retaliatory strike no matter what, then we will be less likely to strike first. And the Russians themselves would be less likely to fire first and ask questions later under a use it or lose it scenario, if they knew they had a backup automated system. PERIMETR meant, to the Kremlin, they wouldn't "lose it," thus would be less likely to "use it," which would make their finger on the nuclear trigger less quick to fire in order to keep their deterrent from being neutralized.

We turned to the subject of the nuclear sub problem—the problem of commanders launching on their own authority. Letters of Last Resort and the like. What makes subs different from land-based nuclear weapons is the difficulty of close communication with vessels that seek to conceal their location in the most remote depths of the ocean. That concealment means they have to carry the targeting software with them on board and cannot depend on getting a burst of codes authorizing a launch through a deep sea barrier. Again the insoluble paradox: the more you centralize, limit the subs' ability to act on their own, the more you make yourself vulnerable to losing the ability to execute a sub launch order in a cutoff scenario. The more you give the sub commander individual authority in case of a cutoff, the more you risk him launching on his own.

I asked Blair, "I've heard or read that submarine commanders had more independent authority to launch than land-based because of the difficulty of communication."

"The procedures would be different but they're not delegated independent authority to fire. They always, from the beginning, have been required to receive a valid launch order to fire."

"They're required," I said, "but they're capable of doing it alone?"

"But they've been capable just like we were capable with the Minuteman into the 1970s. Bombers were capable until 1971. Minuteman until 1976 or 1977."

"What happened in those cases?"

"Locks were installed of various kinds and then on submarines they were finally installed in 1997."

Not till then—why?

"Those locks were installed as a result of the investigation that revealed problems of unauthorized launch possibilities on nuclear submarines that also uncovered an electronic backdoor."

Blair said that in 1998 the Navy came across an electronic backdoor in the naval broadcast communications system network that would allow unauthorized people, including hackers and terrorists, to seize electronic control over the radio stations that were used to transmit launch orders to (nuclear-armed) submarines. If you hacked the right codes, he says "you could inject a valid launch order, you could seize control and transmit a launch command to the submarines."

Has this ever been reported on?

"A little bit. Basically because I've written up stuff in my obscure writings and people like you come along occasionally and pick up on it but nothing really widely circulated."

"It's interesting," I said. "As late as 1998 we're still discovering problems and serious ones. How confident should we be at this point that there aren't as yet undiscovered serious problems. Or do you think there still are?"

"I think there are and," he added, "I think there always will be."

He became convinced of this during his period as a congressional investigator when Congress focused not on the substance of his testimony—there was "fundamental doubt on the ability of the United States to implement . . . [the] doctrine of comprehensive retaliation," he testified—but on his ability to have peered into the secret system in the first place.

Talking to Blair I felt somewhat like Dante being guided by Virgil down into the circles of nuclear chain of command hell. Blair meanwhile looks to Major Hering for his inspiration.

"No one has yet come up with an answer to Major Hering's question," Blair told me, the one about how one could know whether a presidential launch order, however legitimate in every other way, come from a sane president.

And it's become even more urgent now in the multipolar second nuclear age that features regional nuclear powers, rogue states, terrorists, and renewed U.S.–Russian hostility.

"We still have missiles in Montana and in Siberia that will fire as soon as they get a short stream of computer signals," Blair says. "I'm particularly concerned about them continuing to maintain these postures on hair-trigger alert in the context of the new frontier of warfare, which is cyber-space and cyber-warfare. The advent of the computer age has changed everything in the military business. We are so dependent now on computers and on the security of computers—that they can cause war to break out by cyber-attack or cyber-failure."

"That 1998 backdoor launch vulnerability as a harbinger?" I asked.

"That was the leading edge into the realization of vulnerabilities," he says.

It gives additional urgency to plans to bring the still vast nuclear arsenals of the superpowers back from the brink. And one man, Blair's former Russian counterpart, Valery Yarynich, believes he has a solution.

CHAPTER SIX

# COLONEL YARYNICH'S "100 NUCLEAR WARS" AND THE APOCALYPSE EQUATION

## FROM RUSSIA WITH COMPLICATIONS

After spending some time with Colonel Valery E. Yarynich one realizes something: thirty years in the Soviet Strategic Rocket Force and on the Soviet General Staff, its military command hierarchy, can do something to a man. One thing it can do is give him a deep-dyed black-humored sense of the absurd. The man in question was someone, after all, who may have saved the world from nuclear war with a statistical device known as "Monte Carlo runs."

That sense of absurdity is what I found almost endearing about Colonel Yarynich, an otherwise stern and sober-minded high-level strategic nuclear war planner, when we finally met in December 2008. Yarynich was not only one of the architects of the PERIMETR system but the author of a remarkable book—*C3: Nuclear Command, Control, Cooperation*—written during the brief moment after the Cold War when Russians and Americans were working hard to climb down from their respective nuclear ledges. His 2003 book

111

is packed with astonishingly detailed descriptions and diagrams of how the Soviets and their Russian Federation successors for a dozen years after the fall prepared to fight a global nuclear war. It contains the sort of secrets that spies of a previous generation would have given their lives for.

It was through Yarynich's book that the West learned the details of PERIMETR: how it used technology, electronic telemetry (dual phenomenology), and the like to ensure retaliation should the Russians face a decapitated chain of command.

His intent at the time was to encourage us to build our own PERIMETR system with the idea that two such systems facing each other would stabilize deterrence should some mad leader or leaders think they could get away with a successful (retaliation-free) surprise attack decapitation. The cover of his black-bound tech-heavy book about the architectonics of nuclear war features a photo of two hands in a firm handclasp, each hand touchingly identified as, respectively, "United States" and "Russia." Both of the hands are cut off at the wrists—unintentionally, one might suppose.

That fear of decapitation reached its height when the Soviet leader Yuri Andropov raged in the Kremlin in early 1980s, lashing his bleary-eyed former KGB colleagues to stay up all night in every capital of Europe counting the lights in the windows of Western foreign ministries: a sudden increase in lights on would mean, Andropov believed, the imminence of a surprise attack. The successful campaign by the Reagan administration to convince NATO to station advanced intermediate-range ballistic missiles (IRBMs) of the Pershing II class on European soil, had made the Soviets edgy even before the first of the Pershings were to arrive in late November 1983.

To the U.S. and its allies, the missiles were defensive insurance against Western Europe being overwhelmed by Warsaw Pact conventional arms superiority. To Moscow, the Pershings were potential offensive weapons of decapitation, as little as seven minutes from cutting off the head of the nuclear chain of command in Moscow.

Valery Yarynich's work played an important role in defusing a potentially apocalyptic showdown that arose from fear of decapitation and surprise attack.

In November 1983 tensions between nuclear superpowers had reached a fever pitch as NATO prepared for an annual nuclear use drill, Operation Able Archer 83 with the ambition of making it as real as possible, including rushing President Reagan out of the White House to an "undisclosed location." Andropov believed the real plan was to use the cover of a drill to mask real preparations for a surprise attack.

The clash of mutual suspicions ratcheted up tensions to the point where, David Hoffman asserts, "on the night of November 8 or 9, flash telegrams were sent to Soviet intelligence bases across Europe mistakenly reporting an alert at U.S. bases." The British KGB mole, Gordievsky, Hoffman reports, claimed that some in the Kremlin believed this "marked the start of preparations for a nuclear first strike."

Here was the ultimate Cold War close call. On September 6. "We came so close," the *Spectator* had declared about the 2007 Israeli raid on the Syrian nuclear installation. We were never closer than on those nights in November 1983 when the advantage of striking preemptively grew as the tension mounted. But the system worked! Or so we're told, but each time we learn that there was a human factor without which the system was far more likely to have failed cataclysmically.

Here is where Colonel Yarynich and his Monte Carlo runs come in.

The Kremlin higher-ups, quite ominously, demanded to know from their Strategic Rocket Forces savants what chance of success they would have if they decided to order a preemptive surprise nuclear strike against the West before the one they were expecting the West to launch against them. A decapitating attack, of course.

It was, and is, one of the key questions a nuclear power must answer: How do you estimate the probability of success of a nuclear attack when there are so many variables at any given moment? This had become a kind of pseudoscience, devising the best way to start and win a nuclear war. It was not merely the preoccupation of Sovietologists like Richard Pipes—who wrote a piece for *Commentary* in July 1977, entitled "Why the Soviet Union Thinks It Could Fight and Win a Nuclear War" based on Soviet military manuals. It was the ultimate question for nuclear strategist such as Yarynich on both sides of the Wall. What percent of missiles should you fire in a surprise attack? And what percent should you keep in reserve for post-attack blackmail and re-retaliation? What percent will misfire entirely? What percent will be accurate? How do you know what "winning" is?

For instance, how many U.S. missiles in how many silos will be destroyed if a surprise attack catches them still slumbering in their silos, and how many silo-based missiles are likely to remain functional enough for a retaliatory attack? How many nuclear-armed bombers will be armed and in the air, how many destroyed on the ground? What are the chances that communications with U.S. nuclear-armed submarines—the third and supposedly most survivable leg of our nuclear triad—can be knocked out? How many submarines are, at any given time, within striking distance of Russian targets? And what kind of damage could they do? The answers depend on a high number of variables: on the attackers' side, they involve everything from the atmospheric density, temperature, and wind direction to the slight differences in the precision of the precision guidance systems magnified over distance. On the victim side, they involve factors like the alert status of missiles and bombers—how much warning time there was, what percentage of the silos are empty, the airbases deserted, because their weapons have been launched in reaction to a warning.

And what would victory mean in a surprise attack? How disproportionate should the damage be between that caused by the attack and the retaliation? Should it be huge enough to intimidate the enemy into not retaliating at all? What ratio of missiles and warheads would ensure post-attack dominance? How to factor in the human factor in a post-attack blackmail situation—the choice the surviving hand on the nuclear football would make? What would the U.S. do if it is hit first and threatened with a second attack if it strikes back? So many variables, so many branching paths and thickets of decision trees. Was there any way to get an answer?

Assigning a single probability value to each variable and then seeing what comes out by multiplying them just does not compute in any meaningful way when there are so many uncertainties about so many variables. Yarynich and his colleagues believed there was only one way to answer the question: by doing multiple variations of what are known in statistical science as Monte Carlo runs—by randomly configuring more than one cascade of variables for an attack scenario, conducting multiple virtual nuclear wars with a number of possible outcomes to see what if anything can be predicted about the likely outcome from a standing start. Runs, as they called them, meant running each war by a different set of potential variables from a wide array of combinations and permutations.

The modeling process—or at least the racy name for it—originated with Stanislaw Ulam, one of the physicists seeking to find the formula for the amount of energy a given critical mass would release in a chain reaction. He predicted that there would be no one single answer because of the unpredictable behavior of neutrons, among other things. The bottom line: the same weapons might succeed decisively on Monday in a surprise attack or might fail decisively on Tuesday, depending on variations in accuracy, weather conditions, warning time, and the last-minute defenses put up by the U.S.

Ulam named the predictive models Monte Carlo runs after an uncle who repeatedly lost his shirt there. Interesting that the attempt to predict the course of a nuclear chain reaction is as much of a gamble as predicting the course of a nuclear war or predicting the course of a betting streak at a casino.

In any case the message that came back to the Kremlin and its Strategic Rocket Force from Yarynich and his colleagues is that attempting to be confident a surprise attack would succeed would be rolling the dice on a single Monte Carlo run with no more guarantee of success that the average craps player at a real casino. Yarynich's Monte Carlo runs argument helped convince the hothead faction in the Kremlin that a gamble would not always show a winning outcome. That contributed to the decision not to launch a surprise attack at the one moment in nuclear history that came closest to it. But the problem and the paranoia did not end there: Yarynich's conclusion also highlighted the decapitation problem they would have with Pershings seven minutes away once they were deployed.

## "THE PLAY WITH FIRE"

As a result, Yarynich and his colleague set out to design a more solidly based architecture—the semiautomated system known as PERIMETR—to protect against a decapitating strike that would make the Kremlin feel less the need to preempt.

A quarter-century later, Yarynich was coming to America with another plan—another attempt to save the world from accidental nuclear war. Or as he more modestly put it in his halting English, when we finally met for lunch, "reduce tragic mistake in the play with fire." That phrase—"play with fire"—has a double edge to it: it was his way of saying "playing with fire," but it also captures in a theatrical way what we've been doing since the first nuclear age— play with fire, thermonuclear fire, almost like children unaware of how dangerous such playacting is.

This new plan, a seven-page summary of which (entitled "100 Nuclear Wars") Yarynich handed to me when we met for lunch, is designed to solve one of the most difficult and dangerous problems left over from the Cold War balance of terror, Mutually Assured Destruction era: the de facto hair-trigger, launch on warning posture of our nuclear arsenals a problem not addressed in the new START treaty, which was about numbers of warheads, not their alert status. It is meant to solve the problem of de-alerting by shifting the readiness posture of each superpower arsenal from a forward-leaning to a more defensive stance.

At seventy-one, the retired colonel walks with the stiffened gait that bespeaks a lifelong military bearing as well as age. One can imagine a younger version of him goose-stepping behind a missile in the Kremlin's May Day parade. He was—and is—a Russian patriot. But he was—and is—a rationalist in a realm of absurdists. He tells me, as we swerve around DuPont Circle to Connecticut Avenue toward our destination restaurant, La Tomate, that he grew up in a military family, that his father (and family) suffered through the notoriously bloody three-year-long siege of Leningrad by savage Nazi armies. He followed his father into the military and his first posting was as a launch control officer for one of the Soviets' biggest and newest ICBMs. It was its very size that made its use problematic, he tells me.

For instance, he says, with a shrug at the absurdity of things, it was what "saved the world" during the Cuban Missile Crisis.

There was no sunlight in the underground bunker he was occupying that October in 1963, a command module deep beneath the tundra that ministered to the SS-6, a giant, unwieldy liquid-fueled monster of an ICBM, lurking in an underground silo that was, then, the newly commissioned and operational pride of the Soviet Strategic Rocket Forces.

It was the rocket that would have been tasked with taking out New York, Los Angeles, or Washington, some huge population or government center in a retaliatory strike—unless it was used to strike first to incapacitate our silo-based missiles or to decapitate our chain of command, in which case the ground we were walking on would have melted into a literal pit of fire.

But instead this dinosaur, this Tyrannosaurus rex of rockets that ruled the early nuclear ages, may have—in its very monstrous unwieldiness—as Yarynich put it, saved the world.

"Saved the world?" I asked as we continued on Connecticut Avenue, all looking so safe and tidy, newspaper boxes gleaming in the sun.

Yes, saved the world, Yarynich said, because the liquid fuel was a mixture of two unstable substances that were designed to be fed into the missile's devil's maw at the last minute; it was too unstable to sit around with the explosive brew good to go. And once the two elements of the liquid fuel, including super-cooled nitrogen, were mixed inside the missile's storage tanks, the liquid became too unstable to be preserved or reused. So fueling the missile was expensive: if not used after a short period of time the fuel had to be drained and discarded at great, unrecoverable cost.

Thus on Saturday, October 27, 1962, at the height of the Cuban Missile Crisis, when a Soviet freighter approached the imaginary

line in the South Atlantic drawn by President Kennedy, the Kremlin had to make a decision as to whether to resist a U.S stop-and-
search at sea. That blockade operation could have escalated quickly
into conflict, especially since we now know that Soviet and Cuban
teams were moving nuclear-tipped missiles into place above Guan-
tánamo Bay ready to attack the U.S. base there and a Soviet sub
was aiming its nuclear-tipped torpedo at the U.S. blockade ship.
The Kremlin had to decide just how ready it was to stand up to
the Kennedy move: if they ordered their freighter to resist board-
ing and the U.S. Navy struck it, the Soviets would have had their
choice of retaliation points: Berlin, Gitmo, or—why wait—go for
a preemptive first strike knockout blow right away. Any of these
moves would have required Yarynich's missile to be fueled up and
ready to launch.

Fortunately, according to Yarynich, one factor prevailed over
all geopolitical considerations: the Kremlin he told me was "very
cheap." They didn't want to start the expensive process of fueling
the missile—and then draining the unreusable mix—unless they
were determined to use it. So they backed down from a confrontation. The price of fuel may have tipped the balance.

Maybe the argument about cost in the Kremlin was just a fig
leaf for a failure of nerve (they knew, though we didn't, how over-
matched their nuclear arsenal was). Or a belated return to sanity
from the shores of apocalyptic absurdity.

Yarynich laughs now at the triumph of cheapness over all else,
the absurdity of it all. But the issue of readiness and alert, the fact
that thousands of rockets can still be fired with much more decisive
rapidity now than in the days of the liquid-fueled dinosaurs, has
remained on his mind as today's dangerous absurdity.

Up until now, the most public focus of post–Cold War nuclear
deescalation has been on reducing the number of warheads by
using the START treaties. But for serious students of arms control
the greater issue is de-alerting the deadly remaining arsenals from
their hair-trigger, launch on warning posture. Yarynich's book was
an attempt to bring this problem out in the open: it was meant to
let the U.S. know what the Russian launch procedures were, and

to let the U.S. know how much the Russians knew about the U.S. launch procedures, which was quite a lot. The book was like an MRI of the Russian nuclear brain.

But the book didn't change anything. In fact, it came out just as the George W. Bush administration was framing up a new, more aggressive nuclear posture. The hand extended on its cover was cut off in more ways than one.

So both Bruce Blair, the former missile man, and Valery Yarynich, himself a former missile crewman and now Blair's Russian collabo- rator, have devised separate plans that they believe can address the problem of nuclear missiles going off because of unverifiable elec- tronic warnings. They are not incompatible, Blair's is more simpli- fied and less hierarchical than Yarynich's multi-"echelon" strategic architecture.

Blair's plan has four phases, but I'd like to focus on the first two, which seem to me to be the simplest to carry out, the least likely to arouse opposition, and the most likely to reduce anxiety about nuclear "inadvertence," the bland term for blowing the world up unintentionally.

In Phase 1 of Blair's approach, he recommends "revising the nuclear war plans to eliminate massive attack options and launch- on-warning from the repertoire of response options available to nuclear decision-makers." In Blair's vision, massive attacks wouldn't be impossible; they just wouldn't be a one-step option in the president's nuclear football. Neither side has an interest in deliberately annihilating the other and suffering annihilation in return. Why not acknowledge that and remove the capability from instant inadvertent use? Remove it from our football. Remove it from their PERIMETR.

In addition, Blair suggests that "the strategic missile forces could also be de-targeted, stripped of all wartime aim points." At the moment, missiles are de-targeted in the sense that specific targets have been removed from the software in the missiles. But targeting codes can be called up and reinstalled in moments—the coordinates are still programmed into missile-base computers. In Blair's plan, retargeting the missiles would take hours rather than minutes, and missiles would be less subject to a cyber-spoofed launch order.

In Phase 2 of Blair's de-alerting proposals, "strategic missiles in silos would be isolated from external launch control, by flipping a safety switch inside each silo, as was done in 1991 when President Bush de-alerted nearly one-half of the US Minuteman force almost overnight." De-alerting the rest of our missiles would prevent an electronic or physical takeover of a command center on a missile base from being able to cause an immediate unauthorized launch. (That's because re-alerting the missiles would take at least twenty-four hours and could not be done from within the silos.) The Russians would simultaneously match our measures, and the moves on both sides would be subject to verification. Blair also proposes that submarines at sea refrain from installing a crucial element of their launch system, the so-called inverters, the devices that need to be triggered to permit a launch order to be executed. This would also preclude an inadvertent launch.

The combined effect of the two phases of his proposals, if adopted by both superpowers, would be to create a kind of time-delay firewall that would replace the accident-prone, short-fuse, hair-trigger, launch on warning, command and control systems both nuclear arsenals have retained from the Cold War.

Blair's third and fourth phase proposals—separating warheads from missiles, taking them out of the silos and putting them into storage—and then disassembling them, would make accidental nuclear war or surprise attack virtually impossible, although they would likely require more elaborate negotiations about inspection and verification of warhead removal and disassembly. They probably couldn't be adopted as easily as Phases 1 and 2 could be.

But there's no reason the administration couldn't start from there.

## COLONEL YARYNICH'S ECHELONS

Yarynich's seven-page plan is called "100 Nuclear Wars." It is not the only possible solution to the urgent need for de-alerting, but it deserves careful attention because its source is someone who knows technical and strategic issues of command and control from both sides.

The best way to understand Yarynich's "100 Nuclear Wars" is to start with START. The treaty's goal was to reduce the number of actively deployed nuclear warheads (on missiles, bombers, and subs) from more than 5,000 on each side to a number between 1,700 and 2,200 by 2012.

START, which was signed in 1991 and after some travail has achieved both real and sham reductions. In the latter category the Bush administration announced with great fanfare in 2007 that it had reduced the number of operational warheads by two hundred but critics of the Pentagon were able to demonstrate that some of these reductions were a three-card Monte shuffle. That in some cases, the Bush reductions meant detaching the actual nuclear warheads from ballistic missiles and storing them in distant facilities so that quick "break-out" reassembly is not feasible.

But on closer inspection it turned out the storage facilities were at "full capacity" and so the warheads were "temporarily" going to be moved to warehouses on the same missile bases as the silos only minutes or hours away from being ready to be reinstalled.

But even if the reduction of missile numbers were to be carried out in good faith and verifiable on both sides, the readiness question needs to be addressed: how long after a warning signal appeared on Cheyenne Mountain radar screens could warheads be reactivated and retargeted?

And so the question became, how does one step back from the fifteen-minute readiness posture without placing oneself in danger of surprise attack? Just renouncing surprise attacks, as Blair is advocating, is not enough. There must be physical limitations to premature or preemptive firing, and that's where Yarynich's plan comes in. It may sound quixotic and overcomplicated but no one has come up with a simpler solution.

He would first divide all American and Russian missiles into three "echelons" depending on the time it would take to get them ready to launch. The first echelon would be about deterrence and retaliation: it would consist of large but inaccurate missiles for the most part, weapons designed to bring vast swaths of retaliatory wrath down upon a first strike attacking side. They would not be first strike weapons because first strike weapons are targeted on the foe's silos and other military installations, and require accuracy. But when it came to retaliation these first echelon weapons would be big and inaccurate in Yarynich's scheme, but they would be ready to go and reasonably invulnerable, like submarine-launched missiles. They would not be designed for first strikes and would ensure that neither side could get very far with a surprise attack. There would have to be two decisions made by both sides about the first echelon missiles; first, both sides would have to agree on a number and mega-tonnage of missiles that would produce a level of casualties sufficient to deter surprise attack. (I know: estimating millions of deaths per megaton—and how many deaths are acceptable before deterrence takes hold—is likely to be a horrifying task, however necessary.) Secondly, both sides would have to agree on separating in time and in space the warheads from their launchers. In other words, nuclear warheads would have to be taken off ballistic missiles and stored separately from launchers so they couldn't launch on alert, launch on warning, launch on anything but a real attack. But how much of a time delay in mounting an attack would be sufficient?

Yarynich's plan suggests the two sides agree on a three-hour window for the first echelon of missiles to reach readiness. This would mean warheads would be stored at enough of a physical distance from the launchers to require at least three hours for transport and technical rehookup. That's one solution. Another is to install internationally monitored time locks on storage facilities for warheads that wouldn't permit their activation, or release from storage, without raising an alert or warning—no secret race to a middle-of-the-night surprise launch.

Yarynich's second echelon would consist of weapons that are capable of first strike precision accuracy. Until the destruction of these weapons has been negotiated by treaty he wants to make their disassembly and distance from launch site a priority.

The third echelon would consist of all other weapons, which he suggests are mainly candidates for the scrap heap. Both superpowers still have in storage thousands of medium-range and short-range warheads that we've taken out of our war plans but have yet to destroy. He believes work on destroying them would be an easy first step in beginning to move from three echelons to one.

The heart of Yarynich's idea is that he has done Monte Carlo runs of one hundred nuclear wars using the weaponry in his three echelon model, with a range of possibilities and variables they might encounter. He believes that his statistical calculations show that structuring U.S. and Russian nuclear arsenals in this way will make the outbreak of nuclear war by deliberation or inadvertence radically more unlikely.

Of course his modeling, like Blair's proposals, is bipolar and doesn't include the nuclear arsenals of Britain, France, and rogue states like North Korea or dangerous enigmas like Pakistan and Israel. It is limited but, considering the relatively small size of the other nuclear nations' arsenals, it addresses the problem of 90 percent of the nuclear warheads on earth in this "play with fire" interim. And it addresses the possibility that the fire will never be put out.

Yarynich's proposal is perhaps the graphic example of the paradox of nuclear disarmament. The more one applies reason to the matter the more unreasonable it seems to be. Yarynich's plan, the rational division of weapons into echelons, looks impressive on paper, but seems beyond reach as a treaty when you consider how difficult the START negotiations have been for the far simpler goals of reducing the number of launchers and warheads. Sometimes I wonder if "100 Nuclear Wars" is in its way an emblematic document of the new nuclear age, the attempt to restructure the absurd into a simulacrum of reasonableness. Its larger aim is to remove the last vestiges of Cold War surprise attack/decapitation culture. Still, the concept of Monte Carlo runs in itself has an importance all its own. Not only as a way of evaluating nuclear risk—or demonstrating that such risk can vary wildly and, most importantly, unpredictably—it undermines *any* given attack plan and thus helps achieve stability by demonstrating the uncertainty inextricable in any such plans. This seems as persuasive to me as it may well have been to the Soviet Presidium in November 1983, thank God.

And I also like the Monte Carlo run as a metaphor for living with nuclear weapons. Every day is a new Monte Carlo run. So far we've been lucky but what are the chances when we roll the dice today we won't be any longer?

When I first heard the term "Monte Caro run," I had conjured up a misinterpretation of the significance of "Monte Carlo." I had thought first of the road race through the streets of the town, not the casinos. I had an image of all of us in the nuclear age, like a jaywalking pedestrian blithely crossing the road as the burning speedsters whiz by on the macadam of Monte Carlo's roads. We act like there's no chance of getting run over. We act like there's little chance of a crisis getting out of hand. It's a little like the old joke about the guy who jumped from the top of the Empire State Building. As he passes the 64th floor someone calls out "How does it feel?" And the guy whizzing by says, "Okay so far."

In terms of avoiding a nuclear war we've been okay so far for sixty-five years. Are the odds of that continuing calculable? Statistics can perhaps throw some light on how many daily Monte Carlo runs of deterrence we have left before we get smashed.

## THE APOCALYPSE EQUATION

Trying to decide what to make of "100 Nuclear Wars" led me into the arcane field of statistical nuclear war prediction, to look at other statistical approaches to nuclear risk. It's another way of asking the "how close are we" question. Statistics are sometimes a field where the mechanics and morals of nuclear war converge.

For instance, if there were a negligible chance that nuclear deterrence would ever fail, a negligible chance that we'd ever be faced with the genocidal choice, it wouldn't make much of moral difference if we were indifferent to the existence of that negligible chance. Would it permit us to threaten genocide to prevent genocide if we could be almost sure nothing could go wrong. Threaten evil to prevent evil. A negligible chance of non-negligible moral consequences to trouble the soul. But how sure is "almost sure"?

In fact, we would have to cede the moral high ground to those who say that—at virtually negligible risk—nuclear deterrence has saved the lives of as many as 60 million people who would otherwise have died in the conventional wars supposedly deterred by rules. (Recall: pre-Hiroshima twentieth-century war deaths; 100 million. Post-Nagasaki; 40 million.) But how do we calculate the risk now? Is it something we can live with or something we will die of? How do we know we're not merely passing the 64th floor on the way down?

It is on this issue I found the work of the statistician Dr. Martin Hellman of Stanford provocative. Hellman set out in 2008 to research something akin to what Yarynich sought: nuclear war risk quantification. He sought to quantify to an order of magnitude (usually meaning a power of ten) the possibility or probability of a nuclear war occurring—and how soon it is likely—based on what we've learned in the past half-century from nuclear crises.

Hellman is an interesting fellow. As an electrical engineering professor specializing in cryptography and information theory at Stanford, after stints at MIT and IBM's advanced research facility, he became famous in tech circles for being one of the inventors of the "public-key" and "trap-door" methods of encryption, which made (mostly) secure Internet and Web communication possible.

But for the last quarter-century he's been pursuing the question of "the inevitability and prevention of nuclear war" as he called it in an award-winning peer-reviewed 1985 paper. He constructed his mathematical model around the sharpened and limited question: what is the risk nuclear deterrence will fail to deter attack? It is a limited question in the sense that it excludes the very real chance that nuclear war will break out by accident.

He compares his work to estimating the failure rate of a nuclear reactor design that has not yet failed: "In addition to estimating the failure rate, such a study also identifies the most likely event sequences that result in a catastrophic failure. Such a failure is composed of a cascade of small failures and reasonable numbers are often available for many of the variables (e.g., the failure rate of a cooling pump in a reactor)."

He doesn't claim to have solved the problem of catastrophe estimation beyond a reasonable doubt, but his study of failure rate bears a relationship to the Monte Carlo runs in estimating the probability of success of a nuclear attack. Here's how he does it.

He starts with a baseline unavoidable but acceptable risk. He defines acceptably small risk as the chance of extinction by an asteroid. "Such NEO (near earth object) extinction events [such as the one that probably created a fatal global winter for the dinosaurs] have a failure rate on the order of 10 to the minus 8th power per year," astronomers tell us, where "failure rate" means number of expected hits not misses. That's very small. Ten to the minus 8th power is one in 100,000,000 at a given instant. But what about over prolonged time?

"During the next century that failure rate," Hellman wrote in an Engineering Honors Society professional journal in 2008, "corresponds to one chance in a million of humanity being destroyed."

What does that mean? "While ten to the minus 8th power [nuclear war as an asteroid-like danger] is a small probability, the associated cost is so high—infinite from our perspective—that some might argue that a century is too long a delay before working to reduce the threat."

And while no serious efforts have been made to plan for an NEO event—other than a Michael Bay movie about astronauts landing on the asteroid and blowing it up with, you guessed it, nuclear weapons—at those odds we don't really have to hurry. We can wait a decade until the tech gets better space lasers, like those in a James Cameron movie maybe.

He goes down the orders of magnitude: "If the failure rate is ten to the minus fifth power . . . then it's difficult to tolerate even a decade's delay . . . If the failure rate is 10 to the minus fourth the probability of humanity destroying itself during a decade long effort [to prevent it] would be one in a thousand which is much too large. If the failure rate is 10 to the minus 3 power per year the probability increases to approximately one percent over a decade and ten percent over a century and delay is clearly unacceptable." By "delay" he means a delay in nuclear abolition.

If the failure rate is closer than that, "anything short of an all-out effort to change course would be criminally negligent: Each year we delay in reducing the risk brings with it a one percent chance of disaster and a decade's delay entails roughly a ten percent chance."

So how desperate a situation are we in?

In attempting to quantify the risk, Hellman takes a conservative approach, not only excluding accidents, but excluding many well-known near-misses, including the Berlin crisis of 1961, Nixon's newly disclosed nuclear alert of 1969, the shadowy but well-known nuclear threats during the 1973 Yom Kippur War, the Able Archer crisis of 1983, the Norwegian rocket mistake, the assorted "flock of geese" dual phenomenology failures, the training tapes incident Zbigniev Brzezinski relates, and the chilling episode in which Colonel Petrov saved the day. Nor does he include the possibility of a nuclear war that starts regionally at first and escalates to a global one.

Using what statisticians call the "time invariant modeling" procedure, Hellman factors in only one full-blown nuclear crisis in the first fifty years of deterrence—the Cuban Missile Crisis—and two other potential crises: President Reagan's threat to reimpose a naval blockade of Cuba in the 1980s and the planned deployment of an American missile defense system in Eastern Europe. At the end of his study, he concludes, even with this narrow list of crises, that "the projected failure rate of deterrence from all sources is on the order of one percent per year and even the lower level is well above the level that any engineering design review would find acceptable." Here, for the record, is the equation he uses to arrive at his disturbing conclusion.

> The annualized probability of a CMTC [Cuban Missile type crisis] resulting in World War III, denoted $\lambda_{CMTC}(t)$, is
>
> $$\lambda_{CMTC} = \lambda_{IE} \, P_1 \, P_2 \, P_3$$
>
> where $\lambda_{IE}$ is the annualized probability of an initiating event that could lead to a CMTC, $P_1$ is the conditional probability

> that such an initiating event results in a CMTC, $P_2$ is the conditional probability that the CMTC leads to the use of a nuclear weapon, and $P_3$ is the conditional probability that the use of a nuclear weapon results in full-scale nuclear war.

And by the way Hellman is not alone in thinking of the risk this way. A summary of his statement on the level of nuclear risk has received the endorsement of top military and academic luminaries, including Robert Inman, the retired admiral and former NSA director who is known as a no-nonsense technocrat, not a bleeding heart. It is worth noting *Scientific American*'s recent estimate of a 1 in 30 chance of a global nuclear war in which "hundreds of millions" die taking place in the next decade, while smaller than Hellman's 1 in 10, isn't reassuring.

Hellman calls those who don't buy his analysis "nuclear optimists" and denounced one of them, Jonathan Tepperman, in this message sent to those on his e-mail list:

> **How Confident Should a Nuclear Optimist Be?**
>
> Nuclear optimism is a school of thought which argues that more nuclear weapons make the world safer. Given that our nation and Russia each have around ten thousand such weapons in its arsenal, such thinking is more widespread than might be thought. The following assessment is therefore much more than an academic exercise, and has vital implications for humanity's future!
>
> In a five-page essay in the September 7 [2009] issue of *Newsweek*, Jonathan Tepperman explains Why Obama Should Learn to Love the Bomb by quoting the dean of nuclear optimism, Prof. Kenneth Waltz: "We now have 64 years of experience since Hiroshima. It's striking and against all historical precedent that for that substantial period, there has not been any war among nuclear states." Tepperman calls for "cold-blooded calculations about just how dangerous possessing them [nuclear weapons] actually is."

In other words, Tepperman is addressing both the fact of non-use and the brute death toll disparity between the nonnuclear and nuclear halves of the twentieth century.

Hellman counters thusly:

> This response rises to that challenge and shows that the data used to justify nuclear optimism is highly misleading. . . . If we want to be 99% confident about our statements, the 64 years of non-use that we have experienced cannot be used to justify a time horizon of even 14 years. Statistics does not rule out that we might survive significantly longer than these time horizons, but it does say that the data thus far cannot be used to justify such hopes with any degree of confidence.
>
> To understand why we can only be confident of surviving time horizons significantly shorter than the 64 years of non-use already experienced, it helps to consider related space shuttle optimism arguments that led to the loss of Challenger and her crew. The engineers who had designed the shuttle's booster engine tried to delay Challenger's final launch because the weather that morning was unusually cold, and previous cold weather launches had a higher incidence of partial "burn through" on O-rings designed to seal the booster. But those at NASA responsible for the launch decision suffered from the common misperception that the shuttle's prior 23 successful launches provided ample evidence that it was safe to proceed with launch number 24. Instead, as we now know, that launch suffered catastrophic burn through of the O-rings, with resultant loss of the shuttle and her entire crew.
>
> NASA's optimistic reasoning was literally dead wrong. Even 23 perfect launches would not have provided sufficient evidence to confidently predict success for launch number 24, and previous near misses, in the form of partial O-ring burn through, made optimism even more outrageous and unsupportable. The unassailable, cold blooded conclusion provided by statistics and Challenger's deadly lesson is that 64 years

of nuclear non-use, particularly with near misses such as the Cuban missile crisis, is no cause for nuclear optimism.

So what do we make of this fairly frightening ten percent per decade estimate? What percentage of our attention does the possibility of extinction deserve? That's hard to solve with statistics.

One of Hellman's most memorable and impassioned arguments turns on a citation from a Russian scientist named Yuri Zamoshkin whom, Hellman says, he had "the great honor of working with and who made important intellectual contributions to the Soviet reform movement of the 1980s."

He explains that faced with the apocalypse equation or its Russian equivalent, Zamoshkin has turned in anguish to a term used by French and German existentialist writers. Zamoshkin writes:

In the philosophy of twentieth-century German and French existentialists (notably K. Jaspers), the term *grenzsituation* (border situation) has been used to designate an experience in which an individual comes face to face with the real possibility of death. Death is no longer merely an abstract thought, but a distinct possibility. Life and death hang in the balance.

Different human beings respond to the *grenzsituation* in different ways. Some become passive and put their heads on the chopping block, so to speak. Others experience something akin to a revelation and find themselves capable of feats they never before could have thought possible. In a *grenzsituation* some timid individuals have become heroes; some selfish individuals have become Schweitzers. And sometimes in so transcending their normal personalities they cheat the grim reaper where normally they would not.

Until now this not only has been applied only to individuals. But I am convinced that today it can be purposefully applied to the world as a whole. The present day global *grenzsituation* resides in the possibility of global death and global life.

The situation for the first time in history, directly, practically and not purely speculatively confronts human thought with the possibility of death for the entire human race. The continuity of history, which earlier had seemed to be a given suddenly becomes highly questionable. . . .

Of course there is always the possibility that faced with a *grenzsituation*, mankind will go passive and put the collective head on the nuclear chopping block. But before we can learn our true mettle, we must bring the global *grenzsituation* into clear focus for all humanity. Society must see that it has but two possibilities, global life or global death.

Yes. I like it: *grenzsituation*. When I read it I realized that it had been written at a time (1989) when the Cold War balance of terror *grenzsituation* still obtained.

But we are still in a new, less obvious, but equally if not more dangerous *grenzsituation*. And we are acting as if it were not there anymore. Twenty-five thousand nuclear warheads, nine nuclear nations and counting. Regional nuclear wars just a shot away all over the globe.

One of the most restrained and respected of nuclear analysts, Harvard's Graham Allison, head of its Belfer Center for Science and International Affairs, wrote in the January/February 2010 issue of *Foreign Affairs* that "The global nuclear order today could be as fragile as the global financial one was two years ago . . . [and the] collapse of the global nuclear order . . . and the consequences [of the collapse] would make nuclear terrorism and nuclear war so imminent that prudent statesmen must do everything feasible to prevent it.

"The collapse of the existing nuclear order is a real threat," he concludes. He doesn't use the word "*grenzsituation*." But that's what he's saying in plain English.

That is what Yarynich and Hellman have been trying to say with statistics and equations and echelons. You cannot play with fire too long without getting badly burned, if not entirely immolated.

CHAPTER SEVEN

# "THE ASHES ARE STILL WARM": THE SECOND HOLOCAUST, ISRAEL, AND THE MORALITY OF NUCLEAR RETALIATION

"History teaches us that overreaction is preferable to under-reaction."

—SHIMON PERES, PRESIDENT OF ISRAEL, MAY 2009

## HITLER'S CHAIN REACTION

A nuclear Third World War could begin in a variety of ways, which include calculated preemption, a regional war going global, accident, misperception, inadequate command and control, suicidal martyrdom, a madman's hubris. But one other factor makes Israel the most likely initial flashpoint: memory.

Back when I was beginning my book about Hitler, I was talking about memory and revenge with my friend Gus, then a lawyer, now a judge; like me a secular, liberal, nonobservant, non-Zionist

132

American-born Jew with no immediate family members murdered in the Holocaust. We were talking about what the appropriate level of feeling toward the perpetrators and the perpetrator nation should be as the Holocaust receded in time. Is the time coming, I wondered, when some kind of forgiveness or at least forgetfulness will supplant the natural desire for retribution?

He looked at me and said, gravely and definitively, "For me, the ashes are still warm."

It is that kind of memory that makes the phrase "second Holocaust" a powerful *strategic factor* in nuclear war considerations among Israeli Jews and one that may play an incalculable part in defining how the end will begin.

If we are talking about when and how World War III will begin, then we cannot avoid examining the role that is likely to be played by that highly loaded, inevitably inflammatory and grim phrase "second Holocaust." A phrase that has gone from tabooed utterance to an increasingly common rubric in the discourse over nuclear war in the second nuclear age. It is a phrase that has become a potential motive, if not a trigger for, the outbreak of World War III in the Middle East.

It means the potential nuclear immolation of the state of Israel and a substantial portion of the nearly six million Jews who live there. It means memory. Memory in the form of awareness among the Jews of Israel that they are being threatened with extermination a second time in six decades. Memory that raises the stakes in the debate over the morality of nuclear retaliation.

The death toll in a second Holocaust may not be as large as that tragically iconic number, six million, with its fearful symmetry with the first. And the source of the first detonation, the outbreak of nuclear war, is not easy to predict. Will it be a missile attack on Tel Aviv, traceable to the state that launched it? Nuclear devices smuggled in by land or sea with "no return address" or even a "false flag" cover making the target of retaliation hard to define with specificity? Or will it be an Israeli nuclear preemption of what their intelligence signals warn is an imminent nuclear attack and the nuclear retaliation that follows?

In the past the Israelis have not hesitated to attack nonnuclear powers who give evidence of seeking to become one—the 1981 attack on the Iraqi reactor at Osirak, the 2007 attack on the Syrian reactor at al-Kibar. Those were long-term threats.

The threat to Israel now posed by Iran is much more immediate: Israeli and American sources have dropped figures that range from months to two years before Iran will have a bomb ready for delivery, 2012–2013 being the most mentioned early and late dates Iran's Ayatollah Ali Akbar Hashemi Rafsanjani has talked of Iran's willingness to lose millions of lives in a "nuclear exchange" with Israel for the sacred mission of destroying the Jewish state and bringing upon the apocalyptic return of "the hidden imam" called for in radical Shia eschatology. Curiously, he seems to evince little concern for the nearly one million Arab citizens of Israel who could die in this "nuclear exchange," since radiation and firestorms don't discriminate by sect.

The Israeli nuclear arsenal is as many as a hundred times the number of nuclear bombs Iran is likely to have by 2012. But Iran only needs two bombs to destroy the Jewish state depending on their megatonnage. They don't even have to be launched by long-distance missile, just lobbed across the northern, eastern, or southern border of Israel, by Hezbollah, Fatah, or Hamas, respectively—all groups sworn to destroy the Jewish state. No warning time likely at all.

The attempted Israeli preemption of such an attack could succeed in an overwhelming way. But unless Israel does succeed completely and utterly, unless its preemption destroys all potentially hostile nuclear weapons including those sixty-plus "Islamic bombs" in Pakistan, then it faces a retaliation that could easily destroy it. Just one or two bombs and delivery vehicles need to escape the Israeli attack for retaliation to succeed entirely. Israel, therefore, has virtually no margin of error. Its people are damned if they do preempt, and dead if they don't. It doesn't make for a stable situation.

Will there be an Israeli attack before the Iranian bomb goes on-line? If there is, the fire that keeps the ashes of Hitler's Holocaust warm will in some way have lit the fuse.

I don't think it appropriate that I pretend to be dispassionate on this subject, considering my Jewish descent and having spent ten years of my life examining the origin of Hitler's Holocaust. But let us try to be as analytical as possible and begin with some distinctions, for instance, in the way the second Holocaust will differ from Hitler's. The Ghost of Holocaust Future resembles the one of the past in its potential death toll carnage and tragedy. But it could be argued the second one transcends the enormity of the first by its very secondness. In which case history, to modify the line from Karl Marx's *Eighteenth Brumaire of Louis Bonaparte*, unfolds itself as "first time tragedy, second time even more dreadful tragedy." That it should happen again to the same people in the space of sixty years is not merely twice as horrifying but exponentially more tragic. As is the notion that the second time will have been a consequence of an attempt to provide refuge for the victims of the first.

A second Holocaust is still a tragedy waiting to happen. But it's a specter pervasively conjured up, prayed for, on multiple electronic and digital outlets in the landmass surrounding Israel's sliver of seacoast and desert. Israelis can easily find, on their airwaves or on multiple Web sites, imams throughout the Middle East calling for their extermination.

And to have Hitler smiling on the fulfillment of the process he began! In December 2009, Yale University Press published a remarkable book by the historian Jeffrey Herf. Herf had discovered State Department transcripts of Arabic language broadcasts made in Berlin and broadcast to the Middle East during the Hitler days by Haj-al-Amin Husseni, the Grand Mufti of Jerusalem. He claimed to be a spiritual leader of the Arab peoples, as well as a political leader of the Palestine National Council. The Mufti spent the war years in Berlin (after fleeing the failed pro-Hitler regime he'd helped foist on Iraq), broadcasting to his brethen left behind in the Middle East. They gathered around communal radios to hear what the Mufti believed was a "fusion" of Nazism and Islamism, a fusion characterized by an exterminationist hatred for the Jews. A growing school of historians has come to believe that one powerful source of contemporary exterminationist anti-Semitism in the Middle

East was the vast propaganda campaign led by the Nazi-sponsored Mufti. Meanwhile he had Hitler's ear and—by all accounts—spent the war years urging Hitler to kill more and more Jews, faster and faster until he could get to the ones in the Middle East and exterminate them. "Kill the Jews wherever you find them," he urged his listeners.

Herf's book is further evidence of how it is not unrealistic for the Jews of Israel to hear Hitler's voice echo on the airwaves today, because in a sense they are hearing Hitler's ventriloquy. The Mufti set the exterminationist tone of the hatred not just of Israel but of all Jews everywhere. The evil incitements to genocide that are echoed today in the airwaves that bombard parents raising children in Israel are echoes of Hitler and cannot help but influence Israel's nuclear decision makers.

Israelis tell me the use of the phrase "second Holocaust" has become normalized there. When I asked the co-author of the Israel Defense Forces' code of ethics, Moshe Halbertal, whether he thought the secondness of a second Holocaust would be a factor in Israeli's military posture, he shrugged and said, "Of course."

Historians such as Michael Oren have noted that the phrase "second Holocaust" had already been used by ordinary Israeli citizens during the run-up to the 1967 Six Day War to describe the threat to the Jewish state's existence and that of the Jewish people who would perish with it. In that war, the Israelis launched preemptive invasions of Egypt and Syria—though, technically, under international law, the first act of war was the Egyptian blockade of the Straits of Tiran, completing a nooselike encirclement of Israel by cutting off its southernmost port. Preemption, then, is part of their history.

In 2007, Israeli historian Benny Morris published an essay entitled "The Second Holocaust Will Not Be Like the First," which focused on one way the nuclear destruction of the state of Israel will differ in its nature and timeframe from Hitler's Holocaust.

"The second holocaust will not be like the first," he wrote. "The Nazis, of course, industrialized mass murder. But still, the perpetrators had one-on-one contact with the victims. They may have dehumanized them over months and years of appalling debasement and in their minds, before the actual killing. But, still, they were in eye and ear contact, sometimes in tactile contact, with their victims. The Germans, along with their non-German helpers, had to round up the men, women and children from their houses and drag and beat them through the streets and mow them down in nearby woods or push and pack them into cattle cars and transport them to the camps where [they had to] lure them into 'shower' halls and pour in the gas and then take out, or oversee the extraction of, the bodies."

He argues that a second Holocaust will by contrast more likely be launched at a distance. "One bright morning, in five or 10 years, perhaps during a regional crisis, perhaps out of the blue, a day or a year or five years after Iran's acquisition of the Bomb, the mullahs in Qom will convene in secret session, under a portrait of the steely-eyed Ayatollah Khomeini, and give President Mahmoud Ahmadinejad, by then in his second or third term, the go-ahead. The orders will go out and the Şhehab III and IV missiles will take off for Tel Aviv, Beersheba, Haifa and Jerusalem, and probably some military sites, including Israel's half dozen air and (reported) nuclear missile bases. Some of the Shehabs will be nuclear-tipped, perhaps even with multiple warheads. Others will be dupes, packed merely with biological or chemical agents, or old newspapers, to draw off or confuse Israel's anti-missile batteries and Home Front Command units.

"With a country the size and shape of Israel (an elongated 20,000 square kilometers), probably four or five hits will suffice: No more Israel. A million or more Israelis in the greater Tel Aviv, Haifa and Jerusalem areas will die immediately. Millions will be seriously irradiated. Israel has about seven million inhabitants. No Iranian will see or touch an Israeli. It will be quite impersonal." The implication is that push-button impersonality will make the second Holocaust easier to carry out, the work of an instant.

Another key difference about a second Holocaust, when it happens (I suppose I should say "if") is that this one will have been predicted, proclaimed, joyfully heralded in advance by the perpetrators and imams in every nation in the region, announcements made available in Hebrew by the valuable Middle East Media Research Institute transcriptions and translations of Arabic language broadcasts. When it comes to Israel, there is an incessant, open incitement to genocide, as opposed to the secretive if not entirely secret execution of Hitler's Final Solution. Those who seek the extermination of the Jews today have no hesitation in calling for just that in as public and specific a way possible. And so we have a leading Islamist preacher and broadcaster on Al Jazeera, Yusuf al-Qaradawi, praying to Allah to kill the Jews, "Oh Allah, Count their numbers and kill them down to the very last one."

And then there is the founding charter of Hamas, the ruling party in Gaza, a movement that is regarded by many as merely a somewhat extreme Palestinian rights group. Yet the very charter of its existence follows the Muslim Brotherhood's spiritual leader by citing a hadith (a non-Quranic, proverbial remark of Muhammad that can nonetheless carry great weight) that calls for the hunting down and killing of all Jews: not just Israeli Jews or West Bank Jewish settlers, not just Zionists or self-proclaimed anti-Zionists, but all Jews. For Hamas, there is no shyness about a second Holocaust: its platform exceeds Hitler's in Jew hatred, and it cites in its charter such staples of Western anti-Semitism distributed by the Nazis as *The Protocols of the Elders of Zion*.

Supreme Leader of Iran Ayatollah Ali Khamenei is also clear about inflicting a second Holocaust. "Israel is a cancerous tumor," he says. Yes, he is speaking about Israel, not Jews, and yes, he is using a metaphor. But medical metaphors have a bad history. Hitler used them all the time, also likening Jews to a cancer. The implications of the Supreme Leader's cancer metaphor, his Hitler trope, are clear: Jews are the cancer cells in the cancerous tumor. How does one excise a "cancerous lesion"? We have heard the "moderate" former Iranian president Hashemi Rafsanjani speaking glowingly as early as 2001 of a future "nuclear exchange" between Iran and Israel, which would leave "nothing on the ground" in the state of Israel, nothing presumably but a human stain.

The point is, Hitler carried out the Final Solution but was fearful of publicizing it. He never set foot in a death camp, never allowed his signature, so far as we know, on an extermination order. We only have reports of him giving oral orders. He thought the world would be horrified if it found out about the industrialized mass murder. He thought it would be bad for his image. Seriously! As it turns out, when the news began to emerge, the world was not concerned enough to make more than empty gestures. Hitler overestimated the world's conscience.

By contrast many radical Islamists in positions of state and spiritual authority boast of their exterminationist intentions. They want the world to know it. They want the Jews to know it, and the world does nothing about it and tells those concerned, those targeted, don't be affected by it, it's "only rhetoric." Or as most Israelis complete the thought: "Just like Hitler's threats were 'only rhetoric.'"

The world will lament the fate of the Tutsis in Rwanda, say, and pretend that those who incite genocide don't really mean it until they do it and then it's too late. And when the world does decide that rhetoric matters—that incitement to genocide could be a crime—it ignores the incitement to a second genocide of the Jews. Yet international law has recognized that rhetoric can kill. That is one reason that one of the few criminal convictions to emerge from the Rwandan genocide was related to that of a radio station, Radio Mille Collines. Its key personnel were prosecuted and convicted of "inciting to genocide" by the International Criminal Court under a provision of the Rome Treaty on Preventing Genocide—Article 25 (30) (e) to be precise. The radio station hate mongers were convicted for allowing "the genocide planners" to use the station's airwaves to "broadcast murderous instructions directly to the people." It is instructive in two ways: incitement to genocide is now an internationally recognized, successfully prosecutable crime. It does not require the genocide be consummated. The idea is that if you prosecute incitement, execution will be less likely.

And yet there has been no effort to prosecute the incessant incitement to genocide—to a second Holocaust—of the Jewish people. No one outside Israel, and the U.S. has suggested that any of the Iranian leadership, or the leaders of Hamas, be prosecuted under international law for incitement to genocide. Nor have their governments been called to account for it. A "Referral of Iranian President Ahmadinejad on the Charge of Incitement to Commit Genocide," prepared by the Israeli jurist Justus Reid Weiner in 2006, lays out the case for any who care. Not many seem to. These are people who are more forthright in calling for extermination than Adolf Hitler was, and yet the murderous incitement that issues from their mouths is not taken seriously by the world. Israelis and Jews should accommodate themselves to this international call for extermination even when it appears in elementary school textbooks in their neighboring nations. It shouldn't be an obstacle to the "peace process" for God's sake. It certainly shouldn't be cause for Israel to take action against the weapons that would enable the fulfillment of this genocidal vision, should it?

## THE CONSEQUENCES

All this will make it more likely that—sooner or later—Israel will unleash nuclear weapons, risk inaugurating World War III—to prevent what they perceive as an impending nuclear strike. Israelis will not wait for the world to step in. They may not even wait to be sure their intelligence on the strike they wish to preempt is rock-solid certain. They can't afford to take that chance. It is not something I advocate; it is something I forsee.

In 1981, Israel Air Force F-16s attacked and destroyed the Iraqi nuclear reactor at Osirak near Baghdad—a reactor capable of producing weapons-grade plutonium from spent fuel rods near Baghdad. Most of the world outside Israel condemned the attack. When Prime Minister Menachem Begin explained his decision afterward, he said, "We have to defend our nation, after one and a half million of our children were exterminated by the Nazis in the gas chambers in the Second World War." Begin, "who had escaped the Nazi invasion of Poland in September 1939, arrived in Palestine three years later. . . . In his six years as prime minister, he never ceased feeling that it was his personal mission to ensure that a second Holocaust never took place," wrote Anshel Pfeffer of Israel's *Ha'aretz*.

"When Begin sent the Israel Defense Forces into Lebanon to drive out the Palestine Liberation Organization he likened PLO leader Yasser Arafat to 'Hitler in his bunker.'"

Twenty-five years later, Benjamin Netanyahu, despite belonging to a different generation, used a stark historical analogy to describe the Iranian threat to Israel: "It is 1938 and Iran is Germany. And Iran is racing to arm itself with atomic bombs."

Even Shimon Peres, long regarded as the preeminent dovish Israeli statesman and its prime minister from 1986 to 1988, said in May 2009: "History teaches us that overreaction is preferable to under-reaction." He was virtually declaring that he prefers an Israeli preemptive first strike, even nuclear, even if it's an overreaction, to the wait-and-hope passivity of under-reaction that enabled Hitler's Holocaust to reap so many victims.

Would the overreaction have an element of displaced vengeance for Hitler's Holocaust? In other words, might there be an element of retaliation for the first Holocaust in an Israeli nuclear preemption ostensibly to prevent a second? It is only speculation, impossible to read the minds of those who will give the orders. But it wouldn't surprise me. The contemporary Middle East is a Hitler dream come true. The Jews have been compelled by the Holocaust and history to, in effect, round themselves up and may feel compelled by history to inflict an attack with genocidal consequences on others that could well precede a second one for them. Yes, it's an emotional factor, but as they say, feelings are facts. Hitler's Holocaust has shaped Israeli awareness of history, and the implications of the past failure to take Hitler's exterminationist rhetoric seriously will affect Israelis current reaction—or overreaction—to the exterminationist rhetoric and the real threats that rain down on their sliver of land. The very secondness of the second Holocaust carries with it a temptation to abandon all thoughts of proportionality in retaliation, and to punish the whole world for allowing not one but two slaughters of a people.

Abandonment of proportionality is the essence of the so-called Samson Option in all its variants. A Samson Option is made possible by the fact that even if Israel has been obliterated, it can be sure that its Dolphin-class nuclear missile submarines cruising the Red Sea, the Indian Ocean, and the Persian Gulf, at depths impervious to detection, can carry out a genocidal-scaled retaliation virtually anywhere in the world.

It is probably unnecessary to recall the origin of the phrase: Samson's suicidal dying act in the Bible was to pull down the pillars of the Philistine temple around him and kill all those inside including himself. The extreme version of the Samson option presupposes a rage on the part of post–second Holocaust survivors in possession of nuclear weapons determined to reduce the entire temple of civilization to ashes for having complacently allowed two Holocausts to be inflicted on one people.

It is useful to remember that even if Israel strikes first for good reason or bad intelligence, there is no assurance that such action would guarantee prevention of an anticipated nuclear strike. The Washington-based Center for Strategic and International Studies's most recent study of a possible nonnunclear Israeli attack on Iranian nuclear facilities—a one-hundred-page analysis of every plane, missile, weapon, every flight path potential, every estimate of wind-dependent radiation damage—does not give the reader confidence that any nonnuclear strike has more than a 50-50 chance of succeeding, which strongly suggests nuclear strikes at the outset are the only guarantee of success. This is something that must be known to the Israelis but which they may be compelled to gamble their existence on.

Think of it this way: Hitler's Holocaust, the first, increases the likelihood of a second Holocaust by causing the concentration of survivors and refugees in Israel thus making a one- or two-bomb attack genocidal. And Israel, seeking to prevent a second Holocaust, launches a preemptive nuclear strike whose consequences for both sides is genocidal.

And the victim of a second Holocaust is likely to have the weapons or the allies to inflict a third on the party that struck first, and, they, for all we know, could unleash a fourth against the party that struck them until it all goes global and there's no one left to kill.

At a certain point what we will have is a chain reaction of lowercase holocausts, perhaps enough to escalate to the global level, certain to put a smile on Hitler's face in hell. Hitler's nuclear chain reaction.

Would there have been a bomb at all without that fear of Hitler? When Leo Szilard got Einstein to persuade FDR to build a bomb, the argument was that if we didn't move fast Hitler would have a war-winning one first. It has never been clear whether Hitler's scientists had been tasked with making such a weapon, or if they had been, that they had made any significant progress by 1939 when Einstein wrote his letter. The Manhattan Project was an early instance of the exorbitant effects of the ambiguities of warning in nuclear affairs that Thomas Powers has explored in his study of the German bomb question, *Heisenberg's War*. It would be the ultimate irony if the atomic bomb was only invented because of misplaced fears Hitler might get one. A bomb that might ultimately nonetheless serve to finish off Hitler's Final Solution if detonated in Israel.

## SECOND HOLOCAUST DENIAL

Still there are those who resist taking into account the secondness of a second Holocaust as a strategic—triggering—factor or admit the prospect into their worldview at all.

I didn't become aware of the term "second Holocaust," or, in any case, it didn't linger in my memory, until I reread Philip Roth's 1993 novel *Operation Shylock* in 2002, nearly ten years after it was published. Prompted by the events of that year—not just the wave of suicide bombers within Israel but growing awareness of external nuclear threats from Iran. I used the phrase "second Holocaust" in print and found myself under fire—mainly from American Jews—for having broken a taboo. It took me a while to understand the fearful reaction to the phrase. Perhaps it's best to begin with Roth's use of "second Holocaust" in *Operation Shylock*.

In Roth's strange and brilliant book the words "second Holocaust" are spoken through several levels of disguise and impersonation and so one is never clear what Roth's relation to the phrase is; he's such a brilliant ventriloquist who sometimes disguises his own views in a colorfully alien voice. In this case, in a novel that calls itself a true story, the "real" Philip Roth, the American novelist, narrator learns (from a reporter) that someone calling himself "Philip Roth" has been giving lectures in Jerusalem on the philosophy of "Diasporism." It is Roth imagining "Roth" as a prophet of tragic nuclear extermination, a second Holocaust.

The "diasporist" Roth argues that the real glory of the Jewish people has been in exile. However oppressed and persecuted the Jews had been, their civilization and culture flourished and produced great works, but while restricted to, constricted by, Israel, Jews produced little of comparable importance. So the Jewish state was a mistake because Jews no longer engaged in the same kind of stimulating and provoking dialectic with the rest of the world the exiles had, and because Israel had with the help of the world turned itself into a kind of concentration camp that made it all the more vulnerable to . . . a second Holocaust. He used the phrase.

One learns after reading Roth for years—or one thinks one learns—to distinguish when he's impersonating and when he's— for want of a better word—personating—putting his own thoughts into others' words. I couldn't be sure which was happening in the key *Operation Shylock* paragraph, which led to a heated controversy when I quoted it in a column in 2002.

"The meanings of the Holocaust" [says the "diasporist" who calls himself "Philip Roth"] are for us to determine, but one thing is sure—its meaning will be no less tragic than it is now if there is a second Holocaust and the offspring of the European Jews who evacuated Europe for a seemingly safer haven should meet collective annihilation in the Middle East. . . . A second Holocaust could happen here all too easily, and if the conflict between Arab and Jew escalates much longer, it will—it must. . . . The destruction of Israel in a nuclear exchange is a possibility much less farfetched today than was the Holocaust itself fifty years ago."

"It will—it must." That's strong even in the words of an unreliable narrator, an impersonator. Too strong for some.

It seemed clear to me that Roth was using the "diasporist" to break the taboo against uttering the phrase "second Holocaust," but by embedding it in a novel's multiple layers of irony it failed to provoke much of a reaction at the time. When it was proposed as a terrifying but real nonfiction possibility, the reaction suggested that something taboolike was at work in the superstitious fear of the phrase, as if uttering it might somehow bring it closer. I came to think of this phenomenon as second holocaust denial.

There were two main varieties of second Holocaust denial: geographical displacement and Holocaust inconsequentialism. Geographical displacement is the lesser of the two although the more revealing of the fear the phrase inspired. Thus on the talk show *Charlie Rose* one critic indignantly told me it was "nonsense" to say there was likely to be a second Holocaust in Europe, a nonsensical response since I had been writing about the possibility of a second Holocaust in Israel. The geographic displacement seemed more an evasion than a mistake. Let's talk about someplace it's not likely to happen.

I wouldn't have given it a second thought (after correcting him) if it hadn't come up again. This time it came from a columnist for the *New York Times* who, in an even more far-fetched geographical displacement, insisted that I had suggested there would be a second Holocaust in America! The two instances suggested that two intelligent people, both Jews, could not handle a discussion about the likeliest geographical site—the true picture was too distressing and tragic to deal with.

But the geographic displacement variety of second Holocaust denial was far less significant than what I've come to call Holocaust inconsequentialism—the denial of any historical lessons to be learned from the horror—which surfaced in the dispute between the well-known American novelist and essayist Cynthia Ozick and the prominent Anglo-Dutch intellectual Ian Buruma over the Israeli attack on the Iraqi nuclear reactor at Osirak in 1981. Menachem Begin's frank explanation that Hitler's Holocaust was a key factor in his decision did not sit well with some who were uncomfortable with the Holocaust having historical consequences. Cynthia Ozick takes up the story, telling us:

"In a [2003] *New York Times Magazine* piece called 'How to Talk About Israel,' Ian Buruma, alluding to Israel's demolishment of Iraq's nuclear installation, contends that it might have been justified in 'many legitimate ways . . . but [Buruma] derides Menachem Begin's appeal to the memory of the one and a half million Jewish children who were annihilated' as illegitimate, even 'shameful.'"

Yes, that's where the shame inheres—in speaking of it and in drawing lessons from it, not in perpetrating it. Or so one might imagine reading Buruma's outrage.

To Buruma's charge that a Holocaust reference was "shameful" Ozick replies, in an Afterword to an anthology on the question of contemporary anti-Semitism I compiled: "Is the imagination's capacity to connect Hitler's Holocaust to a potential second one as Begin did worthy of such scorn or is this how human beings ought to think and feel?"

Some writers have accused Jews of making too much of the Holocaust, even exploiting it to justify Israeli actions they disagree with by giving the Holocaust a sacralized ahistorical status. I'd argue that in fact all the Holocaust museums in the world don't make a difference if the Holocaust is made ahistorical in the other extreme—deprived of real-world, contemporary consequences from "the imagination's capacity to connect events." It bears some relation to what the philosopher Berel Lang was thinking about when he spoke to me about Heidegger's silence after the Holocaust. The German philosopher and godfather of postmodernist theory continued to write for three decades after the Holocaust, but the former Nazi Party rector of Freiburg University who offered his ruminations on just about everything else on heaven and earth never found the time or the interest to reflect in print on his role as a Nazi Party member who did his part to make his lecture halls *Judenrein* and who defended Nazism for the "organic" mentality of its blood-and-soil ideology. (Indeed what exercised him most in his postwar work was mechanized agriculture—not the mechanized killing that he had enabled.) "The Holocaust happened," as Berel Lang put it. "It just didn't have any consequences for Heidegger." Nor should it have for Begin, for Israel, for us, according to Buruma.

Are there are other "no-go" periods in history peremptorily off-limits to those who want to put the current situation in perspective? Do we banish the history of slavery from our minds when discussing affirmative action? The Supreme Court just reaffirmed the Voting Rights Act, which makes certain that areas that exhibited racist behavior in the past are subject to special inspections. This accords history a place in the conduct of current affairs.

In many ways, Holocaust inconsequentialism is worse than Holocaust denial, because inconsequentialism doesn't deny it happened; it acknowledges the mass murder but adds insult to injury by depriving those murdered lives of any possible meaning for the living. Actually, the wish to "banish" it is not even second Holocaust denial: it's a call for erasure of the first Holocaust, for elimination. The Final Solution to the Final Solution: forget it, eradicate it for all practical purposes.

Why the irrational fear of according Hitler's Holocaust a place in historically based deliberations? If you ask me I think it's because it's an unbearable reminder of the shamefulness of human conduct. This willed memory erasure stems from an all too intense fear that it's going to happen again and there's no way to prevent it, so better to delegitimize or abolish recognition of the relevance of the original unbearable truth. In the end, the Holocaust is sacralized out of history by some, shamed out of history by others.

In America in particular, to speak of a second Holocaust as a serious possibility contravenes one of our most cherished beliefs: there is a solution to every problem, even the Middle East. Perhaps it is the absence of a tragic sense of history here, and perhaps also the absence of daily death threats. The idea of a second Holocaust has disturbed some American Jews such as *New Republic* literary editor Leon Wieseltier, who called concern about a second Holocaust "ethnic panic," evidently too tribal for his lofty literary universalism.

I suppose I can understand they are not eager to have their comfortable American assimilation disrupted by association with victimhood halfway around the world. No ghetto mentality here! There is also a superstitious reluctance by these second Holocaust deniers to utter it—as if, like a voodoo spell, speaking it aloud would bring it to life, and with it, a monumental golem of grief. Unfortunately such obtuseness feeds into the Israeli perception that they have no friends in the West willing to speak of the kind of peril they face—all the more reason to go it alone in the case of ambiguity of warning.

Compare this Holocaust inconsequentialism with the resurgence of flat-out Holocaust denial exemplified in the 2006 Tehran Holocaust deniers conference. It was an important event because it demonstrated how Holocaust denial—once the province of a few crackpots—has morphed into an instrument, a central strategic rationale, for those who want to perpetrate one "for real." Delegitimizing Israel's existence by making it seem the product of a "Jewish trick"—inventing a Holocaust to guilt-trip the world into letting them take over in Palestine. But Holocaust inconsequentialism is worse because it doesn't wear its anti-Semitism on its sleeve. Because all too many who wouldn't go within miles of a Holocaust denier share a negationism with the Holocaust inconsequentialists on this issue. A negation of consequences, most saliently nuclear war.

To understand how deep emotion might determine our nuclear future, consider the words of Louisiana State University professor David Perlmutter in an op ed piece in the *Los Angeles Times* that goes so far as to justify a Samson Option type response.

"What would serve the Jew-hating world better," Perlmutter asks, "in repayment for thousands of years of massacres but a Nuclear Winter? Or invite all those tut-tutting European statesmen and peace activists to join us in the ovens? For the first time in history, a people facing extermination while the world either cackles or looks away—unlike the Armenians, Tibetans, World War II European Jews or Rwandans—have the power to destroy the world. The ultimate justice?"

Justice or vengeance? Or just pure rage at the world's unconcern about incitement to genocide. It may be wrong, not proportional. But it's there, that emotion. What role should emotion play in nuclear decisions? Isn't the entire deterrent system designed to be based on an emotional dynamic, that of fear? Fear of attack leads to threatening a more fearsome retaliation that is designed to inspire fear of attacking in the first place.

What is the moral status of such retaliation? A friend familiar with the faculty of New York's Jewish Theological Seminary offered to put me in contact with three of the sages there most familiar with such difficult ethical questions such as justice and retaliation and the history of Jewish thinking on the question.

I asked them, separately, to put themselves in the place of a Jewish submarine commander who learns of a nuclear Holocaust in Israel, and, cut off from his home base chain of command by the destruction of land-based communications links, must decide for himself what is the just response. What, in effect, would the sages' Letter of Last Resort say?

The results played out almost as in some biblical story, or perhaps as if I were the wicked son asking the wicked question at the Passover feast. First one sage, then a second, pronounced himself unwilling to confront the question. Almost as if it were an affront to have been asked. One just wouldn't comment, the other claimed a lack of expertise. I hate to say it, but I had a feeling they were afraid to commit themselves. These are literally explosive issues. Better to stay in their safe tenured little patch of academia than risk saying something on urgent but controversial questions where their purported wisdom might help ordinary people wrestle with huge life-or-death decisions. Academic timidity, don't get me started. These are the ethics of genocide and you have nothing to say?

The third sage at least left me with a memorable phrase that I felt justified the quest. When I asked him my forbidden question about the morality of retaliation, particularly in the event of second Holocaust in Israel, he said, "You're asking something new under the sun."

"Something new under the sun." He understood! These are not questions that have had to be asked before the nuclear age. Perhaps the principles applied are older but the alternatives, genocide on each side of the question—this is "something new under the sun."

And so you're left with me to think about it and to ask you to think about it. One thing I want to think about is the possibility of nonretaliation. No striking back. Not necessarily to advocate it, but to describe my encounter with an advocate of it.

One of the saddest, most provocative things I've heard about the history of the Jews is the notion that while Christians preach turning the other cheek Jews are the ones who, through history, have actually done it. Berel Lang, one of the few scholars unafraid to face such questions, wrote an essay for a Jewish quarterly that he called "Why No Retaliation?" for Hitler's Holocaust. Some Jews did attempt postwar to poison a few German POWs, a haphazard scheme that didn't result in many deaths. There were virtually no Jews left in Europe to do any retaliating, and even those who tried to return to their old homes and might have been in a position to do so were forced to flee again by pogroms throughout Eastern Europe.

So it was more by default, not really by choice, that there was no retaliation. There was justice of a limited sort, the Nazi hunting of Simon Wiesenthal for instance. But no retaliation, just memory.

Next time, should there be a second Holocaust, Jews will have the means to inflict massive retaliation, they will have the choice at least, it will be by choice and that choice may well come down to a submarine commander. The last resort of choice.

Should he retaliate, regardless of his orders? Several years ago I gave a talk to a seminar sponsored by the Yale Interdisciplinary Initiative for the Study of Anti-Semitism about the idea of a second Holocaust and the controversy over it. And, at the end, the issue of retaliation came up.

One speaker addressed the question of whether the Israelis had provided for it and shielded their retaliatory forces. He told the story of the Isaiah scroll in Jerusalem's Shrine of the Book, the repository for the most ancient and revered manuscripts of the Jewish people, and how the Isaiah scroll, after a brief period of being on display in a super-hardened glass case, retracts deep, deep into the earth, into the titanium steel alloy silo you might say, that reaches far beneath the surface and is said to be able to survive a direct nuclear blast. They care about books there. You can't use your library card to get the Isaiah scroll. The point he was making was that the Israelis guarded their retaliatory capacity with the same care as the Isaiah scroll and that was saying something.

Until the very end of the question and comment period no voices had been raised to question the fact that there would or should be retaliation. Then a grad-student-looking fellow at the back of the room spoke up and in a halting, tentative voice framed his question this way:

What if the Jews didn't retaliate at all? What if they, the survivors, somehow declared there would be nothing to be gained, only a preponderance of innocent lives to be lost among the guilty perpetrators. Wouldn't the Jews—however few were left alive—be honored then and for centuries afterward for this forbearance?

Interesting choice of words: honored. I thought of Falstaff: "What is honor?"

Before I could answer, a fellow on the side of the room spoke up and said such talk, or a public airing of it, would be dangerous because it would undermine the credibility of Israel's deterrent, which depended on the certainty of retaliation. Not that anyone in that room was going to be giving the order.

I didn't have an answer for either one of them. I felt in part the terror the Jewish Theological Seminarians felt. What if you don't know what to think about the question of retaliation.

It just so happened that on July 3, 2009, the *Jerusalem Post* printed a dispatch about one of Israelis nuclear-capable Dolphin-class submarines. Israeli papers are not allowed to acknowledge possession of nuclear weapons by the state and so the dispatch was muted, although the reverberations must have been pronounced for those in the know about the role of the Dolphins as the Israeli launchers of last resort. "After a long hiatus the Israeli Navy has returned to sail through the Suez Canal," the story said, "recently sending one of its advanced Dolphin class submarines through the waterway to participate in naval maneuvers off the Eilat Coast in the Red Sea."

A message was being sent. A message about retaliation. And the means to do it. But what about the will to do it, the morality of the choice? And so as I write this a submarine that could start (or end)

World War III is cruising into range. And no one knows what the commander thinks about the consequences of a second Holocaust. Or whether he carries a Letter of Last Resort.

It took me a while, but at last I found someone who was an authority on the ethics of the question and the military implications there of someone who was willing to talk about what was "new under the sun."

## MOSHE HALBERTAL: THE DETERMINATE VERSUS THE IMMEASURABLE

"Do you think it's wrong to write about this?" I asked Moshe Halbertal toward the end of our talk.

We were sitting in his office at NYU Law School where he spends half the academic year teaching ethics and the international law of war; the other half he does the same at Hebrew University in Jerusalem. He is one of the most widely respected thinkers on the moral and ethical dilemmas of modern warfare. He was influenced by the writings of Michael Walzer, the author of the influential book *Just and Unjust Wars: A Moral Argument with Historical Illustrations*. And Halbertal's gotten involved in a way that is more difficult and perilous than academic: he's co-written the code of ethics for the IDF, the Israel Defense Forces.

He admitted he had not written about how just war ethics apply to nuclear war questions. He admitted he felt he was entering into a "no-man's-land . . . beyond the law." Occasionally he would say variations of "but you can't say that" after he'd said it. Which is why I asked him if I should write about it.

We had been speaking as well about his shocking-at-first notion that a preemptive nuclear strike might be a morally justifiable act under certain restrictive conditions involving "thresholds" and "supreme emergencies." We had been talking about submarines, the retaliatory weapons of last resort. And so I found myself asking in a guilty way whether deterrence was—or should be—a bluff, something you threaten but aren't allowed to carry out, as Walzer believes. But of course even to discuss it is to make an attack by a foe more tempting should he think the threat might be a bluff.

"Wrong to write about it?" I asked. "Not that anyone is going to pay attention," I hastily added, not wishing to risk being held responsible for a nuclear cataclysm, "but—"

"No, not at all, you should, you should definitely—"

"No one in Iran is going to say—"

"No I don't think you'll break the . . ."

He trails off but I think he means to break the veil of secrecy or the shroud of ambiguity that cloaks Israeli nuclear war plans, even nuclear weapons possession.

Halbertal was just the person I had been seeking to talk to, a much admired Talmudic scholar most well known among the Talmudists for his book on idolatry who had brought his immersion in the wisdom of the sages to contemporary military ethics. He is deeply knowledgeable about the whole tradition of just war theory, but willing to acknowledge that nuclear weapons presented new challenges to ancient conundrums. Something new under the sun.

He is a modest shirt-sleeved fiftyish guy who says dramatic things in an offhand undramatic manner and is frank about his hesitancy, uncertainty, and agony on certain matters. He comes across as a someone of genuine humility who admits to being tentative. He's a serious and courageous man.

I began by asking Halbertal to describe how his military experience led him to his current position. He told me that he had enlisted in the Israeli army and served as an artillery spotter. In other words his task was both military and ethical: to make distinctions—often difficult and immensely consequential ones—between civilian and military targets in the grim struggles of "irregular warfare" where decisions were not always possible with precision. The artillery spotter is a battlefield ethicist who puts his life on the line getting to the forward-most position for the sake of saving innocents. A position where to make the wrong choice is to risk killing innocents.

He told me our conversation was his "first extended" one on

something he had been thinking about but had not addressed formally. "All this has become unfortunately very real," he said. He's talking about Iran and what Israel will have to do about it. Ten days after Halbertal and I spoke the following report appeared on a Web site called DEBKAfile known to be a conduit for Israeli information and disinformation. It's not clear which this was, but since Israel does not officially admit to having nuclear weapons, it was remarkably detailed technically. That doesn't mean the voyage described wasn't manufactured out of whole cloth. But if so it was designed to paint a picture for the Iranians of a voyage that *could* take place:

> 04 Oct. [2009] Western naval sources report that Israel's German-made Dolphin submarines have been heavily modified: its torpedo tubes enlarged to accommodate missiles, new electronics installed and its fuel capacity expanded to keep the vessel at sea for 50 days without refueling. Eight years after receiving the first three Dolphin subs from Germany and two more last month, naval sources rate them the most modern non-nuclear [-powered] subs in any world navy. Israel has equipped the new Dolphin-class subs with homemade 1,500-km range cruise missiles carrying 200 kiloton nuclear warheads and 135-km range US-made Harpoon missiles also fitted with nuclear warheads. These missiles, fired through the newly-enlarged 650mm-26-inch tubes, can reach Iranian coastal targets including its nuclear sites as well as naval, port and Revolutionary Guards facilities. The Dolphins' expanded fuel tanks enable them to cover distances of up to 10,000 kilometers from their Mediterranean home port (instead of 8,000 kilometers heretofore) and spend more time—up to 50 days—off the Iranian coast.

DEBKAfile's military sources note: "Their presence outside Israeli waters is a powerful deterrent to any surprise nuclear or conventional attack, endowing Israel with an instantaneous second-strike nuclear capability."

It seems likely someone in the Israeli high command authorized this leak, wanted to paint a detailed picture for most likely the Iranians—and for anyone else who thought a nuclear strike on Israel would go unpunished. There's no point in Israel having five German-made submarines unless it were for the purpose of having an invulnerable second strike retaliatory capacity. I certainly think DEBKAfile's sources wanted its readers in Islamic capitals to believe that nuclear retaliation was inevitable.

I asked Halbertal, "Does nuclear war change traditional just war thinking?"

"Yes," he says. But adds, "I must say I'm in agony about it. I don't have a clear answer to it. I'll tell you what's my dilemma. I don't think that 'Supreme Emergency' is a reason for intentional killing of all civilians. I don't think you are allowed to do it, morally."

"Now, 'Supreme Emergency'—that's Walzer's term, right?" I asked him.

"Exactly."

"And when you say 'intentional killing of all civilians' with regard to nuclear war that would mean either a preemptive or a retaliatory strike?"

"Right, but leave nuclear war aside for a moment and look at the difficulty of 'supreme emergency.'"

"Supreme Emergency" is a phrase adopted by Walzer from a 1939 speech by Winston Churchill in an attempt to reconcile just war ethics with the killing of innocent civilians entailed in the nighttime bombing of German cities. Halbertal began contextualizing his views on nuclear war by tracing the differences he and Walzer have over what recent historical events qualify as supreme emergencies.

He points out that Walzer first used the term "supreme emergency" when discussing Churchill's decision to bomb German cities and the civilians who lived in them in 1940.

"Here was a supreme emergency," Walzer writes, referring to the period after the fall of France before the entrance of the U.S. in the war, "when the victory of Hitler's evil seemed assured, where one might well be required to override the rights of innocent people and shatter the [Geneva] war convention" that requires distinguishing between combatants and noncombatants.

Walzer concedes that its morality is not a sure bet: "Should I wager this determinate crime against immeasurable evil [of a Nazi victory]?," he asks. His answer: yes.

Walzer's use of the word "wager" is almost shocking in its lack of conviction. It's just a bet that bombing civilians might be the right thing to do when weighing the determinate against the immeasurable. He chooses his words carefully and tentatively because he knows he's treading on a minefield. This is the kind of wager in which one just can't calculate odds. Only in hindsight, but not when the choice is made. Then one must trust in "moral luck."

Halbertal too is troubled by the fact that "supreme emergency" is a subjective judgment. And there are some moral minefields he's not willing to follow Walzer into, including Churchill's decision to bomb those German cities in 1940. It's not an easy question. In hindsight one can understand the rationale for Churchill's orders even if one does not accept it: Hitler's victory in France in 1940 and the paucity of British defenses at the time made it seem like the conquest of England would be short work and would subjugate the entire continent to a thousand-year reign of evil. Does this imminent threat not count as a supreme emergency, even if the purpose of bombing German cities is morale-building mass slaughter? Even if it's based on weighing the immeasurable more heavily than the determinate? Could England have survived without it? Churchill didn't think so but he couldn't know.

"No, you cannot save your life at the expense of actual targeting of innocent people," Halbertal says, emphatically disagreeing with Walzer—and Churchill.

This is the unshakable foundation of Halbertal's thinking. "You cannot save your life at the expense of actual targeting of innocent people." But his thinking can lead to some surprising conclusions such as his argument that in certain cases a preemptive nuclear strike can be moral while retaliation after being struck by nuclear weapons cannot be.

He accepts the supreme emergency exception but locates the moral problem, the one that may be impossible to find an objective answer to, in the "threshold" issue. What is the threshold of a supreme emergency? What makes an ordinary emergency so supreme, so urgent that it justifies lowering the threshold of the distinction between combatants and noncombatants? Is it timing, the imminence of threat, or is the magnitude of threat or some algorithm that links them? Alas, problems of morals are not soluble the way problems of mathematics are.

"Now when it comes to nuclear weapons," Halbertal says, "that's where I think [Walzer] is rightfully very critical of the way nuclear weapons were used to end the Second World War." He's talking about Hiroshima and Nagasaki. "He's [Walzer] right that there could have been a cease-fire, or a treaty without actually the absolute surrender of Japan." What Walzer says is that "to use the atomic bomb without even attempting such an experiment was a double crime."

Halbertal takes issue as well with another argument in favor of dropping the bomb—that it would save the lives of soldiers who would otherwise die in an invasion of the Japanese home islands. "Something he [Walzer] doesn't raise, but I don't think he'd approve of, is the argument that you save even a hundred or two hundred thousand soldiers of our stripe by absolute indiscriminate intent of killing Japanese children."

Actually most estimates are higher for U.S. invasion casualties. (And those numbers don't include the million or more Japanese civilians who might die in an invasion, five times more than in Hiroshima and Nagasaki.) Note though, the uncompromising language of his description of the indiscriminate killing of the innocent in Hiroshima and Nagasaki—"absolute indiscriminate intent of killing Japanese children."

It wasn't really the main intent, to kill *children*, but it was the effect. And Halbertal's way of thinking about these things demands that states take responsibility for the effect as well as the intent of their acts—as if the effects were included in the intent.

So it didn't entirely surprise me when he said, "So when we

come to nuclear war things are a little bit changed. Now when it comes to strategic deterrence, you might threaten it as a strategic thing, that's fine as long as you're not going to use it—or then you're going to have an esoteric morality for strategic reasons."

An "esoteric morality?" I asked him.

"You construct the principle where you say 'Well I'm not going to use these weapons [to retaliate] because I'm not going to save my life by killing innocent people, but I shouldn't tell it to the enemy because this [the threat of use] is the only thing that would protect me.'"

"Shouldn't tell it to the enemy"? Isn't he doing just that? Not really: he's not an official representative of the Israeli government. He says he's not been involved in official discussions of nuclear ethics. And yet he's not entirely unofficial. He did, after all, co-author the IDF code of ethics and it is the IDF, the Israeli military command, that controls the nuclear weapons capacity everyone knows they have, although they won't admit because of nuclear ambiguity.

So he is casting ambiguity on ambiguity? A veil over a veil? A fence around a fence? The entire notion of an "esoteric strategy"— the idea that secretly, esoterically, we don't plan to retaliate, at least as Halbertal defines "esoteric strategy" here—something I've been reading reference to for decades (recall Thomas Schelling's parenthetical remark, "Why retaliate once you are wiped out?") seems more of a construct to make nuclear ethicists feel comfortable with allowing the morality of threatening deterrence without having to weigh as heavily the likelihood that the deterrent threat would be carried out.

The response of the British Ministry of Defence to my inquiry about the Letter of Last Resort discussed in an earlier chapter seems to bear on this: there is no ambiguity in what the Ministry of Defence thinks the letter will say. The Ministry of Defence believes it will ensure retaliation should the submarine be cut off by a "bolt from the blue." The ministry seems to believe the letter removes ambiguity about retaliation when in fact to most it seems to *introduce* ambiguity. But the official position is certainty. The American missile crewmen I talked to devised the spoon-and-string workaround to be sure they would *not* be prevented from launching a genocidal retaliatory attack by some crewman turning peacenik.

Of course there has always been, always will be ambiguity. The point is that no enemy can be certain that they will not be obliterated in retaliation for a major strike by those following well-established orders. It's unlikely a foe contemplating a surprise attack is going to rely on the existence of an esoteric strategy (if there ever was one).

Halbertal's doctrine, his thinking on these questions, always returns to the principle of distinction—distinction between military and noncombatant casualties of a military operation—and the way nuclear weapons obliterate the distinction. "The principle of distinction has to stay firm even in moments of supreme emergency. I cannot see a world in which you are allowed to actually kill an innocent person intentionally. I cannot see a world where that is allowed."

"But you must be allowed to threaten it?" I asked him.

"Okay, then it must be allowed to threaten to do this in order for the other side not to do the same."

"And also you must not reveal to the other side that you will not carry out the threat?"

"Exactly, and so with Walzer we talk about this kind of esoteric morality. But, and here, that's where my doubts begin with Walzer. And it brings me to paradoxical thinking. There is a way in which the aim of a nuclear attack is to destroy the capacity of collective action of the other side."

I wasn't sure what he was getting at exactly. But then he made it specific when he dropped what I regard as a kind of bombshell for an ethicist: "allowing" a preemptive nuclear first strike in certain circumstances.

"Are you talking about a retaliatory attack or possibly even preemption?" I asked him.

"Even preemption," he said.

I found the fact that Halbertal was making an argument in favor of nuclear preemption a little shocking.

I asked him to elaborate and he said, "Let's play out the case of

Israel because my thinking now is about Israel. There is, I can see that there is a real threat of nuclear attack on Israel if Iran does get nuclear weapons. I think it a serious problem. They talk about the destruction of Israel and also they might well be outsourcing them and giving them to Hezbollah, it's hard to know what we have here, but it's very problematic. Now Israel can be wiped out with one or two bombs. It's very small. You hit its center, you hit Tel Aviv and the area, there's no Israel."

Then he adds another somewhat shocking remark: "I am against—strangely enough—I am against retaliation."

"Really?" It was a remarkably definitive and unexpected declaration coming almost out of context. It was one thing hearing it from a grad student in a Yale seminar room but from one of the writers of the Israeli military code of ethics . . .

"Israel is gone," he says, beginning to elaborate a scenario. "And let's say we have submarines, and I imagine that we do have, we must have them, strategically, because they [hostile nations] have to have a feeling that we can retaliate even if Israel was destroyed."

"Right," I said, wondering where this was leading, which was to a reiteration, almost an incantation.

"I am against retaliation. I don't see the point in retaliation. But I can see a preventive strike."

Not that he doesn't have doubts.

"My doubts about possible preemptive strikes have to do with the following, and I'm saying it after I claim that I am against intentional killing of civilians in emergencies. So I'm working within the two moral boundaries that I have: first of all I am against retaliation, second I am against the collapse of the principle of distinction in supreme emergency.

"And yet I have doubts about a preventive nuclear strike—not whether it would be a good thing or not a good thing [in other words it can never be a good thing] but whether it might be necessary and justified."

I'm tempted to say: Wow! I was fascinated following his thought process though horrified at where it seemed to be leading. I remember at this point in the conversation I nervously stopped my tape recorder to make sure I was getting all of this, something that I usually hate to do, then when I started it up I pushed it closer to him. He didn't seem fazed.

"So the preemption issue is the following," he said. "There might be a situation in which the only way to prevent a nuclear attack on Israel will be to destroy the Iranian state. By that I mean to destroy its capacity to act like a state. And here it would be a very strange thing to say, but it's a case almost of a collateral killing of civilians. It's not aimed at innocent civilians, it's not Hiroshima or Nagasaki. It might be either aimed at nuclear laboratories, factories, reactors whatever they have. Or the state apparatus that is necessary for ordering and forming such a thing."

Should such matters even be open for public discussion? Or was this public discussion a kind of warning, a preemptive admonition to those who need to listen up: that Israel's leading ethicist could find grounds, if not the precise threshold, to justify a preemptive nuclear attack. Don't give them grounds, don't approach that threshold. Halbertal, a revered ethicist, giving his blessing however ambiguous or esoteric to a preemptive strike: almost like a mullah blessing a "martyrdom action" in which children will die. Could he have meant it to send an admonitory message, one that might perhaps make such action unnecessary? Perhaps it will just add another layer of ambiguity.

I decided to ask Halbertal about Israel's nuclear "opacity," the refusal of Israel to admit officially that it had nuclear weapons. The carefully worded, scarcely plausible statement by the Israel Ministry of Defense that "Israel would not be the first to introduce nuclear weapons" into the Middle East. This has often been decoded to mean, at best, a situation in which not all components of Israeli nuclear weapons had been joined together, although readiness to fire was a few bolts and a few minutes away, for an arsenal most estimated at some two hundred warheads ready to "introduced." Not counting the ones on subs.

One group of Israeli and American nuclear strategists led by Louis René Beres of Purdue, who had formed Project Daniel, a kind of informal extra-governmental Team B for reassessing Israeli nuclear strategy, issued a report in 2007 that argued it was time to end Israeli nuclear ambiguity, that "bringing the bomb out of the basement" would enhance deterrence. Their argument was that declaring Israel's nuclear capacity would remind the populations of the hostile states surrounding Israel of the consequences of rash acts by their leaders.

Halbertal had what I thought was an important refinement, a middle ground between opacity and full disclosure.

"I think what should be known is that there is a submarine [nuclear] capacity. Because then they know that we will retaliate. I think the problem is they might be tempted to think that nobody will survive to retaliate."

Notice that he says it's important "they know that we will retaliate," even though he opposes retaliation. He seems to be saying, "it's going to happen whether I like it or not." It's almost a fatalistic admission that it will. A feeling similar to the one I have about the U.S. Those missile crewmen will turn the keys.

"I would allow for the preemptive nuclear attack aimed at the capacity for a state to form a nuclear attack, while being also against retaliatory attacks because I don't see much point. Though this should be secret."

"This should be secret"—the esoteric strategy of nonretaliation. One he does not say exists but one he favors. It seemed to me his views would make news. I feel it is news: Leading Israeli military ethics adviser calls for disclosure of nuclear capacity. Defends preemption. Opposes retaliation.

Again: should this be talked about? I'm conflicted. But I feel the case against retaliation has not been discussed openly enough. That the case against retaliation has not been made precisely because of the argument that it must be kept secret, "esoteric," which has lulled some people into a belief that it's not going to happen, an attack, then a choice. But it *is* going to happen, an attack, then a choice. A choice to retaliate or not. I'm in favor of bringing whatever is esoteric out into the open in a case like this.

I asked him if the fact that a nuclear attack on Israel, the one or two bombs that would be necessary for the destruction of Israel, would represent a second Holocaust affected the threshold. Meaning crossing the bright line to nuclear use. He had previously discussed the threshold across which one is in "Supreme Emergency" territory and the ordinary just war restrictions don't apply.

"Yes. Sure," he says without hesitation.

"The decision about the threshold is affected [by the secondness of a second Holocaust]? Should the threshold be more clearly defined?"

"Yes. I don't think we can only think about it in the abstract. It means a particular commitment to Israel growing out of its history, facing a sworn enemy that is using and abusing the Holocaust in a very complex way. [He's referring to Holocaust denial by would-be Holocaust perpetrators in Iran who use the denial as strategic weapon, an excuse to perpetrate a Holocaust.] Yes, it factors in. And it's not merely emotional, I can see the moral weight."

"It [that secondness] becomes a strategic fact?"

"Yes."

"When it comes down to the decision: has the threshold been crossed . . ."

He speaks about past instances in which nuclear use by Israel has been contemplated. "I would be very, very careful with this threshold," he says, "Very careful. Here is another scenario. This was quite real in 1973. Moshe Dayan had big doubts about what should be played out in 1973. [The Yom Kippur War in October of that year, which began with an Egyptian surprise attack that along with a Syrian attack from the north seemed about to overwhelm the state of Israel.] At least in the eyes of Moshe Dyan, you know and others in the military and political leadership of Israel, there was a feeling that we are on the verge of collapse. The first few days. Now let's say that you are on the verge of collapse and you know the Syrian forces are already entering the Galilee and soon taking Haifa. Can you, at last resort, use a nuclear bomb?"

Last resort here—in the 1973 example—means a situation in which the nuclear decision is not one of preemption (too late) or pure retaliation (too soon), but one made in the fog of war, one that crosses the nuclear threshold in the heat of battle, not an opening but a closing act. He is discussing what others, most recently Benny Morris, have reported as well about the opening days of the 1973 war, an actual moment of nuclear decision, much closer than we came in Cuba.

"This [use of a bomb when in peril of national collapse from conventional war] is clearly 'first use' if not technically preemptive," Halbertal says. "It's preempting being completely destroyed, but the preemptive level of the threshold is clearly serious because now we have lost our capacity to defend ourselves.

"And the question is whether it's justified. Now what we are speaking of here is not really preemption of nuclear attack. But preemption against loss of independence. Loss of the state. If not loss of existence itself, then a homeless people again, perhaps vulnerable to slaughter again." What a choice.

"An existential threat," I interposed.

"Right, to the state, to the Zionist project, etc. etc. etc. And I read somewhere that Dayan gave the order to be ready with them [the nukes]. Whether that was the case or not there is a dispute. But it's a dilemma, a real dilemma."

He was speaking about then but he was of course speaking about now as well. A real dilemma, no good answer. No good choices.

Halbertal became particularly eloquent when I asked him the "species" question that Ellsberg had raised. Is there something fatally flawed in human nature that brought us to this point? A question I had asked scholars of Hitler and the Holocaust: "Do you wonder about the nature of human nature when you contemplate these kind of questions?" I asked him. His answer was both memorable and tragic.

"I think, you know, I didn't realize what I always knew, but it's become more clear: that humans are capable of the best and the worst, and the gap within humanity is so big. I mean I'm not—I didn't turn cynical, because I see cases of goodwill and piety and altruistic sentiment that are so genuine, and then you know, just to see manifestations of radical evil.

"And then what I learn is, I come back in that respect to the Jewish teaching that the options are open. There are very different options and choices that are open to human beings and what they should do and they can shape themselves in very different radically diametrically opposed directions, and that humans have a choice in how they do it. But when you confront the spectrum of humanity you understand the potential of freedom that exists, and human responsibility for what it makes out of itself."

At the end of the interview I must admit I found myself feeling somewhat emotional. I had been searching throughout the course of this book for someone in a position of responsibility, or at least inside knowledge, to entertain the notion that I had fixated upon that nuclear retaliation was immoral. I thought his willingness to speak frankly was courageous, not least because he was likely to die in any nuclear exchange.

"It's rare to find someone," I found myself telling Halbertal, as I prepared to leave, "who takes the question of the morality of retaliation seriously. I've always thought that in focusing on this that I was an outlier or something like that, or beyond the pale, whatever, but retaliation never made any sense to me. On the other hand there is the paradox that one shouldn't talk about the possibility of an esoteric morality because it invites an immoral attack."

This was when I asked him if it was wrong to write about this, and this was when he said I should.

# CHAPTER EIGHT

# IRAN: THE "ENIGMATIC BOX" AND THE NIE

A nd so everyone is waiting for it to happen. Or war-gaming what will happen when it happens. Or even what will happen in the interval before it happens: before Iran goes nuclear, before Iran successfully tests a bomb and signals it has more. Or in the new scare phrase for the new nuclear age, before Iran is "nuclear-capable." That is, if it has manufactured the three elements of a nuclear weapon: the fissionable material, either U-235 or plutonium; the bomb or warhead designed to carry the separated segments of critical mass along with a triggering mechanism for the implosion necessary to create the critical mass for detonation; and finally the delivery vehicle—the missile with the range for the target. CIA Chief Leon Panetta reported in June 2010 that Iran has enough enrichable uranium to produce two bombs in two years.

How long will that interval be, between the shadow and the act, with the fog of war obscuring the true state of things? I haven't found many who believe it won't happen soon. I have found few who believe the new (June 2010) U.N. sanctions will work.

Recall those Israeli submarines? Every month or so this phantom flotilla seems to be proceeding at unfathomable depths toward Iran. And then suddenly the notional journey of the phantom flotilla appears, in the *London Sunday Times* for May 30, 2010, off the coast of Iran.

Again we can't be sure how much of any of these reports of the submarine flotilla are genuine or meant to deter without having to exist, because submarines are undetectable anyway and so you might as well say they're there as not. The *Times* dispatch offered some seductive specifics such as the alleged names of the subs— *Tekuma, Leviathan,* and *Dolphin*—and claimed that "a decision has now been taken to ensure a permanent presence of at least one of the vessels" off the coast of Iran. More chillingly we are told "each of the submarines [is] capable of launching a nuclear cruise missile."

And in the third week of August 2010, Iran announced that its nuclear energy reactor at Bushehr would begin being loaded with uranium fuel supplied by the Russians. Such a plant offers a "second path" to a nuclear weapon: it produces bomb-capable plutonium as a "waste product."

There are a few people on the planet who sincerely don't believe Iran is seeking the ability to produce nuclear weapons. The stone age tribesmen of Papua New Guinea, for instance, are perhaps blessedly unaware of the possibility. And then there are those who believed or misread the 2007 National Intelligence Estimate on the question. These people came away believing that Iran had stopped their nuclear program in 2003. Because of that misreading, many people stopped paying attention to the question, considered it settled.

The misbegotten, misunderstood 2007 NIE on Iran allowed the urgency of the situation to be denied. That there are still those who believe the way the NIE was reported, even cite its supposed conclusions, suggests they do so because of wish-fulfillment: it accords with the way they'd prefer to view the world—as less threatening, offering less cause for alarm.

But sooner or later the report, having done its damage, will be cast upon the junk heap of history and we will be forced to face the question it allowed us to avoid: just how close are the Iranians to the bomb; how much time is left? Few believe that the Israelis will wait till the Iranians have enough bombs to destroy them and rely on deterrence to prevent it.

One writer who follows this matter closely observed shrewdly to me that no nation that has gone nuclear has taken longer to do so than Iran. While the Israelis publicly leak threatened plans for air strikes on buried Iranian nuclear facilities, they (with undoubtedly some U.S. intelligence help) have been quietly pursuing another path to put off the day of reckoning: sabotage. Planes carrying Iranian nuclear scientists mysteriously crash-land, equipment for the highly sensitive centrifuging operation to separate the highly fissionable but rare isotope U-235 from the relatively inert but far more plentiful U-238 has mysteriously malfunctioned, occasionally blowing up. Iranian physicists have mysteriously disappeared, defected, or—according to the Iranians—been kidnapped by the West. And now, as was widely reported in September 2010, attacks from cyberworms such as STUXNET have played havoc with Iranian nuclear computers.

It has slowed things down, kicked the can down the road by a factor of several years. "How Much Time Do We Have?" is a chapter title in a 2009 book called *Red Cloud at Dawn* by Princeton historian Michael Gordin. This is his study of the period between August 1945 and August 1949 when the U.S. had a nuclear monopoly and was anxiously seeking to know what to do with it and how long it would last before the Soviets got the bomb. Reading the chapter one comes across the following questions about the Soviets back then: "How hard is it to build an atomic bomb? . . . How smart are the Soviets? . . . When did the Soviets begin?" The fog of information and disinformation that obscures the answers to such urgent questions has a certain similarity with the fog now surrounding Iran.

This book—this odyssey into the realm of the new nuclear age—began with the mysterious Israeli raid on the alleged Syrian nuclear reactor. The enigma extended to who had built the reactor and for what purposes, what the apparent involvement of North Korean in its construction meant, whether it had a relation to Iranian nuclear ambitions as an outsourced generator of bomb-making fissionable material. Why the silence from Syria and Israel about what took place in al-Kibar on the night of September 6, 2007? And—most salient of all—what was the source of the senior ministry official's alarmed account that "we came so close to World War III."

As I discovered, the attempt to form a reliable picture of what a nuclear close call involved was to enter a labyrinth of rumors and leaks, a landscape of conflicting conjectures, spin, and speculation. Emblematic of the mysterious nature of the target was that satellite imaging before the raid showed a large featureless boxlike structure. The Israelis said the structure, which was nicknamed the "Enigmatic Box on the Euphrates" by the armscontrolwonk.com blog, initially clouded evidence the box screened a reactor. The cloud of uncertainty that still hovers over the raid on Syria's al-Kibar reactor could stand for the situation in the Middle East now, which might be called the fog of prewar.

As historians of the war to come peer back through the mists, the raid and the potential consequenced escaped that night, it will likely be seen as a harbinger of the unavoidable tragedy to come. The Israel–Iran nuclear-related hostilities are the closest thing to the balance of terror, Mutually Assured Destruction standoff of the first nuclear age—except more unstable and with a lower threshold for preemptive action. After the raid, Syria first denied it had happened, then issued a tersely worded statement that conceded that Israeli munitions may have been "dropped" (by accident?) on Syrian soil. Israel remained silent. Attempts to glean the truth from myriad conflicting reports and statements were disorienting. It was unclear which anonymous source was quoting which other anonymous source nor where the conjectures appeared first. Reports later surfaced of an informal Israeli-Syrian agreement to avoid official acknowledgment that an attack had taken place, thereby minimizing Syrian embarrassment and the need to retaliate; and allowing Israel to avoid confessing to what was, on the face of it, a violation of international law.

Then, a few days after the raid, virtually out of the blue, North Korea, not having been asked, issued a strident protest—almost as if it wished to incriminate itself in the incident. Up till then no one without top secret clearance, nobody publicly, had connected the North Koreans with the alleged reactor, or the reactor's similarity to one made in North Korea. Stories emerged of a North Korean freighter docking in the northern Syrian port of Tartous shortly before the raid. Some speculated the North Korean freighter's cargo might have been fuel for the supposed reactor. And another sharp-eyed blogospheric investigator noted that the Web site of the port of Tartous changed the registration of the freighter docking from North Korea to South Korea. It was a change that looked more like a post facto deception than a correction.

The freighter in the fogbank off Tartous: it began to seem like an Eric Ambler espionage novel. Then Hersh wrote a *New Yorker* piece giving vent to almost all previous varied and conflicting cloak-and-dagger speculations from unnamed sources: there was no reactor, the raid wasn't targeted on Syria at all, but designed to test electronic countermeasures against Russian-made antiaircraft systems of the sort both Syria and Iran used. Israel wanted to demonstrate to Iran that it could blind their electronic warning and antiaircraft radar defenses with cyber-war measures. Iran may have been the initial target. Take your pick.

What really went on?

Everyone in the know went silent until April 2008, when for some reason (most likely congressional pressure) the heads of the U.S. intelligence community—the CIA head and the new Director of National Intelligence ("connect the dots")—took it upon themselves to reveal what their agencies knew about this mysterious raid, the enigma of the box-shaped structure it destroyed, and what it meant. And while they were at it, they just happened to want to correct a misinterpretation of the 2007 National Intelligence Estimate on Iran, with its high-profile declaration that—contrary to its previous (2005) NIE on Iran—the intelligence community believed Iran had shut down its nuclear weapons program in 2003.

It was hard to tell which part of their presentation was a cover for the other—the Enigmatic Box or Iran—in this unprecedented briefing for a small group of reporters later released at full length by the intelligence chiefs. It's a rare inside glimpse into the way the highest U.S. intelligence officials wrestled with the problem of the Enigmatic Box—and their view of the seriousness of the interlocking array of potential nuclear flashpoints triggered by the attack on it. It was a glimpse into the deadly serious business of making estimates about nuclear capabilities and intentions where mistakes can be catastrophic.

The transcript is a remarkable document that reads like a scene from a spy novel, but is even more fascinating for the questions it leaves unanswered. It helps explain why I consider the raid on the enigmatic box the paradigmatic crisis of the second nuclear age, and helps answer the question—if we came so close that night to World War III, what "close" really means.

At the time of the briefing the Israelis still had not admitted the raid took place. The Syrians still denied the enigmatic box concealed a reactor. And Iran—the silent player lurking behind the scenes throughout the crisis—was still denying any designs on an atomic bomb.

The two "senior US intelligence officials" who delivered the briefing were later identified as Mike McConnell, head of the National Intelligence Council (the entity that supervises the CIA), the Defense Department's DIA (Defence Intelligence Agency), the State Departments NSA (National Security Agency)—every intelligence entity in the U.S. government, and Michael Hayden, the head of the CIA. The briefing was given at CIA headquarters first on a background only basis; the transcript was later declassified. Think of it as a kind of one-act stage play. (Look for the surprising dramatic twist toward the end. Take my bracketed comments as combination stage directions and critic's notes.)

A note here about the design of the nuclear reactor in question—a "Calder Hall" model. Calder Hall is the name of a small town in West Cumbria, the section of Great Britain that faces the Irish Sea. I happened to be aware of an episode of violence that took place in that West Cumbrian backwater in June 2010, a killing spree by the "PSYCHO CABBIE," as the tabloid *News of the World* called him. An ordinary cabdriver, a West Cumbrian Homer Simpson, who in fact had worked at and been fired from the Calder Hall reactor, one morning got up and shot his twin brother, his lawyer, and killed twelve people before shooting himself.

No one could figure out why. But somehow that event connected for me with the problem of the continued existence of nukes. It takes just one deranged human to launch a missile, just one unpredictable neutron split to make a critical mass. That is why every nuclear close call, including the Israeli raid on the Syrian reactor, should be examined carefully for the language used to analyze it. That's why it is valuable to hear how "senior intelligence officials" speak when they talk shop about nuclear possibilities.

### O.D.N.I. (Office of the Director of National Intelligence)

*Background Briefing with Senior US Officials on Syria's Covert Nuclear Reactor and North Korea's Involvement*

APRIL 24, 2008

**SENIOR INTELLIGENCE OFFICIAL 1:** Hello. My name is *[Senior Intelligence Official 1]. [Later identified as Mike McConnell, the chief of the entire U.S. intelligence establishment.]* And I have the start-off role. It's been a pretty busy morning and afternoon, as you might imagine. We've been on the Hill having dialogue with our committees. *[The congressional intelligence committees basically blackmailed them with a threat of budgetary cut off if they didn't explain more fully what went on at al-Kibar in the first battlefield nuclear incident of the second nuclear age.]*

What I want to do is just frame the issue. . . . What we're going to discuss is a nuclear reactor. It was constructed by the Syrians in the eastern desert of Syria along the Euphrates River on the east side. The Syrians constructed this reactor for the production of plutonium with the assistance of the North Koreans. *[This—the fact that it was a reactor—had come in for skeptical questioning most prominently by Seymour Hersh in* The New Yorker, *who seems to have relied on sources out of the loop. The key judgment here is not just that it was a nuclear reactor, but that it was the type of reactor designed to produce plutonium as a by-product that could be used to make nuclear bombs. But the key judgment was buttressed with post-Iraq precision.]*

Our evidence goes back an extended period of time. We have had insights to what was going on since very late '90s, early 2000, 2001 that something was happening. Our issue was pinning it down and being more precise. We had increasing appreciation for what was happening in the 2003, 2006 timeframe. But we still couldn't quite pin it down, as will become apparent to you when we show you more of the physical evidence that you'll see in just a moment.

In the spring of last year, we were able to obtain some additional information that made it conclusive. *[Note the careful wording of "we were able to obtain." Most would translate this to: "The Israelis showed us photos taken inside the reactor either by one of their spies or by a bribed or blackmailed Syrian worker.]* And so, we engaged in this policy process of now that we have the evidence, what do we do about it? The evidence concluded a nuclear reactor, as I mentioned, constructed by the Syrians, started probably in 2001, completed in the summer of 2007. And it was nearing operational capability. *[More than a year later the International Atomic Energy Agency (IAEA) found evidence in soil samples taken from the al-Kibar area of "the presence of uranium."]*

So from that point of departure, I am joined by *[Senior Intelligence Official 2] [Michael Hayden, head of the CIA]* who will provide details on the intelligence and what we knew and so on. We will show you a video of the evidence, so give you a chance to ask questions about that. And then *[a senior administration official]*, seated to my right will be available for responding to any policy questions you might have. So with that, I'll turn it over to *[Senior Intelligence Official 2]*.

**SENIOR INTELLIGENCE OFFICIAL 2:** The format I've got, I'll talk a bit; I've got some slides that will show up behind me that shows some data. And then, we'll run the video. . . .

As *[Senior Intelligence Official 1]* said, information we

acquired since 2001 has indicated cooperation between North Korean nuclear entities and high-level Syrian officials. And we went to the 2001 data, and I know this is true in your business, when you learn something, it doesn't just illuminate the future; it illuminates the past.

*[I was reminded of something that the legendary CIA counter-intelligence chief James Angleton had once told me with an air of mysterious knowingness: "The past telescopes into the future."]*

And when we acquired information in 2001 and then were able to look backward on information that had been collected but not quite understood, it's clear to us that this cooperation between North Korean nuclear-related personalities and entities and high-level Syrian officials began probably as early as 1997 which, and now this is an estimate now, all right, not court-of-law evidence, puts it into the Hafez al Assad regime in terms of the original decision to begin this cooperation.

Now, as early as 2003, we judged that the interactions probably were nuclear-related, again, because of who it was we were seeing in these interactions. But we had no details on the nature or location of the cooperative projects. We assessed the cooperation involved work at sites probably within Syria. But again, we didn't know exactly where. So we had this body of evidence, kind of, almost like a cloud of, boy, there's something going on here but we can't get a whole lot of precision about it.

We received indications in '05 that the Syrians and North Koreans were involved in a project in the Dayr az Zawr region of eastern Syria, but again, no specific information on the nature or the exact location of the work. But you can see, as evidence mounts, more confident there is cooperation, more confident it involves nuclear-related people. And now, we've got a fairly good sense as to where the center point of the cooperation might be.

*[The emphasis on the North Korean partnership here is significant in the light of the Obama administration's April 2010*

*Nuclear Posture Review, which singles out North Korea and Iran as exceptions to its policy of not threatening non-nuclear states with nuclear attack.]*

Imagery searches *[satellite mapping]* of the region revealed a large unidentified building under construction in a remote area near the Euphrates River near a point that we call al Kibar. And there you see the photo. The first time we saw it was after this evidence look out there remember '05, '06 timeframe. Take a look there. We identified the facility. And once again, sometimes the present illuminates not just the future but can illuminate the past. We looked back on historical imagery that found that the only high-quality imagery we had was of a building that looked pretty much like this. It was externally complete. *[This is the "Enigmatic Box."]*

And it's hard to figure out looking at that building what its purpose is. *[The enigmatic nature of the Enigmatic Box!]* And it certainly didn't have any observable, externally observable characteristics that would say, oh, yeah, you got yourself a nuclear reactor here. Things like a massive electrical-supply system, massive ventilation, and most importantly a cooling system. We acquired information, though, in the spring of '07 that enabled us to conclude that this non-descript-looking building in al Wadi, near the Euphrates River in eastern Syria *[to avoid confusion, al Wadi is a geologic formation, a dry stream bed; al Kibar was the closest inhabited town]* was indeed a covert nuclear reactor. . . .

Now, we carefully compared these photos *[of the interior of the reactor]*, which are obviously handheld and we've got a certain volume of them measured in the dozens, these handheld photos with the overhead photos. And I'm here to assure you that all the windows, doors, holes in the wall, and so on, matched up; i.e., these handheld photos are of that building we showed you in the overhead photo. *[In other words the photographic details of the interior of the building confirmed that it was the same building photographed by surveillance satellites. Note how careful they are to avoid the trap Colin Powell fell into when he showed misleading CIA photographic evidence at his pre-invasion U.N. presentation on weapons of mass destruction in Iraq, which turned out to be false.]* And that's very important because the handheld photos reveal construction activity at the site in a period of time prior to the external completion of the building. Does that make sense? Okay, good.

The reactor inside that building was clearly not configured to produce electricity. We saw no way and there are no power lines coming out of it, none of all the switching facilities that you would need, and frankly was less well-suited for research. I mean, obviously, we're holding up hypotheses here, right? Less well-suited for research than some existing nuclear facilities that we and the Syrians know about and have been made public in Syria. *[In other words it was not a reactor meant for the peaceful uses of atomic energy.]*

Now, we assess that North Korea has assisted Syria with this reactor because, one, it uses North Korean–type technology. The building resembles North Korea's Yongbyon plutonium power reactor. That's Yongbyon on the left. That's that non-descript building in the eastern Syrian Desert before the curtain walls and false roof *[the boxing that made it enigmatic by hiding its actual shape]* were put on the top of it to hide its shape, which, without those curtain walls and false roofs seem to carry the telltale signatures similar to the facility at Yongbyon.

Internal photographs of the reactor vessel under construction show that it's a gas-cooled graphite-moderated reactor similar in technology and configuration to the Yongbyon reactor. *[These photos are the decisive and rather astonishing intelligence coup that made all the difference.]* And you can see that more clearly in this photo that compares the control rods and the refueling-tube arrangements of both reactors. That's internal imagery of al Kibar on the left and Yongbyon on the right. . . .

Our information also indicates involvement of nuclear-related North Koreans in a project somewhere in the area.

And we also have evidence of cargo being transferred from North Korea, most likely to this reactor site in 2006. *[The same year—probably not coincidentally—North Korea exploded its first nuclear bomb.]* The reactor was destroyed in an Israeli air strike early in the morning of 6 September 2007 as it was nearing completion but before it had been operated and before it was charged with uranium fuel.

### Now the Hasty, Incriminating Cover-up Begins.

Shortly after the attack, the Syrians began, this is mid-September now, a massive effort to destroy the ruined reactor building and to remove all potentially incriminating nuclear-related equipment and structures. Much of the work was done at night or was hidden by tarps in an attempt to conceal it from our overhead observation.

The Syrian efforts to dismantle and destroy the building revealed features of the internal arrangements and structure that corroborated what we saw before and were consistent with the ground photos that we had obtained. *[It's the cover-up, not the crime, that's most incriminating.]* If you understand what we're doing here, you have the building. There were real hard reinforced concrete things in there like the sarcophagus *[the Enigmatic Box]* around the reactor and as you can see heat exchanges and so on. The Israeli strike make it inoperable; Syrians decide, okay, we've got to take it down. As you begin to blow it up, what remains, the hard, reinforced concrete structures, which are the guts of the reactor. And that's what you're seeing. This is after the Syrians had begun to dismantle what the Israelis destroyed and the telltale signs of it being a nuclear reactor become even more visible as they go about the destruction.

*[The lights go down and the video shows computer graphics reconstruction of the interior in simulated operation from the photos. It's an expensive-sounding production with narration, we are told.*

*The key features are "the top of the reactor vessel," which "we judged [to be] a spent fuel holding pool." This is key since the spent fuel from a working nuclear reactor is the chief source of plutonium for bomb making and some observers had not seen any plutonium-reprocessing capability in the aerial photos of the site.*

*And there's this: "Only North Korea has built such gas cooled graphite moderated reactors in the past 35 years."*

*And finally the clincher: "When the pipeline and pump house were externally completed in early August 2007, no further observable construction was necessary before the reactor could begin operations. We assess that the reactor could have been complete and that start of operations could have begun at any time."*

*And then the North Korean freighter arrived at the port of Tartous. We may never know its cargo since it slipped away into the night, but that was the night the Israelis struck. The moment when the reactor was about to become nuclear capable.*

*The film concludes with satellite and aerial imagery of the cover-up attempts: the Enigmatic Box over the reactor, now in ruins.*

*These actions probably were intended to forestall identification of reactor debris by international inspectors and are inconsistent with peaceful nuclear intentions.]*

"In conclusion, our information shows that Syria was building a gas-cooled, graphite-moderated reactor that was nearing operational capability in August 2007. The reactor would have been capable of producing plutonium for nuclear weapons. It was not configured to produce electricity and was ill-suited for research. The reactor was destroyed in early September 2007 before it was loaded with nuclear fuel or operated. We are convinced based on a variety of information that North Korea assisted Syria's covert nuclear activities both before and after the reactor was destroyed. Only North Korea has built this type of reactor in the past 35 years."

**SENIOR ADMINISTRATION OFFICIAL:** Just like to make a couple of points. One of the questions you may have is why are we making this disclosure now and why not before.

*[Yes!]* Our first concern was to prevent conflict and perhaps an even broader confrontation in the Middle East region. We were concerned that if knowledge of the existence and then destruction of the reactor became public and was confirmed by sources that the information would spread quickly and Syria would feel great pressure to retaliate. And, obviously, that would have been a threat to Israel and risked the possibility of a broader regional confrontation which we hoped to avoid.

*[Here is a crucial connection between the Israeli attack and the potential for a regional nuclear war, should Syria, Iran, or Pakistan seek to retaliate with chemical or nuclear weapons and Israel either preempts them with nuclear weapons or retaliates with nuclear weapons. It's an instance of everyone pretending something didn't happen for the sake of preventing something worse from happening. Once we have reached the threshold of regional nuclear war, it is one step—a giant step, yes, but not an inconceivable one—to globalizing it, considering the range of Iranian and Pakistani ballistic missiles. It is here at least that the very senior British ministry official's invocation of World War III can be found. This explains the eerie silence that followed the raid on the part of all parties. Syria did not wish to appear to be deterred from retaliation by fear of Israel's nuclear arsenal. Nor did it wish to be forced to retaliate, and create, in the words of* The Spectator's *source, "Armageddon and the bloody Book of Revelation."]*

As time has passed, our assessment is that that risk has receded. . . .

*[Recent developments suggest that Iran is not responding to either international pressure or the strike against an ally's nuclear facilities. Which suggests the Israelis have no alternative but to strike Iran itself, as they did Iraq and Syria, before it becomes nuclear-capable. A nightmare scenario that seems more and more inevitable.]*

For example, first let me take North Korea. *[He's continuing to answer the "why now?" question.]* We are at the point in the Six-Party talks where we believe going public will strengthen our negotiators as they try to get an accurate accounting of North Korea's nuclear programs. We believe and hope that it will encourage North Korea to acknowledge its proliferation activity, but also to provide a more complete and accurate disclosure of their plutonium activities and their enrichment activities as well.

With respect to Iran, the Syrian episode reminds us of the ability of states to obtain nuclear capability covertly and how destabilizing the proliferation of nuclear weapons in the Middle East would be. *[Here he suggests that the raid, with its implicit blessing by the U.S., was about Iran—a bad cop/good cop way of encouraging Iran to expedite a diplomatic solution to its nuclear activities, because it now had an example of what might happen if it didn't.]* And obviously everyone is concerned about that with respect to Iran, and we hope that disclosure will underscore that the international community needs to rededicate itself to ending Iran's nuclear enrichment activities, and needs to take further steps to ensure that Iran does not obtain nuclear weapons. And countries can start by the full implementation of the U.N. Security Council resolutions already dealing with Iranian nuclear activities, which are not being implemented as aggressively and fully as they should. *[Yes, that will certainly take care of the problem.]*

One of the things that I'm sure also people are wondering is whether there was any discussion between us and the Israelis about policy options and how to respond to these facts. We did discuss policy options with Israel. Israel considered a Syrian nuclear capability to be an existential threat to the state of Israel. *[Here we have—slipped into the language of the briefing—the explosive phrase: "existential threat." It is the justification the Israelis use for their forward-leaning, preemptive stance. Some suggest the use of the term "existential threat" is an exaggeration when it comes to the capability of Israel's Middle East antagonists, but the Israelis don't want to be the testing ground for this counterhypothesis. In any case, note the subtle* distinction between the urgency for immediate action attributed to the Israelis and the "other options" Senior Intelligence Official 2 will later suggest the U.S. was considering.] After these discussions, at the end of the day Israel made its own decision to take action. It did so without any green light from us, so-called green light from us; none was asked for, none was given. [The whole "green light" rhetoric is somewhat dodgy. In the summer of 2008 there were leaked reports that Israel had asked President Bush for a green light to attack the Iranian nuclear facilities and had been turned down. In fact most insiders read this as a kind of green light in itself. It gave the U.S. the ability to deny any connection to an Israeli strike while making it seem like plans for just such a strike were moving toward execution, U.S. green light or not.] We understand the Israeli action. We believe this clandestine reactor was a threat to regional peace and security, and we have stated before that we cannot allow the world's most dangerous regimes to acquire the world's most dangerous weapons.

Thank you.

**SENIOR INTELLIGENCE OFFICIAL 2:** Okay, are you going to moderate for us? Go ahead.

*[Reporters begin asking questions.]*

**Q:** Yeah. [Is] there is no other photographic evidence or video that shows North Koreans at the facility?

**SENIOR INTELLIGENCE OFFICIAL 2:** There are some, there's none more compelling that what we showed you.

**SENIOR INTELLIGENCE OFFICIAL 1:** There are also some things that you're going to ask questions about, sources, and so we're not going to be able to answer those. There's a rich level of information here that we can't discuss—the sources or methods, and that's what we're going to try to work around to let you see what we can show you, which we have showed you, and we just won't comment on specificity, about [what] we knew [at] this point or that point or when.

Q: I just have a follow-up. The information I had earlier today is that at least one of the images . . . was [of] North Korean nuclear scientist Chon Chibu, who was linked directly to Yongbyon.

SENIOR INTELLIGENCE OFFICIAL 2: That's him.

Q: That's him? And then my other question is a very basic question. This video presentation I would assume was put together by the CIA or—

SENIOR INTELLIGENCE OFFICIAL 2: [Senior Intelligence Official 1] The President asked us, when this all started breaking about a year ago, really picked up pace, to marshall the resources of the entire community. So what you've seen here was constructed here, that's right.

Q: And this was shown on the Hill today.

SENIOR INTELLIGENCE OFFICIAL 2: Yes.

Q: It has been a while. Syria kind of committed to trying to counterbalance the Israeli nuclear program several years ago and started working on that, and Syria has been a crossroad for all types of unsavory activity for many years, so are you fairly certain that this is the only type of activity going on there?

SENIOR INTELLIGENCE OFFICIAL 2: In terms of the nuclear program? Clearly, it's something we'll continue to keep a full-court press on, all right? Let me say that. But with the destruction of this facility, this is, I'll use the word, an achievement; I don't have time to think of a better one in terms of ending that kind of behavior. There is cooperation that continues, however, between North Korea and the Syrians with regard to the Syrian missile program, and we see that same kind of cooperation between North Korea and Iran. *[This is not a casual, thrown-in line but rather significant: the North Koreans, who have the bomb, are helping the Iranians and so all the attention focused on the underground Iranian centrifuges, reportedly producing bomb-grade uranium, may be a red herring: the North Koreans could just hand one to the Iranians, who have plenty of cash to pay the cash-starved North Koreans. Two years later the degree of cooperation between what Obama's Nuclear Posture Review called the two "outlier" nations continues to be—ominously—shrouded in mystery, baffling the experts.]*

**Q:** A quick follow-on: Would the U.S. have considered any kind of activity had the Israelis not?

**SENIOR ADMINISTRATION OFFICIAL:** We obviously were looking very closely at options, and we had looked at some approaches that involved a mix of diplomacy and the threat of military force with the goal of trying to ensure that the reactor was either dismantled or permanently disabled, and therefore never became operational. We looked at those options. There were, as I mentioned to you, conversations with the Israelis. Israel felt that this reactor posed such an existential threat that a different approach was required. And as a sovereign country, Israel had to make its own evaluation of the threat and the immediacy of the threat, and what actions it should take. And it did so. . . .

**Q:** Can you give us an assessment and tell us what kind of information you might have about the existence . . . of a Syrian nuclear weapons design program? And secondly, can you tell us whether these pictures from inside the building are at different stages or are they all at one particular point in time?

**SENIOR INTELLIGENCE OFFICIAL 2:** The pictures inside of the building are over a period of time, okay? And I really don't have anything more to add with regard to a Syrian weapons program. *[A very conspicuous evasion, probably designed either to imply they know more than they do, or to con-*

*ceal how much they do know. Ambiguity suggests he has more, just does not want to add it.]*

Q: Two questions along those same lines. While there is similarity with the Yongbyon plant, there is no reprocessor *[near the Syrian facility]*. It's unclear from your presentation how they would have obtained the fuel . . . *[A key question; the absence of an adjacent reprocessor to turn the spent fuel containing plutonium into bomb-grade material doesn't mean there was no reprocessor elsewhere in Syria or that the spent fuel couldn't have been reprocessed by the North Koreans or the Iranians.]* And you note the similarity with the North Korean reactor and said no reactor like that had been made in some time, but this is a Calder Hall reactor whose design has been sort of out there for a long while, so could they have obtained the technology as opposed to needing help from individuals?

SENIOR INTELLIGENCE OFFICIAL 2: The body of evidence that we have over a period that spans a decade gives us very high confidence that, A, this is a nuclear reactor; B, that there was long-term, detailed cooperation between the North Koreans and the Syrians in terms of nuclear cooperation; and if anything, the actions since the strike that we have been able to detect reinforce our belief that North Koreans were actually involved not just in kind of a theoretical or a broad-based nuclear cooperative effort with the Syrians, but were cooperating at this site.

Q: And the reprocessor and the fuel?

SENIOR INTELLIGENCE OFFICIAL 2: There is no reprocessing facility in the region of al Kibar. *[A carefully delimited answer.]*

*We Begin to See the Perils of Estimative Language*
SENIOR INTELLIGENCE OFFICIAL 1: I might add something that would be helpful here. These are lessons learned

that . . . came out of previous experience about how to put more rigor into our process. So there's a difference between evidence and an assessment. *[We are now entering the all-important ambiguous territory of what is known in intelligence circles as "estimative language." That language has often been the source of confusion for even some of the more sophisticated journalists covering intelligence issues. In this context, the language in question spans the spectrum of meanings attached to "low," "medium," and "high confidence."]* And when we examined this information, and what [Senior Intelligence Official 2] alluded to, let me just reinforce: very sensitive; everybody wants to know; everybody wants to have a part of the decision. So the decision was taken by the President to restrict access significantly. So we made this CIA-centric to restrict those who were aware and it worked.

The entire community participated. The entire community contributed. And you know who is in the community. You know we take pictures; you know we listen, and so on. So I'll just leave it at that. *[Note the out-of-the-blue, casual-to-the-point-of-hiding-in-plain-sight "you know we listen" suggesting that the National Security Agency has eavesdropping capability on the Syrians, which added to the confidence of the judgment that this reactor was designed to produce plutonium for weapons but which couldn't be spelled out without giving away our methods.]* We had very rich, rich information. So when we worked through the data, in large part what you saw here, we concluded with high confidence it is a nuclear reactor of the design that was described for plutonium. We had, at that time, medium confidence that the North Koreans were and are participating. *[Note distinction between high and medium confidence. Both mean generally, very confident. But—and here is the source of confusion—as we shall see, "low confidence" doesn't mean no confidence or even necessarily little confidence as generally colloquially used. It's the difference between evidence and assessment or judgment—the difference between direct evidence and circumstantial evidence.]*

SENIOR INTELLIGENCE OFFICIAL 2: At the reactor, not in generalized nuclear cooperation.

SENIOR INTELLIGENCE OFFICIAL 1: To go with the question you're asking [about] weapons. We said, we believe it. There's no other reason for it. *["No other reason" sounds like dead certainty but ends up being described as "low confidence" in estimative language because it's an assessment not direct evidence such as a Syrian official saying, "Why else do you think we're building this reactor?"]* But our confidence level that it's weapons is low at this point. We believe it, but it's low based on the physical evidence *[i.e., the absence of a plutonium reprocessing facility in the vicinity]*.

Q: Even at the time of the destruction of the reactor?

SENIOR INTELLIGENCE OFFICIAL 1: Even at the time. *[Because "even at the time" there was "no other reason" than weapons fuel production, but no weapons fuel had yet been produced.]* So now, what that asks is, in a nuclear program, it's complex. There are a series of steps and stages. So was that something evidence that would be uncovered at a point in time? And I'll just leave it right there as to where it is at the moment, other than to say we have reasonable confidence that we have, that the Israelis have destroyed a [weapons-producing] capability. And we are monitoring everything to see if there's anything subsequent to that.

Q: Do we have any reason to believe that the Syrians now have or are building a reprocessing capability?

SENIOR INTELLIGENCE OFFICIAL 1: Just let me leave it with what I described. *[Another interesting evasion. For all we know the reprocessing could have been designed to take place in Iran.]*

SENIOR INTELLIGENCE OFFICIAL 2: And as you say, this makes no sense without that. *[In other words, yes, there is a reprocessing capability but we can't for whatever reason say any-thing more about what we know or how we know it without giv-ing the reprocessors a clue that someone may know where they are, and be coming after them.]*

Q: This does make no sense without that. And that's my hard-est part with the evidence that you've shown. And I think it's interesting that you have a low-confidence level that they . . . *[An example of a reporter just not getting that "low confidence" doesn't mean deep doubt. An understandable confusion, created by the—let's come out and say it—stupidity of the "confidence" hier-archy the intelligence community may have adopted after the Iraqi WMD debacle. In other words, it allows them to say things they believe as fact, but assign them "low confidence" if they turn out to be disproven later. And ingenious bureaucratic trick.]*

Q: Did you tell the Israelis you have low confidence it was for weapons? *[Another reporter, or the same one, still doesn't get it.]*

**SENIOR INTELLIGENCE OFFICIAL 2:** No, you need to understand. I'm sorry to dwell on the point. This is very, very important. *[Yes!]*

**SENIOR INTELLIGENCE OFFICIAL 1:** This is very impor-tant. *[Double yes!]*

**SENIOR INTELLIGENCE OFFICIAL 2:** We told our Presi-dent four things: This is a reactor; the North Koreans and the Syrians are cooperating on nuclear activities; the North Kore-ans and Syrians are cooperating on the construction of this reactor; and this reactor, its purpose, is to create fuel for a nuclear weapons program. Those are the things we concluded.

Now, when you look at the body of evidence of those four sentences and begin to sort out how much of that is based on an overwhelming body of evidence as opposed to a more lim-ited body of evidence and therefore more reliant on assess-ment, the fact that it was a nuclear reactor—absolutely high confidence; the fact of Syrian-Korean nuclear cooperation spanning a decade at an intense level—high confidence. At the time of the strike, fact of North Korean–Syrian cooperation in the building of that reactor—medium confidence that then got higher because of events, some of which we have alluded to in the briefing, okay. *[What others? He doesn't say.]* The fact that that material was going to be used for a weapons program—we believe that to be true, but because we did not have, as [Senior Intelligence Official 1] points out, additional clinical evidence of other activities, we could only give it a low confidence level. *[It would be so much simpler to say "we could only make an absolute judgment based on the evidence, but you can't prove a negative—i.e., you can't prove it wouldn't be used for something other than weapons."]* But you need to, and I think you understand what I'm trying to say. *[Nudge, nudge, hint, hint, wink, wink.]* That's not more or less sure; it's just that it's a way of communicating that for which you have a large body of evidence and that for which you may not.

Q: Where is that confidence level now?

SENIOR INTELLIGENCE OFFICIAL 2: In terms of—

Q: On the last one you said a low confidence level that this was for weapons or has that changed in the aftermath of. *[The guy still doesn't get it.]*

SENIOR INTELLIGENCE OFFICIAL 2: No. No, that has not changed. However actually, David, we haven't addressed it, but I would suggest to you that the Syrian behavior after the strike keeping it secret, destroying it, not allowing the IAEA, if anything, it certainly doesn't weaken that there were nefarious purposes for the reactor. *[That is, doesn't weaken their belief that they were highly confident about the low confidence judgment.]*

Q: Three questions. Did the United States military aid in any way this Israeli strike through reconnaissance or through targeting help? Did the US obtain these photos or were they from another country's intelligence agency? And what is the intention of North Korea's cooperation here? Is it cash-motivated? Are they looking to get plutonium themselves for their own reprocessing?

SENIOR INTELLIGENCE OFFICIAL 2: What was one?

Q: One was did the US military aid in any way the Israelis? with targeting or some other—

SENIOR INTELLIGENCE OFFICIAL 2: Let me talk a little bit obliquely here, okay. There is a rich intelligence exchange with a body of partners around the world that included an exchange on this information here. There is [a] difference between a rich exchange of intelligence and providing information that would actually enable the targeting and strike of this kind of target.

Q: So you shared information. You didn't give them targeting information.

SENIOR INTELLIGENCE OFFICIAL 2: We were in A, not B on this. The second one?

Q: And the second one is did the US intelligence agencies obtain these photos or did they come through another nation's intelligence?

SENIOR INTELLIGENCE OFFICIAL 2: I'm only free to say that we acquired the photos, and we have, and I tried to communicate to you under whatever guise we acquired them the confidence level we have in them.

Q: And North Korean intentions? Cash?

SENIOR INTELLIGENCE OFFICIAL 1: Cash.

SENIOR INTELLIGENCE OFFICIAL 2: It's cash.

SENIOR INTELLIGENCE OFFICIAL 1: Cash. *[The certainty here—the "confidence"—is puzzling unless based on hard eavesdropping or other evidence.]*

**Q:** So they weren't going to be taking this—

**SENIOR INTELLIGENCE OFFICIAL 2:** We don't—

**SENIOR INTELLIGENCE OFFICIAL 1:** We examined—

**SENIOR INTELLIGENCE OFFICIAL 2:** We examined that. We examined that hypothesis. This just wasn't.

**SENIOR INTELLIGENCE OFFICIAL 1:** Probably not.

**SENIOR INTELLIGENCE OFFICIAL 2:** You know, a reactor in Syria for Syria, that it may be outsourcing. And our judgment based on the overwhelming body of evidence is it was A, not B. That it was in Syria for Syria.

**SENIOR INTELLIGENCE OFFICIAL 2:** I'm sorry. Yeah, you're right. *[The Senior Administration Official]* is correcting me. Option A was in Syria for North Korea; option B was in Syria for Syria. We think it was in Syria for Syria, although we examined both options and held it up to the light with the available evidence. *[Here is where they should say they have low confidence. They have no way of knowing where the prospective plutonium would have ended up, unless they're not telling us something about how they know this, which is entirely possible.]*

**Q:** How much money is in it for North Korea?

**SENIOR INTELLIGENCE OFFICIAL 2:** Not at liberty to say. *[Suggests pretty hard evidence of a known sum.]*

**Q:** I believe a Calder Hall reactor is fueled with naturally occurring uranium. Is there such deposits in Syria? Have you looked to see whether or not the Syrians were actually mining their own uranium, and if so, again, have you located that site? And if not, where were they going to get the uranium from?

**SENIOR INTELLIGENCE OFFICIAL 2:** *[to Senior Intelligence Official 3]* Is there anything that you know that we can share?

**SENIOR INTELLIGENCE OFFICIAL 3:** No, sir. *[i.e., We may know a lot.]*

**SENIOR INTELLIGENCE OFFICIAL 2:** Okay.

**Q:** Can I just ask to be clear what you mean when you're talking about low confidence . . . how that compares to, in the talking points here that you lay out, the nearing operational capability? Can you just walk me through what exactly that means?

**Q:** So I'm trying understand, then, okay, so they were nearing operational capability but then can you compare what that means.

**SENIOR INTELLIGENCE OFFICIAL 2:** Okay, I got it.

**Q:** The low confidence. I want to be clear on that.

**SENIOR INTELLIGENCE OFFICIAL 2:** Yeah. Again, this is a bit arcane *[by this point it shouldn't be]*, and I'm trying to be very precise with our language here, okay. We were certain, okay, this was a reactor and that it was going to produce plutonium. We saw no other logical use for that plutonium based upon, no other use for the reactor other than creating plutonium. And then our judgment was that the Syrians would only have done this, with the great expense and perhaps political risk involved, for a weapons program, although we had not yet detected the detailed and constituent elements of such a weapons program. That is, and therefore, we said, we believe, Mr. President, that is what this is for.

**SENIOR INTELLIGENCE OFFICIAL 1:** It may be—

**SENIOR INTELLIGENCE OFFICIAL 2:** But the body of evidence on which we're basing that is more limited than some of the other things we're telling you.

**SENIOR INTELLIGENCE OFFICIAL 1:** It may be useful, too, to separate it in pieces. Go to the question that was asked about natural uranium. You can take natural uranium, get access to it, build a plant like this, and cause a reactor to operate, which would produce plutonium. So natural uranium in one place, a reactor to produce plutonium, and now you have to reprocess it to turn it into the kinds of material that would be used for weapons, so what we're describing to you with regard to our confidence level, plus with the regard to the reactor in the middle piece.

*The briefing suddenly shifts to the subject of Iran.*
*Senior Official 1 clearly wants to correct the record.*

**SENIOR OFFICIAL 1:** Can I just make a comment on Iran because I know that's eventually, if we stayed long enough you're eventually going to get there. And I think it's useful to talk about nuclear weapons and Iran in this context because this all is potentially interrelated.

*[This is almost funny—his attempt to make it seem as if he is only talking about Iran because he knows that eventually the reporters would ask him about Iran when, in fact, he is impatient with the fact that they haven't. McConnell is about to explain— as I heard him say at a private dinner forum some weeks later— that a misunderstanding about confidence levels was responsible for a worldwide misunderstanding of the 2007 National Intelligence Estimate on Iran's nuclear program. That misunderstanding fatally weakened the attempt by the U.S. and the European Union and other anti-proliferation forces to halt by peaceful means— through sanctions—the Iranian nuclear weapons program by misleading the entire world into thinking it had already been halted when the opposite was true. The 2005 NIE on Iran depicted an ambitious program for acquiring nuclear weapons involving the three components of such a program, getting highly enriched uranium (HEU) fuel for the fissile component, developing missile delivery systems capable of carrying a nuclear warhead long distances, and designing and engineering the nuclear warhead itself. Then in November 2007 a new NIE essentially reversed the judgments of the 2005 NIE and said, in its declassified summary of*

*"key judgments." "We judge with high confidence, that in fall 2003, Tehran halted its nuclear weapons program." That sentence made front-page headlines all over the world.*

*The problem was that the sentence was scandalously inaccurate, knowingly inaccurate, contradicted by a footnote that the authors must have trusted the media to ignore—as they did almost universally in writing their "Iran/no nukes" front-pagers. The footnote keyed to that statement read thus: "For purpose of this estimate, by 'nuclear weapons program' we mean Iran's nuclear weapons design and weaponization work and covert uranium conversion-related work. . . . We do not mean Iran's declared civil work related to uranium conversion and enrichment."*

*In other words, the executive summary of the 2007 NIE that was handed out to the press said it believed Tehran had halted one of three aspects of its nuclear weapons program in 2003, not the entire program, just the actual warhead design. But Iran had not halted uranium enrichment, even though it had declared they were only enriching the fissile material for peaceful reactor use. It had not halted work on long-range missile delivery systems, including the Shehab-3.*

*And as far as the warhead weapons design itself Iran may have halted work in 2003 because such work had already reached completion. Its leaders could easily have bought the plans from A. Q. Khan; they were ready to build the bomb—they just needed the fuel.*

*As it turns out, the intelligence that lay behind even the judgment about Iran halting work on the warhead was eventually called into question. It was based on electronic intercepts of conversations between Iranian scientists and managers of the nuclear program who were overheard complaining about the halt in the program—which led many to suspect the conversations were crafted by Iranians who wanted to disguise the fact that work was continuing but knew they were being overheard.*

*Intelligence officials appeared shocked that the 2007 NIE was misunderstood. When I heard Mike McConnell at a private gathering a few months later, he seemed genuinely hurt or puzzled at the laxity of the media for not reading the footnote. Two and half years later, after just about every intelligence service in the world was coming up with evidence of Iran working away feverishly on its weapons design, the U.S. intelligence community was still trying to clean up the mess it had made—a mess attributable in part to State Department partisans who felt their no-WMD advice had been ignored in the run-up to the Iraq War and were intent this time to err on the side of the false but reassuring wording to defuse a potential confrontation with Iran. This was a history-making intelligence error, which may have more devastating and tragic consequences than the WMD mistake—a regional nuclear war, after all, will cause a bigger death toll than the one continuing in Iraq.]*

**SENIOR OFFICIAL 1:** They [Iran] continue with ballistic missiles and they continue with fissile material pursuit. It was a secret program that they halted. They have never admitted that. So one of our concerns is, is there a connection with North Korea? If there is, we don't know it. But is there something going on there that resembles this program that we we're talking about in Syria in Iran?

*[One is tempted to say, "No shit, Sherlock." But the key words here are "They have never admitted that." The Iranians continue to deny that they have any nuclear weapons programs or designs, even after the discovery of the secret reactor beneath the holy city of Qom (or the announcement of the discovery) in September 2009.*

*The fact that the program that Iran allegedly halted was a secret, illegal program should have led a capable intelligence community not to fist-pump in triumph but to question what Iran's real game was and how many other secret illegal programs and facilities had not been shut down or discovered. Indeed, was the Syrian reactor designed to outsource fuel making for its ally Iran, for instance?]*

**SENOR INTELLIGENCE OFFICIAL 1:** That is a very large concern of ours, a major problem that we're attempting to address. But our unfortunate choice of words in our NIE caused you all in the press to misrepresent what we were trying to explain. *[They are right at least in part to blame it on their "unfortunate choice of words" just as they continue to use an "unfortunate choice of words." They repeat the mistake in not seeming to realize how deceptive estimative language is in the world outside their spy caves. While saying they have "low confidence" that Syria was engaged in a weapons program inside the Enigmatic Box, the entire briefing demonstrated what almost anyone else would call high confidence that the Syrians were building a reactor designed to make weapons with North Korean help because they don't have a notarized confession from the plant manager. If nothing else the briefing demonstrated that intelligence officials should try to use the same language as planet earth in their briefings. It is no exaggeration that the nuclear future of the world may be at stake in these semantic confusions.]* Three parts of the program; they halted one narrow piece of it, which was a secret program. Weapons-head design. They continue with fissile material; they continue with ballistic missile systems for delivery. So we don't know where it is at the moment. *[And the more we learn the less we really know?]*

Q: No Iran–North Korea connection?

SENIOR INTELLIGENCE OFFICIAL 1: None.

SENIOR INTELLIGENCE OFFICIAL 2: On nuclear issues.

Q: On nuclear issues.

SENIOR INTELLIGENCE OFFICIAL 2: Robust connection on—

SENIOR INTELLIGENCE OFFICIAL 1: Other places, yes.

SENIOR INTELLIGENCE OFFICIAL 2: Missile issues. *[This "robust connection" is big news, again lost in the misinterpretation of the NIE: North Korea is helping Iran design and build long-range missiles.]*

Q: Just to follow up on the Six-Party [North Korean] talks. The assumption now on what is being said is that the negotiators are really focusing on plutonium equation and the HEU [highly enriched uranium] and the Syrian assistance is kind of being pushed down the road a little bit. Does this briefing and this information that is coming out now shift that equation? Is that no longer what the White House wants?

SENIOR ADMINISTRATION OFFICIAL: Well, we have said that North Korea needs to do a full accounting of its plutonium activities, its enrichment activities and its proliferation activities. And that's what we are pursuing now. In addition, one of the things that this has done, and I think we'll encourage, is to supplement, in some sense, the Six-Party framework by building in a capacity to verify the disclosures that North Korea is hopefully going to make so that if, down the road, there is evidence that suggests that disclosures are inaccurate or not full and complete that there will be a verification mechanism available in the framework of the Six-Party talks to pursue that issue. So we think we have constructed a framework in the Six-Party talks for dealing with this issue. Thank you. *[In other words, discovery of a blatant North Korean lie hampers their ability (but not overly much) to continue lying about that specific piece of blatant proliferation. But North Korea has neither admitted nor disclosed anything further and has learned that it suffers no consequences for what may have been an attempt to outsource the making of bomb-grade fuel. And perhaps the single most shocking word, the most deeply disturbing evidence of naïveté on the part of the entire U.S. intelligence community, is contained in the word "hopefully." Hopefully the North Koreans will come clean, and be forthcoming with the truth just like the Iranians. These people are the best and brightest the intelligence community can muster and they are an insult to our intelligence.]*

MODERATOR: Thanks, everybody, for coming. *[Thanks for allowing us finally to tell you how badly you screwed up in the past with our inadvertent clumsy help.]*

I found the whole NIE scandal and the Enigmatic Box briefing so scandalous and such a manifestly incompetent demonstration of our intelligence community and its way of thinking that I had to check my perceptions with Dr. Jeffrey Lewis, one of the most respected arms control analysts, no Iran hawk, now a fellow at the New America Foundation where I met him across a table in an empty conference room. He was one of the first to pursue the al-Kibar raid mystery and coined the term "Enigmatic Box."

Here's what he said about the NIE:

"Well, I have listened now to multiple people from ODNI [Mike McConnell's Office of the Director of National Intelligence]. Let's see. The following things I believe to be true. I believe that the analysts who wrote the 2007 NIE . . . live in their own little world and have only a vague connection to what the rest of us are doing including people who are informed and likely to be their consumers. . . . So they wrote a product that had very little chance of being understood by Congress and no chance of being understood by the general public. So to blame the press for reporting it is a little bit feeling sorry for themselves."

"So they [the 2007 NIE analysts]," I asked, "didn't mean the weapons program had been halted in 2003, just the clandestine aspect of the warhead design and not fuel enrichment and ballistics?"

"See this is because of bad writing. What it actually said was halted in 2003 was 'clandestine conversion, enrichment, weapons design.'"

"Which meant they could continue dual use enrichment and ballistics and for all we know the weapons design program was already completed in 2003?"

"Yes."

The misreading of the NIE had serious consequences for the chance of an Israeli-Iranian war, as turns out. The *New York Times* has reported that Israel's efforts during the 2008–2009 period to obtain the weapons, refueling capacity, and permission to fly over Iraq for an attack on Iran grew out of its disbelief and anger at the 2007 NIE. The Israelis rebutted the American report as soon as it was released, and recurrently as new information developed in the years since the 2007 NIE, providing American intelligence officials and Admiral Mike Mullen, the chairman of the Joint Chiefs of Staff, with evidence that they said indicated the Iranians were still working on a weapon. And sure enough, the world eventually caught up to their assessment: in January 2009, the *Wall Street Journal* reported there was fresh evidence of recent efforts by Iran to evade sanctions and acquire metals from China used in high-tech weaponry, including long-range missiles. That evidence came by way of the United Arab Emirates, which informed the U.S. in September 2009 that it had "intercepted a Chinese shipment headed to Iran of specialized aluminum sheets that can be used to make ballistic missiles. A month earlier, UAE officials had also intercepted an Iran-bound shipment of titanium sheets that could be used in long-range missiles," according to the *Wall Street Journal*.

The Israelis were not the only ones highly critical of the United States report. Robert Gates, who was Bush's secretary of defense and stayed on in that role to serve President Obama, said in 2009 that the 2007 NIE had presented the evidence poorly, underemphasizing the importance of Iran's enrichment activity and overemphasizing the suspension of a weapons design effort that could easily be turned back on. In an interview, he said that in his whole career he had never seen "an NIE that had such an impact on U.S. diplomacy," because "people figured, well, the military option is now off the table." What Gates was doing is drawing a straight line between the misleading NIE and a regional nuclear war involving Iran and Israel. It was Gates who, in late January 2010, was reported (first by *The Guardian*) to be suddenly rushing U.S. missile interceptor ships to the Persian Gulf ostensibly to reassure the Gulf sheikdoms, but in fact as almost everyone surmised to prevent an Israeli preemptive attack on Iran by providing them with a more credible nuclear umbrella.

He did not need to get deeper into how such a matter was perceived on the Israeli side, how much tighter it made their hair trigger.

## THE KILLER QUESTION

The U.S. intelligence briefing about the case of the Enigmatic Box was one perspective on what "close" meant in terms of proximity to a regional nuclear war. But the question of what "close" means also arose during my discussion with a professional war gamer, Air Force Colonel (ret.) Sam Gardiner, who has participated in real-world war game exercises during the height of the Cold War and still teaches and practices simulations of nuclear war scenarios at the Army's National War College in Washington, D.C. I had sought him out because I wanted his expertise in tracing the branches of the decision trees that might have led from the Israeli raid on the Syrian nuclear facility to the global outbreak of nuclear war.

Gardiner is the human face of nuclear war gaming, perhaps the most high-profile human war gamer to be found. You could think of him as a doomsday film director, an auteur of Armageddon, doing remake after remake of endless variations on potential World Wars. How many long-range nuclear-armed subs, for instance, do we have and available on active duty—four according to Hans Kristensen of the Federation of American Scientists—ready for instant retaliation or preemption? How many megatons can they fire with what degree of accuracy at any given moment? (The number of nuclear warheads we have in total was finally divulged by the Obama Pentagon: 5,133 as of September 30, 2009.)

Gardiner uses computer-generated information to simulate reality. But his preferred technique is to bring living breathing fallible human beings to the table. Literally, to a large conference table, to explore what actual decision making in high-pressure nuclear war contexts might be like. The human factor where decisions are unpredictable, irrevocable, and consequences are ineradicable.

Gardiner gathers together military and diplomatic experts, supplies them with all the data they need, sets up imaginary but realistic prewar crisis scenarios, and gets them to role-play real-world decision makers—presidents, secretaries of defense and state, defense ministers of Russia, Iran, Israel, and other nations—to see how they would make their decisions, what factors in each crisis scenario would weigh most heavily, what the alternative decisions and alternative outcomes might be, depending on choices that can take place in war games often played in real time over the course of days or weeks.

There are of course academic treatises on deterrence and brinkmanship of the likes of *Nuclear Deterrence and the Search for Credibility* by mathematician Robert Powell, which employ immensely complicated equations of risk and probability. But it's hard to believe real-time decisions will be made just by examining the array of solutions to such equations in the diminishing minutes or seconds that a president has to decide whether to launch.

What I didn't realize about Gardiner until I spent some time talking with him was that he had played war games for real on the plains of Central Europe. Fresh out of the Air Force Academy he was assigned to SHAFE (Supreme Headquarters Allied Forces Europe) in Brussels in the 1970s where he found himself deeply enmeshed in the deployment of nuclear weapons in what was regarded as the most likely flashpoint of any U.S.–Soviet nuclear war.

What he found was a tangled web of nuclear command and control complexity due to several factors, which he says, have still not been sorted out.

First the system of shared control of the nuclear trigger made everything more complex at SHAFE. The nuclear weapons under SHAFE/NATO were mainly of U.S. origin and official ownership, but in order to get a release to fire a nuclear weapon or salvo from European territory a NATO commander had to have the unanimous consent of all sixteen NATO treaty members.

"I remember during one exercise," Gardiner told me, "I ended up frantically trying to convince a Parisian telephone operator who didn't speak English to put me through to SACEUR [Supreme Allied Command, Europe, which controlled the "safety catch" on all U.S.-origin nuclear weapons] to give me permission to fire a nuclear weapon."

"Did you succeed?" I asked.

"What do you think?" he said.

"Have things improved? By now?"

"What do you think?" he said again, laughing, acknowledging that while public telephone switchboards were no longer required, the degree of difficulty, the number of complications had not diminished.

Another complicating factor—with serious relevance to the situation today—was that NATO had a "first use" policy, meaning it reserved to itself the right to use nuclear weapons should a conflict break out in Europe. The initial reason for retaining first use dates back to the time the Soviet and Eastern European Warsaw Pact forces faced off against NATO divisions across the border between East and West Germany. For most of that time, the Soviets had NATO outmanned and outgunned with conventional forces and so most war games envisioned some kind of Warsaw Pact breakthrough that would lead its forces to overrun the rest of Europe all the way to the English Channel. They had to be deterred from such an attack by the possibility that NATO would use nuclear weapons. In most war games, this would result in a global nuclear war, presuming the Soviet Union then retaliated against NATO's nukes with nuclear weapons of its own, leading to a U.S. attempt to take out all Soviet nukes. Gardiner believes that one of the first things a U.S. administration should do is push NATO to renounce its first use policy, which would have the effect of taking the Russians off their high-alert status and make both sides less vulnerable to accidental nuclear war.

Gardiner had more chilling stories from his days as a NATO war gamer. "There was always a two-man team attached to every firing unit. Everyone had one American. I was technically executive officer to a German colonel who outranked me but there was an informal, unspoken rule that no German would be allowed to launch on his own authority."

No German . . . Unspoken was the implication that no German, however democratically inclined, would be permitted to be in a position to perpetrate on his own authority what would amount to, in body count, a holocaust. A reminder that any study of nuclear war is a study of genocide, that any given missile launch in the Cold War tinderbox of Central Europe bristling with short-range and long-range nuclear weapons could touch off slaughter on a scale beyond anything Hitler was able to accomplish. Not the same kind of slaughter that singled out a religious ethnic group, but in sheer magnitude a number of dead far beyond Hitler's imagination. No German . . .

It raised the question of whether such slaughter, even if carried in a "good cause" for the "good guy" democracies, could be justified. Gardiner has a book on his shelf at home, he says, that used to be required reading for all those involved in targeting and release (launch) exercises. It was a book that detailed the casualties any given nuclear weapons or combinations thereof could cause, depending on mega-tonnage, population density, blast height, and so forth. It was used to calculate what percent of a given blast damage would eliminate military-industrial infrastructure and how many civilian deaths that would necessarily entail.

"It used to be required reading," Gardiner told me. "It isn't anymore."

It was in this context that Colonel Gardiner made, in an almost offhand way, before we even began to war-game the Enigmatic Box on the Euphrates, a stunning allusion to an overlooked aspect of the Georgia crisis of August 2008, which had just then come to an uneasy, unstable pause. Gardiner pointed to a moment in the Georgia military conflict with the Russian Federation in August 2008, maneuvering that suggested we had already passed through the first—virtual but serious—superpower nuclear skirmish of the new nuclear age.

"Did you notice," Gardiner asked me, "a reference by [Bush National Security Adviser Stephen] Hadley to the fact that in the midst of the fighting in Georgia the Russians had drawn up SS-26s to the battle front?"

SS-26, he explained, is the NATO designation for what the Russians call the Iskander missile, a mobile short- to medium-range ballistic missile launcher system that—and this is the crucial point—is capable of being equipped with either conventional or nuclear warheads.

"Hadley gave this briefing when Bush was in Beijing for the

Olympics and the Russians were rolling into Georgia and the Georgians were calling on us to back them up," Gardiner told me.

"And the point is not just that Hadley said they were moving nukes to the front, the point is the ambiguity—we didn't know whether these SS-26s were nuclear-tipped or not, and they knew we didn't know, so in fact, any strategist on our side would have to make the conservative assumption that any countermove we made could be initiating nuclear combat."

Which means?

"Which means that this may well have been the first instance of nuclear deterrence between the superpowers in the post–Cold War era. Not that we backed down necessarily, because we may well have had no plans to back the Georgians with military power, but the Russians couldn't have known that for sure, and what they saw—at least one interpretation they could put on it—was 'SS-26s move up, U.S. backs down.' Deterrence!"

He—and others—have said nuclear deterrence came into play more than once between the U.S. and other nonnuclear powers. The most specific: the First Gulf War. Kristensen of the Federation of American Scientists has pointed to a moment in the run-up to the U.S. invasion of Iraq in 1991 in which Secretary of State James Baker handed a letter to Tariq Aziz, Saddam Hussein's henchman.

According to a background briefing by a Pentagon official in 2002: "He [Hussein] didn't cross the line of using chemical or biological weapons [against U.S. troops]. The Iraqis have told us that they interpreted that letter as meaning that the United States would use nuclear weapons [if he did], and it was a powerful deterrent."

But this was a threat to use nukes against a nonnuclear power. What Gardiner was saying was that the movement of the SS-26s, ambiguous as it might have been, was a different story; one nuclear superpower making a chess move against another to deter it from coming to the aid of a quasi-client state.

Was the U.S. then deterred? Was this the first instance of post–Cold War nuclear deterrence in operation as Colonel Gardiner suggested? One way of looking at it is that the U.S. wasn't deterred

because the U.S. had no plans to come to the military aid of Georgia however much Georgia might have imagined such might be
the case.

I presented Colonel Gardiner's SS-26 analysis to a smart nuclear
deterrence theorist, Elbridge "Bridge" Colby, the grandson of the
legendary CIA head William Egan Colby, whom the State Department under Obama had hired to work on the START treaty as part
of a team of negotiators.

This was his reply:

"I played no role in that crisis, so am totally an outside observer.
My sense is that nuclear weapons played no role other than as they
always do in U.S.–Russia relations—as an omnipresent sobering
backdrop. I would speculate (again, no inside information) that
there was no serious—if any at all—consideration of air operations
on behalf of the Georgians not because of the SS-26s but because
the U.S. did not even want to consider getting in a shooting war
with the Russians over such a peripheral interest."

All pro forma nonalarmist so far. But I found Colby's addendum
alarming:

"This caution was likely compounded by the knowledge that
the Russians have quite publicly and deliberately lowered their
nuclear threshold over the last fifteen years, have retained substantial nonstrategic nuclear forces, and have developed doctrine
to employ such weapons in their near-abroad [meaning the former
soviet states or satellite nations]. U.S. decision makers [one would
hope!] took this into account. My guess is that Hadley mentioned
the SS-26s, then, simply to highlight alleged Russian irresponsibility in the matter, specifically the willingness to employ potentially
nuclear-capable forces in the conflict."

In other words Colby comes around to concurring with Gardiner: this taking into account the potential presence of Russian
nukes—and our recognition of the Russian lowering their nuclear
threshold—is one reason for our lack of interest in fighting over
Georgia. This could also be called being deterred by nukes. "Caution . . . compounded" is another way of saying "deterred."

Colby also raises the interesting question of why Hadley made public the SS-26 chess move. If he went public to the highlight Russian irresponsibility, then for whom was that message intended: not to Putin and Medvedev but rather, perhaps, to the rest of the world's leadership, to let them know the Russians were playing with fire.

Or it could have been a message to the European Union whose purpose could have been twofold: to make them aware of the urgency and the stakes in the confrontation and encourage them to use whatever leverage they had with the Russian leadership to hold back from the risk, however small, of touching off a wider war.

It could simultaneously have been a message to the military establishment in the U.S. and those in Congress with budgetary power that nuclear weapons of all sizes still play a role now and that we had better be prepared for them to play a role in the future. The downside of this is that, in view of the fact that we did not hurl anything at the Russians but words, it could be taken as an admission that nuclear weapons had deterred us from coming to the aid of Georgia. (Another reason why we were lucky—it was a close call—that Georgia's application to join NATO, which would have required us to confront the Russians had their admission been complete and accepted, had not been completed at the time of the crisis.)

On the other hand we don't know what secret communications about the situation had been conveyed to the Russians in addition to Hadley's public statement. We may have made it clear that arming the SS-26s with nuclear warheads would risk turning the confrontation into a nuclear standoff, or that we were aware of their nukes but were prepared to match them if the Russians rolled over the rest of Georgia as it looked for a day or so they might. The fact they didn't take advantage of this easy opportunity to eliminate a thorn in their side might be an indication that it was they who were deterred.

The SS-26s have surfaced more than once in the last three years. Just hours after Obama was elected president, Russia announced it would base them within range of our planned missile defense site in Poland. This move was meant to "neutralize" the planned missile defense system that the Bush administration had wanted to deploy in Eastern Europe. Was it deterrence that caused the Obama administration to abandon the Polish interceptor plan?

Both the Bush and Obama Pentagon have stated repeatedly that the defensive shield is designed to protect the continent from missiles launched from rogue states, such as Iran. But Moscow rejects that argument, claiming that the system is actually aimed at Russia. So Russia also made it clear in December 2009 that it had plans to jam a radar located in the Czech Republic used to detect in-bound missiles and intended to guide the projected Polish-based interceptors. The Bush plan was thankfully revoked when Obama came into office, (but replaced by a sea-based system and a Romanian land-based interceptor installation, that are no less objectionable to the Russians) and that may have been Putin and Medvedev's intention all along. The Russians were clearly mounting a challenge to Bush's successor, who has said he is opposed to "unproven" missile defense systems. The Associated Press story describing the nuclear brinkmanship was a concatenation of Cold War clichés: "In some respects," it said, "the SS-26 movement to Kaliningrad [the Russian outpost closest to the proposed Polish interceptor base] is the first 'shot across the bow' of the incoming administration. Moscow is waiting to see if Obama has 'steel in his spine,' and will stand up to a deliberate Russian provocation. So are our Eastern European allies, who wonder if the new president will stand with them against the Russian bear."

These are strong words: "Shot across the bow," "steel in his spine," "stand with them against the Russian bear." World War III is back in words if not yet in deed.

When I asked Colonel Gardiner what he'd learned about wargaming over the years of engaging in it, he told me that it often comes down to finding out "What is the killer question."

He gave an example from his experience in war game exercises he participated in during the Cold War: "Could the Belgian core hold?" The Belgian core was the weak spot in the north–south dividing line between NATO and the Warsaw Pact powers. The geographical weak spot. The likely attack point.

Would we have the credibility to convince the Soviets that we could hold the Belgian core with conventional forces without having to resort to nukes to stop a breakthrough?

Colonel Gardiner had a fascinating account of how we sought to make the Soviets believe that our Fifth Corps would "move up to reinforce the Seventh Corps" in holding the Belgian core, thus discouraging the Warsaw Pact from focusing its forces on the apparent weakness. The killer question was: did they believe us? Apparently. According to Gardiner, we leaked plans through a spy that we'd make that move, thereby implying that we were inviting them into a trap. Then we acted out the move during a war game exercise Gardiner participated in and incorporated the Seventh Corps deception into our actual war plan. "Deception was the essence of credibility," was his way of summing it up.

But in terms of today's war-gaming the new nuclear age flashpoints, Gardiner was most concerned about the urgency of the Pakistan problem. "You want to know where the Pakistani nukes are? I can show you on Google maps," he said.

"You mean they're not exactly secure."

"What do you think?" he said.

In the Iranian-American war game Gardiner ran for *The Atlantic* magazine, the killer question was whether Iran would credibly retaliate against an American attack on its nuclear facilities. Or would they refrain because any retaliation would certainly bring on the kind of obliteration promised Iran by Secretary of State Hillary Clinton, who used that formulation in one of the primary debates. She was referring to our willingness to provide Israel with a nuclear umbrella: a pledge to obliterate Iran if it nuked Israel.

In that war game, the conclusion was that Iran would retaliate, in the Persian Gulf, taking out U.S. aircraft carriers and battleships with Chinese Silkworm missiles, obliterating shipping in the Strait of Hormuz, destroying the Saudi oil refineries and with them much of the West's energy supplies, not to mention—depending on the time frame—sending a Shehab-3 ballistic missile or two or more heading toward Israel, Western Europe, and, for all we knew, the Western Hemisphere as well. The fact that some of the best-informed Western experts on Iran discounted the potency of deterrence is an ominous indication that a global nuclear war could erupt from supposed surgical strikes on Iran.

Syria however, was deterred on the night of September 6, 2007. An attack on its territory left a key nearly completed nuclear facility of some kind obliterated and the Syrians were silent. And the Iranians may have had some kind of mutual defense pact with the Syrians, but did nothing. The Syrians are known to possess missiles with the capacity to deliver chemical weapons into the heart of Israel's major cities and they didn't use them because, they knew— they were deterred by—Israeli nuclear capacity to leave Damascus a radioactive ruin.

The night we came so close to World War III we danced on the knife's edge of deterrence and lived to see another day. But what if things had played out just a little bit differently?

When I think about the Enigmatic Box and the close call it represented I can't help thinking of Pandora's box, which, in the myth, when opened against warnings, released all the evils of the world. At the bottom of Pandora's box of course there was said to be one remaining thing: hope. Did the events of April 2010 recounted in the next chapter represent hope? That's the killer question.

# CHAPTER NINE

# ENDGAME

## THE SURPRISING REBIRTH OF ZERO

Hope springs eternal; but so does false hope. President Barack Obama and Russian president Dmitri Medvedev finally signed the much delayed "follow-on" of the START treaty—"New START" as the optimistic Obama press releases called it. But the treaty was a tacit recognition that nukes are here to stay. It leaves thousands of them on hair-trigger alert and perpetuates the ideology at the heart of deterrence theory: threaten genocide to prevent genocide. The day before the president departed for the Prague signing, the Pentagon released the first Obama administration Nuclear Posture Review (or NPR), a fifty-page document whose departure from the previous one by the Bush administration was hailed by some for its stated intention to make nuclear weapons less central to U.S. military strategy. But it was a rhetorical reset rather than a breakaway from the straitjacket of deterrence theory. "A status quo document," Bruce Blair told the *Wall Street Journal*. In fact, both the treaty and the NPR were status quo documents that left open the question of whether the status quo was sustainable.

There were those who pointed out that in terms of sheer numbers the new treaty could prove to be a step backward. While the treaty officially reduced the maximum number of warheads from 2,200 on each side to 1,500, "Because of quirks in counting warheads aboard heavy bombers" Jonathan Weisman and Peter Spiegel wrote in the April 9 *Wall Street Journal*, "the actual number of nuclear weapons could be considerably higher in seven years." Each "heavy" nuclear bomber—"heavy" as defined by capacity—was counted as a single weapon, just as if it were the single warhead of a missile, despite the fact that each bomber could be loaded up with a dozen or more warheads and bombs, and up to seven hundred of them were permitted.

Even more demoralizing, nothing at all was done to change the alert status of missiles on either side of the standoff. Anyone who spent more than ten minutes studying the document would discover the alert problem was addressed in a highly disingenuous way. In the Introduction to the NPR there is on page x, a section with the astonishingly misleading title "Maximizing Presidential Decision Time." But does the new NPR actually do anything to maximize presidential decision time? No. It flatly declares that nothing will change. "The NPR concluded that the current alert posture of U.S. Strategic Forces—with . . . nearly all ICBMs on alert and a significant number of SSBN's on alert at sea at any given time—*should be maintained for the present* [italics mine]," the executive summary heading of the report says.

In other words despite titling the section as if it were actually doing something to maximize presidential warning time, like getting those ICBMs off hair-trigger alert, it committed us to the current destabilizing situation more deeply and defiantly.

The only way the authors of the NPR justify that title is by weakly suggesting "efforts should continue to further diminish the possibility of nuclear launches resulting from accidents, unauthorized actions or misperceptions and to maximize the time available to the president to consider whether to authorize the use of nuclear weapons." But in its effect the NPR has made it acceptable for those efforts to be disregarded.

General Kevin Chilton, head of STRATCOM, had told me months earlier in Omaha that he lost sleep over the morality of retaliation, but in fact it seemed more like the wily warrior worked sleeplessly to mobilize the Pentagon and Defense Secretary Gates against incorporating Obama's campaign pledge to take missiles off hair-trigger alert into the NPR. In the end, he won the fight he had picked with his commander-in-chief.

The Obama defenders have argued the administration didn't want to go too far with changes in the Nuclear Posture Review because they didn't want to jeopardize chances of ratification of the new START treaty, which depends on a two-thirds majority in the Senate, sixty-seven votes.

And there were those who said that whatever one thought of the treaty agreement specifics, just the act of having come to some agreement with the Russians established a framework for further rational reductions that could eventually lead us significantly closer to Zero. On the other hand there were those who said new START was really an end because any further treaty would have to consider Russian demands to limit ballistic missile defense, an issue upon which the two sides seemed unalterably divided.

Meanwhile, while all this U.S. and Russia nuclear peacemaking was making headlines, Iran was boasting of a new generation of nuclear fuel enrichment centrifuges whirling somewhere beneath the ancient hills of Persia. Israel announced a stepped-up program of building underground shelters under public buildings such as theaters and sports arenas throughout the land, and its Dolphin-class submarines cruised somewhere in the Persian Gulf carrying what the world supposed were nuclear missiles.

And then there was the dog that didn't bark. No throngs of people in the streets of the cities of the world joyously celebrating the Prague treaty the way throngs had filled the cities to support a nuclear freeze in the 1980s when there had been a nuclear peace movement. That movement didn't stop the deployment of Pershing II intermediate-range missiles, but may have led ultimately to the intermediate-range ballistic missile treaty, which eventually removed them as well as their close-range Soviet counterparts. Thirty years later, the little left of that movement was just a bunch of extremely thoughtful and articulate arms control and Zero advocates located in several think tank buildings off DuPont Circle in Washington, D.C. Meanwhile General Chilton has the Pentagon, and the missile crewmen on hair-trigger alert still have the keys.

## CULTISTS OR VISIONARIES?

Are the nuclear abolitionists cultists or visionaries?

It has been nearly three decades since the no-nukes and nuclear freeze movements reached its high-water mark at the height of the Cold War with the international marches and 1979's celebrity-saturated nuclear Woodstock of the Jackson Browne–led No Nukes concert in Madison Square Garden. And an undergrad at Columbia, Barack Obama, wrote an essay for the school paper supporting the nuclear freeze.

Since the freeze fizzled and the Cold War did too, nuclear abolition had become at best a low-priority impossible dream concern for the left, at worst little more than a nostalgic memory associated with tie-dyed T-shirts and hippie communes. But a quarter-century after the No Nukes concert, in January 2007, two years before President Barack Obama declared "a world without nuclear weapons" a national goal, who should come riding to the rescue of the no nukes movement but that ol' peacenik Henry Kissinger in that tie-dyed hippie venue, the op-ed page of the *Wall Street Journal*.

It could be said that the history of the nuclear abolition movement in the second nuclear age began with a kind of bolt from the blue: a manifesto entitled "A World Free of Nuclear Weapons" signed by Kissinger, the legendary master of Machiavellian realpolitik, along with Reagan-era Secretary of State George Shultz and two former Democratic Party nuclear policy luminaries, Clinton-era Secretary of Defense William Perry and Senator Sam Nunn. Jointly these four defense-credentialed realists called not just for nuclear "freeze," not just for nuclear reductions, but for nuclear abolition, for specific steps to be taken to eliminate all nuclear weapons from the world's arsenals. To many it was shocking, even mystifying.

Kissinger, after all, came to prominence as the author of one of the texts that shaped our accumulation and maintenance of a vast nuclear arsenal, his 1957 book *Nuclear Weapons and Foreign Policy*. And as secretary of state, he and Shultz had presided over the seemingly endless SALT talks that for two decades had both stabilized and entrenched the nuclear balance of terror. But there was no mistaking the seriousness of their unexpected plea for nuclear abolition.

In the manifesto they go beyond strategic and tactical considerations to argue that the continuing possession of nuclear weapons is a profound threat to the psyche and soul of civilized society:

> Unless urgent new actions are taken, the US soon will be compelled to enter a new nuclear era that will be more precarious, psychologically disorienting, and economically even more costly than was Cold War deterrence. It is far from certain that we can successfully replicate the old Soviet-American 'mutually assured destruction' with an increasing number of potential nuclear enemies world-wide without dramatically increasing the risk that nuclear weapons will be used. New nuclear states do not have the benefit of years of step-by-step safeguards put in effect during the Cold War to prevent nuclear accidents, misjudgments or unauthorized launches. The United States and the Soviet Union learned from mistakes that were less than fatal. Both countries were diligent to ensure that no nuclear weapon was used during the Cold War by design or by accident. Will new nuclear nations and the world be as fortunate in the next 50 years as we were during the Cold War?

For those who argue that concern about the potential for nuclear annihilation is alarmism, the declaration from these Cold War characters that there is a new nuclear era whose instabilities dramatically increase the risk of nuclear war is a fairly strong and alarming refutation of that complaint. And they did more than wring their hands over it. They laid out an eight-step program to make the new nuclear order safer:

- Change the Cold War posture of deployed nuclear weapons to increase warning time and thereby reduce the danger of an accidental or unauthorized use of a nuclear weapon.
- Continue to reduce substantially the size of nuclear forces in all states that possess them.

- Eliminate short-range nuclear weapons designed to be forward-deployed.
- Initiate a bipartisan process with the Senate to achieve ratification of the Comprehensive Test Ban Treaty, taking advantage of recent technical advances, and working to secure ratification by other key states.
- Provide the highest possible standards of security for all stocks of weapons, weapons-usable plutonium, and highly enriched uranium everywhere in the world.
- Get control of the uranium enrichment process, combined with the guarantee that uranium for nuclear power reactors could be obtained at a reasonable price, first from the Nuclear Suppliers Group and then from the International Atomic Energy Agency (IAEA) or other controlled international reserves.
- Halt the production of fissile material for weapons globally; phase out the use of highly enriched uranium in civil commerce and remove weapons-usable uranium from research facilities around the world and render the materials safe.
- Redouble our efforts to resolve regional confrontations and conflicts that give rise to new nuclear powers.

Without these actions, they argued, "the vision of a nuclear free world will not be perceived as realistic or possible."

What they accomplished was to say to policymakers worldwide: nuclear abolition is not just for Kumbaya-singing pacifists. Nuclear abolition is for grown-ups. For conservatives as well as liberals, even for foreign policy realists. Their manifesto gave cover to nuclear abolitionists who took up the cause again, and to President Obama, who made it his goal two years later.

Of course there were doubters: Kissinger must be up to something, he's trying to burnish a tarnished image with a final legacy of peacemaking; he knows it will never happen anyway and even if it did, nuclear abolition would just allow the U.S. to rule the globe with its superior conventional weaponry.

These doubts could not be imputed to another one of the signatories, former senator Sam Nunn. I had a brief exchange him with him in July 2010 at a screening of a documentary, *Nuclear Tipping Point*, which centered around the conversion to Zero of Nunn and his cohorts Shultz, Kissinger, and Perry. The film was prefaced with a declaration for Zero by another convert to abolition, Colin Powell.

Nunn will be recognized by history—should there be a post-nuclear history—as one of the prime movers of the abolition movement. An unlikely one too. He'd been a protégé of Richard Russell, the late long-serving senator from Georgia and hawkish avatar of that state's prominent role in promoting military spending and armaments ramp-ups.

But after the Cold War ended, Nunn, an otherwise conservative Democrat, had joined with Republican senator Richard Lugar to push through legislation that addressed the profoundly serious situation in which tens of thousands of nuclear warheads in the collapsing Soviet empire were poorly guarded, unaccounted for, or otherwise easy targets for black-market crooks and terrorists. The Nunn-Lugar law provided the new Russian Federation with billions to collect and destroy tens of thousands of warheads (often reprocessing the fissile material in them to power nuclear reactors in the U.S.; 13 percent of our electrical supply, Nunn claimed, came from reprocessed Soviet-era nukes. Yes: swords into ploughshares.).

Nunn-Lugar saved us from the nightmare scenarios involving "loose nukes" and that staple of low-grade thrillers and international con men, the mythical "suitcase nuke" (much talked about, never reliably reported to have been glimpsed). After he left the Senate, Nunn teamed up with Ted Turner to form the Nuclear Threat Initiative to continue nuclear security work. It is now dedicated not just to securing nukes but to abolishing them all. Nunn claims two thirds of living former secretaries of state, defense, and national security advisers are on board with his abolition ambition.

But he is another one who argues, as Bruce Blair has (see chapter 5), that de-alerting nukes from hair-trigger status is even more important than radically reducing the number of warheads. Nunn used the word "hair-trigger," the word General Chilton our nuclear commander has sought to banish.

Nunn told me it was an early encounter with an even more hairy hair-trigger situation that put him on the long path to abolitionism. I had wondered why a conservative Georgia senator had turned into a nuclear abolitionist and in the talk that followed the documentary screening he told the story.

On a congressional junket to NATO installations in the 1970s, he found himself in conversation with one of the Air Force wing commanders in charge of what were then our most forward-based hair-trigger weapons, the fighter jet squadrons in Europe that carried nuclear bombs and could reach Moscow in minutes. They would be the first, most vulnerable target of any Soviet first strike.

The commander told Nunn that when he got an order to send his jets east to deliver their nuclear payloads in what would inevitably be the beginning of a cataclysmic global nuclear war, he estimated he had forty-five to seventy-five *seconds* to make the decision to verify and validate the takeoff order before his jets would likely be destroyed on the ground. A hair trigger's hair trigger. The potentiality for catastrophic, planet-destroying error in that thinnest of decision windows shocked Nunn. From that moment he began a lifelong personal investigation and legislative intervention into nuclear deployment and strategy questions. The endpoint was his advocacy of Zero: the hair-trigger problem had not been solved. Now the decision window was minutes rather than seconds, but seven, ten, fifteen minutes at most, and vulnerability to hackers spoofing an attack made those minutes even more precarious.

One of the strongest points Nunn made in his talk was a critique of the Obama administration's failure in its Nuclear Posture Review to deal with the problem of de-alerting, the kind of steps Bruce Blair had outlined. Nunn suggested he had been given assurances that the NPR would make practical de-alerting suggestions, but that the Pentagon overrode them. He theorized that part of the problem was semantic: the phrase "de-alerting" grated on military culture; military men were trained all their careers that everything depended on maximum alertness. Nunn argued that abandoning the *word* "de-alerting" and speaking instead about "increasing warning and decision time" might make a difference. On such semantic distinctions the future of the planet may depend. Which of course is unacceptable to any rational being.

I sensed there was more to Nunn's nuclear abolitionism than concerns about alert times. After his talk I asked him the question that had obsessed me for so long.

"Senator," I said, "what's your attitude toward the morality of nuclear retaliation: if deterrence fails, what's the morality of carrying out our threat and killing tens of millions of innocents to punish the acts of their leaders?"

It was something he'd thought about.

"Well, I wouldn't want the response to be automatic," he said. "I'd want there to be time for questions to be asked."

"But what if you were president and you were faced with that choice? What would you do?"

"I wouldn't want to answer that question publicly," he said. "But I know we shouldn't allow machines to make the decision, which has become the tendency."

It was the damnable paradox of deterrence again. I sensed that he would in that moment of Last Resort not choose willingly to kill tens, hundreds of millions. But even he, nuclear abolitionist, couldn't say that such genocidal vengeance was wrong because it might undermine deterrence if he gave the impression his thinking was widespread among U.S. leadership.

And so he fell back on what the generals at Omaha had offered: ambiguity. He might have had an answer in mind, but an attacker could not be sure what it was. Meanwhile despite all the ambiguity they sought to convince us of, the hair-trigger configuration, the training of the people with the codes and the keys did not factor in ambiguity. They were hair-trigger-trained, ready to twist the keys. Use it or lose it.

I suspect that for Nunn it is the impossibility of solving the nuclear deterrence paradox—that we must give the impression we will commit genocide to avoid genocide—that has forced this plain-spoken moral man to be afraid to say he won't commit genocide. For that reason alone nuclear weapons must go.

But Nunn, Kissinger, and their cohorts were not the only veterans of the Cold War to convert to abolitionism. I was particularly impressed by the deeply penitent response of one of the most hard-nosed nuclear advocates, Sir Peregrine Worsthorne. The man who had been editor of the influential Tory *Sunday Telegraph* at the height of the Cold War and a confidant to Prime Minister Margaret Thatcher and President Ronald Reagan had delivered himself of what seemed an agonized recantation. In 1996 he had claimed to a certainty that Thatcher and Reagan were not bluffing about nuclear retaliation; they would have pushed the button even if there had been no point but the promised punishment left. And, he added, to do so, he now believed, was obscenely immoral.

He has also changed his view of the acceptability of the nuclear deterrence: "Would some historian emerging centuries later from the post thermonuclear war Dark Ages have judged [pressing the button] morally justified, or so evil as to dwarf even the most monstrous inequities of Hitler, Stalin and Mao? . . . How could we have believed anything so preposterous?"

## A CONVERSION NARRATIVE

In the last ten years, abolition had brought to its side not only some prominent hawks, but a significant segment of the liberal, dovish arms control community, which up until then had favored radical reductions in nuclear weapons and "minimal deterrence." One of the key figures in this shift was Bruce Blair. His conversion from arms controller to abolitionist was surprisingly recent, just "a few years ago," he told me. And when he speaks about it, one is able to witness its emotional power. In most of our previous conversations Blair had been calm, cool, very much the well-informed unemotional analyst, comfortable talking the jargon of the nuclear command and control community from which he came. He was an arms control advocate, and personally controlled as well.

But on our third visit, we found ourselves talking about nuclear weapons and war crimes. We were in the cafeteria of the Brookings Institution next door to his office in the Carnegie Endowment for International Peace building.

I asked Blair what I'd asked the missile crewmen I'd met about "having the power of twisting the keys and thereby killing 10, 20 million people." I recalled that most of them seemed to deliberately speak lightly about it but sensed in their forced levity that they were troubled by it.

"Were you?" I asked Blair. "How did you feel about that when you had that power?"

"I felt important," he said. "For someone who is young in their early twenties and to have this sort of responsibility is fairly sobering and self-empowering, but not a matter of conscience for me at the time. I didn't struggle with that. And never dwelled on it either. I think there was some denial mechanism at work, and let's face it, millions of people—that's an abstraction. The training was designed to screen out people who had serious issues with that, so they never were in the position of giving—so you [the ones not screened out] were at best in the kind of somewhat troubled category, not deeply."

The "somewhat troubled category, not deeply": an interesting way of putting it. "Has it changed for you?"

"Oh, heck . . . of course. Everything changed for me."

"At what point?"

"I turned completely against the idea of a world with nuclear weapons. There were so many factors that sank in over time for me that suddenly tipped me into the 'this is totally unacceptable' camp."

"How long after you got out did this begin to happen?"

"I didn't really tip over into this camp until a few years ago."

This came as a surprise. "So up until then you felt your task was making it [deterrence] rational."

"Yeah. Safer. I came to realize over time just how dangerous it was. That doesn't mean that I didn't think we could alleviate those damages satisfactorily through things like de-alerting.

"When I wrote the article [in 1997] with [Sam] Nunn, we were not for the elimination of nuclear weapons." (He's referring to an influential *Washington Post* piece that led to the Nunn-Lugar nuclear demolition program.)

He pauses. "Now I'm seriously, sincerely, urgently for Zero. It's the realization of the danger, not only launch on warning but the extent of delegation [of launch authority] to multiple people lower down the chain of command which I learned really much more later on. I knew [some of] that at the time—"

"That's in your 1985 book, right?" I asked, referring to *Strategic Command and Control.*

"Yeah and I learned more over time. I knew a little bit at the time but all of these dangers, the three-minute drill [where Cheyenne Mountain threat assessment specialists are asked to judge the reliability of nuclear attack warnings from radar and satellite sensors within three minutes], the thirty-second briefing [where specialists give an assessment to the chief of STRATCOM in Omaha, who then transmits it immediately to the president]."

But it was more than the severe urgent localized instabilities in the command and control structure. It was the system itself, he says, which—on an issue of potential life or death for the entire populace of the U.S. and billions elsewhere—was profoundly undemocratic. "What it tells you is that the democratic system isn't very functional in the control of nuclear weapons, because the timeliness—the emphasis on preemption, quick decision making, rote decision making—just denies any possibility of national leadership, much less some kind of semi-democratic—"

"No people's choice when it comes to nuclear targeting?"

"And then you realize, Jesus, even if democracy's functioning properly under our Constitution it still gives the power to, really, to one person. The president's commander-in-chief and by God you realize as you get older, that these people have deep flaws. For chrissake Nixon was drunk during the Yom Kippur whirlwind [the 1973 Egyptian invasion of Israel in which threats and counterthreats of nuclear intervention rocketed between Israel, Cairo, Washington, and Moscow]. I was in a launch control center and was told to go to DEFCON-3, take my launch keys out of the safe and the launch codes. And Nixon was asleep in a stupor. And that was [Secretary of Defense James] Schlesinger and [National Security Adviser Henry] Kissinger and the gang who were making these decisions. They told him about it later after he came to."

"Is that well known?"

"No, but it's . . . I think, a few people have. It's been out there, but never—you know how these things are—never really crystallized . . ."

It's not just that the decision to launch rests with one person, the president, it's the fact that the president's choices are predetermined or at least preselected by a nuclear priesthood.

"There's so much kept secret by the nuclear priesthood that even secretaries of defense and presidents don't even know what's going on."

He speaks of an encounter with Robert McNamara in 1980. As secretary of defense, McNamara had become obsessed with installing Permissive Action Links (PALs) on every American nuclear warhead, which meant they couldn't be launched without an explicit properly encoded order from above. Blair portrays McNamara as shocked upon learning from Blair that they had not been installed or made operational until long after he left office, after 1976.

"Think of this example, of McNamara thinking they had installed those PAL links [which require affirmative order from above to release launch codes] on the system—it's just one of the examples.

"Then the fact that it's not necessary anymore to have these arsenals. It's in our national interest to get rid of them. If we could get rid of a lot them in particular it would clearly be empowering. We have so much soft power and conventional military power that nuclear weapons in the possession of other countries, counteracts, doesn't neutralize but severely levels the field."

In other words, our strengths would be even more overwhelming in a nonnuclear world because we couldn't be threatened by nukes.

"Not that I'm in favor of having preponderant power over the world, but nuclear weapons clearly don't help us, they're not usable. We can't use them against terrorists if we want to because we can't identify their location and if we could we wouldn't need nuclear weapons to get them out. If you just do this sort of net assessment off the military utility, nuclear weapons come up, really, Zero."

Zero. It has become, since his revelation, his one word, his watchword. I can't help thinking of the serendipity of the name of his partner in Zero: Nunn.

"Was this something that came to you cumulatively and then—"

"Yeah, yeah, right," he says. "In just the last few years I've been doing the calculations of the lethality of conventional forces and what nuclear missions can now be carried out with conventional weapons. And it's clear they can do virtually everything a nuclear weapon can do."

He hesitates. "And there's this . . . the Cold War is over it's hard to justify it. There's the morality issue. I mean it's one thing to rationalize the threat to use nuclear weapons that could kill hundreds of millions of people during the Cold War. I mean that rationale for the threat is something to debate, but to actually carry it out would have been clearly, clearly in my mind now in retrospect, not only immoral but illegal."

"It would have been a war crime?"

"It would have been a war crime. So, you can't carry it out and now I don't even think you can even threaten to carry it out. At the end of the Cold War there's no logic to this, no rationale to it. We're trying to get ourselves into some new deterrent relationship with China to provide a . . . to refresh the rationale for deterrence, but that's totally misguided and unnecessary, huge mistake. And we've got to sort of clamp down on this kind of expansion of Mutually Assured Destruction deterrence."

"What are the signs," I asked, "that we're using China that way. It was restored to the SIOP [Single Integrated Operations Plan] in—"

"January of '98. And increasing the focus on China, adding more and more targets all the time, trying to justify our large nuclear force, even though China has like twenty long-range missiles capable of reaching the United States."

It is personal for him. "The immorality of . . . I think of my daughter . . . there are women now who are launch officers and I think of my children being put in a position today of doing what I did and I just don't think the rationale stands up, and deterrence is not a plausible argument. There's no plausible argument. And it's immoral for us and totally lacking in vision for us to be putting our kids in this position today, twenty years after the fall of the Wall."

"So looking back at your role," I asked him, "when you were a crewman, going down the checklists, you now think that what you were being asked to do was profoundly immoral?"

"Yeah. To launch nuclear—"

"To be part of this system?"

"—armed missiles which would kill millions of people."

"And you didn't necessarily think that until recently because you thought it might have been a flawed system but the system in some way had some rationale . . ."

"It was the rationale of deterrence that you would never have to do that."

"It did seem to work, but we don't know whether it worked because of luck or design."

"Yes, all these counterfactual problems and history . . . I think the absence of a nuclear attack against the United State was probably over-determined by a range of forces including nuclear deterrence to some extent. You know you can make a case that there was a deterrent effect but it's that deterrent effect in retrospect was not sufficient, I think, to justify ever actually using nuclear weapons, implementing the war plan."

Few of us will ever know what it was like to hold operational launch keys. But in a sense Bruce Blair and his successors at the Minuteman consoles have been our surrogates, carrying out what the policy of officials we have elected and reelected for more than half a century have designed. But we were all at a distance. They were there, people like Blair, our stand-ins, heavy metal keys in their hands. Still weighing heavily on Blair's conscience.

"We're still asking people, young kids, to do what you were asked to do," I said to him.

"Yeah, and the justification has just completely disappeared," he said. "I would have to tell my daughter, a sophomore in engineering at Michigan who once considered, not too long ago, going to one of the military academies, getting a free education and good education. Might have wound up doing this and I would have to say, 'You can't do that.' You would have to sign the thing saying this is against my conscience [to get out], which some people [did] even back during the Cold War."

"They offered it to everyone who had access to a key?"

"You had to sign [something else], by the end of your training at Vandenberg Air Force Base, to learn how to carry out nuclear war plans, before you graduated and went on to a combat assignment, places like Montana. You had to sign a piece of paper saying you would carry out the order."

"Not just carry out orders, but . . ."

"No, it was specific to the job that we would carry out the order to fire nuclear missiles. I don't know exactly what the wording was but it clearly—"

"You are joining our nuclear strike force and you agree that you have no res—"

"And I seem to recall that we actually were asked to sign that after the first week or so of training where we were presented some of the, I think, very watered down—"

"Films? I remember one of the crewmen talking about films."

"Films. They showed films. It was very . . . showed the films of nuclear bombs going off and blowing over—you know [shacks] at the Nevada test site, or else they were blowing over sand and little garages. They were designed to test your stamina, endurance. And we signed that and went on. I mean it was never any really true deep conversation. This was as you can imagine just about as superficial as it could possibly be."

"But some did decide at that point not to sign?"

"Some would not, some could not do it."

"Did you talk to them about it?"

"I didn't personally know anyone. Some people signed and were willing to do it, but they were so rattled by the sort of colossal weightiness of the responsibility that they couldn't even turn the keys in training. I mean they would lose their composure in these simulators at Vandenberg, where you're just going through computer-based mock simulation training, on everything from fighting a fire in the capsule to implementing a DEFCON order that puts you on a higher alert to actually launching missiles. And as you know it's a very straight, checklist-driven process. For the final launch there's decode the message, compare the codes in the message with the codes in your safe, and figure out the war order that you have to then carry out very, very quickly.

"And that's a culmination of a 'ride' as we call it. A simulated ride, which would take sometimes hours but certainly an hour or two longer. It starts out with some innocuous event like maintenance—a missile breaks down and you have to call in maintenance and then it turns out there's a security breach and you kind of go on higher alert locally . . ."

"It's a checklist-driven process where launch is just the last item."

"Yeah. Absolutely. You have to use some judgment, though, to decide which checklist you ran and which one to break away from, what the priorities are, things like that. But it gets very tense, very nerve-racking even for the calmest of people. Lights and warning sirens and warble tones and all that going off. Maybe you have to put on a mask, stuff like that. And you walk up through this escalation of commands like Pavlov's dog. You literally go through it and you know what's coming next and I did this scores of times.

"Some people just couldn't do any of that. They got so rattled, particularly when it reached the point where you have to carry out a war plan even though it's mostly make-believe."

"Even just in the simulator?"

"Some of the calmest, I mean I knew people when they were washing out. They were seasoned officers. The training reproduced the tension of it some way, of what it was like. The pressures . . ."

"Made it so it functions as a simulacrum of the real thing, if it made people wash out."

"Yeah at some level it succeeded in that. What they came to appreciate was how sterile and formulaic that really is and how unrealistic it really is and how you're sort of protected from the real human buzz and confusion that we actually have happening in the real world, because there were always, you know, these unexpected things and they surprised people."

"Right, and that Russian Colonel Petrov who saved the world I guess . . . ?" I was speaking of the Colonel Petrov who reacted to what seemed like definitive electronic sensor data that a nuclear attack from the U.S. was under way in 1983.

"Yeah, he completely violated all the human checklists."

"And Major Hering, here. He asked a question that wasn't on the checklists."

"How do we know that a launch code comes from a sane person? It cost him his career," said Blair, who had been aware of Major Hering's case and in touch with him sporadically.

"And we still don't have an answer."

"We still don't have an answer."

## THE DREAM OF ZERO AND THE PLAN: RICHARD BURT'S CONVERSION

Is Zero realistic, possible? One could get carried away with the force and fervor of Blair's argument that there is no middle ground. But to really assess the realism of the abolitionists' dream, it makes a difference whether you argue backward from Zero or forward toward it.

If you argue backward from the imagined achievement of Zero, you are forced to picture a moment, however distant in time, in which the last remaining possessors of the last remaining nuclear weapons willingly hand them over to some international authority that proceeds to disable and destroy them. Or holds on to them as enforcement tools.

You have to imagine an inspection and surveillance regime with powers so forceful and intrusive it can break down doors anywhere in the world without notice, find and seize clandestine nukes before they can be used, and arrest and try violators in some international tribunal to enforce Zero.

You have to imagine that no nations have the capacity to evade inspection, hide weapons, or to put in place a plan to reassemble components and rearm themselves with nuclear weapons at a moment's notice.

You have to imagine that there will be no conventional wars in which the side in danger of losing will, in a desperate last-ditch resort, seek to reassemble nukes. Conceivably you would have to suppress publications that instruct how to construct a nuclear weapon. A dictatorship of Zero.

Which compels you to imagine that there will be no unsettled regional or national, ideological or theological conflicts that will result in conventional wars in which it is more than likely a losing side would somehow quickly find a way to assemble or reassemble nuclear weapons, the ones they haven't managed to hide in the first place.

All of which requires you to imagine a virtual transformation of human nature and a voluntary transfer of national power to what in effect will be the unappealable judgments of a world government.

Doesn't sound likely, does it, as a practical matter? The anti-Zero case is strengthened beyond the practical to the moral dimension: there were 60 million more deaths from wars in the twentieth century before Hiroshima than in the same span of years after.

But the Zero advocates have answers. They concede that the moment of Zero won't arrive instantaneously tomorrow, that the world as it is, is not ready for Zero. That a case can be made that things look different if you argue going forward toward Zero. For instance, there is the case that James Acton and George Perkovich make in their book, *Abolishing Nuclear Weapons*, a 130-page study published in 2008 by the London-based International Institute for Strategic Studies. Acton—formerly one of the co-writers of the influential armscontrolwonk.com blog, is a fellow at the Carnegie Endowment for International Peace. Acton and Perkovich are unflinching in their intellectual honesty about the difficulty of ever achieving abolition. They admit it would require a virtual world government and for all current regional conflicts—India–Pakistan, China–Taiwan, Israel–Palestine to be resolved—plus methods in place for defusing any future conflicts.

But the most persuasive argument they make is a cultural one: that as the world moves toward Zero by means of sharper and sharper reductions, and works together each step of the way toward solving the problems of inspection and verification procedures, presumably including the development of advanced detection technology, this diminution of the role of nukes and concomitant cooperation will draw the world into a different mind-set.

Bruce Blair's Global Zero Initiative is meant to achieve exactly that. It offers a four-step plan for reductions and destruction of warheads over a twenty-year timetable to get to Zero. Can human nature, much less human governance and culture, change so radically in that period of time? On the other hand, if it doesn't, can we be sure human nature, human civilization will survive that long?

In a review of the Acton-Perkovich pro-abolition book, Elbridge Colby, recently a START-follow-on-treaty negotiator, wondered whether Zero was an unquestioned good: "Such a prospect seems neither plausible nor particularly appealing. Which leads to the question: why again are we trying to do this? The authors state that their 'ultimate reason' is to try to 'reduce the danger of sudden mass annihilation.' But opponents of abolition share that goal— they just think that retaining nuclear weapons is more likely to prevent that unfortunate outcome."

Colby argues: "To those who believe we are perpetually only a minute away from the midnight of nuclear darkness, such a tradeoff [giving up national sovereignty for nuclear abolition] may be, if not appealing, simply a necessity. To those who value the independence of nations or who see world government as a recipe for gross inefficiency and unresponsiveness if not tyranny, and who can bear the tension of a cold peace, the abolition project is to be resisted."

It's a strong counterargument to Zero. But before agreeing with Colby, and his "cold peace" alternative to Zero, it's worth listening to the arguments of one of the most prominent and unexpected Zero advocates. He is Ambassador Richard R. Burt, former *New York Times* defense correspondent, Reagan-Bush–era nuclear arms negotiator, widely regarded by both sides as one of the smartest, most lucid Cold War nuclear advocates. And he does not consider himself a penitent for his role in speaking up for nuclear readiness when he was in the State Department. It's not a warm and fuzzy thing for Burt, nuclear abolition, but a cold-blooded national interest calculation.

Burt had cogent reasons he gave me. But it still mystified some.

"Rick Burt! An abolitionist?" was the reaction I got from one of his former colleagues at the *New York Times*.

My talk with Burt about his conversion to Zero was illuminating.

"I'm just a tool of Bruce Blair," Burt began jocularly over the phone from his Washington office in June 2009. He was trying to explain why he'd just gone public as the most well-known nuclear diplomacy expert backing the Global Zero Initiative at a press conference at Washington's St. Regis Hotel ballroom. He and an international panel unveiled Global Zero's four-step blueprint for getting to Zero before 2030. It was a week before Obama's summit with Medvedev in London and Blair and Burt had had conversations with Obama's nuclear negotiators and Russian technical advisers to the START treaty. Among an array of international luminaries endorsing the Zero nukes plan was one of Medvedev's top nuclear advisers, Igor Yurgens.

But more surprising in a way was the presence—the dominance at the conference—of Burt, who brought all his intellectual and rhetorical skills, his years of nuclear negotiation expertise to the challenge Obama had set out. His role was particularly ironic, almost shocking since he had been as responsible as anyone for killing any hope of making Zero an objective in the Reagan administration as Reagan occasionally, fitfully, probably sentimentally sought to do. Just a week before I spoke to Burt there appeared an op-ed reminiscence of Burt's role in body-blocking Zero at a crucial moment in Reagan's second term. It was an anti-Zero op-ed written by one of Burt's former State Department colleagues, John Hughes, who had left the State Department to become editor of *The Christian Science Monitor* (now retired). In his June 18, 2009, piece, Hughes offered this shocked-sounding recollection of new Zero point man Burt in his previous anti-Zero incarnation:

> When Ronald Reagan was president, he scheduled a weekly one-on-one meeting in the White House with Secretary of State George Shultz. Nobody else was present, so when Shultz returned to the State Department, four or five of us senior advisers were always eager for a debriefing on what had been discussed and decided.
> On one of these occasions, Shultz returned to announce that Reagan had become committed to ridding the world of

nuclear weapons. A startled Richard Burt, then assistant secretary for European affairs, blurted out: "He can't do that!" following up with the conviction that replacing the US nuclear deterrent with conventional weaponry and troops would be of astronomical cost.

Shultz stared at us with those pale, impassive blue eyes that had served him so well as a negotiator in private life and government. You guys "had better get on the ball," he said. The president meant it, he said, and we were to work toward it.

Instead they killed it.

"I remember long arguments with George Shultz," Burt told me when I spoke with him, "in which I made the case, this [abolishing nukes] is destabilizing, counterproductive, it will weaken our alliance system. I saw nukes as a stabilizing factor."

I asked Burt what he thought about the recent trend in popular biographies and histories that makes Reagan seem like a secret peacenik, a tender no nukes dove whose dream of Zero was strangled in its cradle by a sinister cabal of hawks that included Burt. He laughed and diplomatically found a way of saying that, yes, Reagan cared passionately about the weight of responsibility contained in the nuclear football that followed him around (so appropriate, a football for the Gipper). But the subtext I got pretty strongly from Burt was that this posture was fuzzy and sentimental—a not serious wish that was not very consistently or powerfully pushed by the president and was quickly abandoned when Soviet leader Mikhail Gorbachev wouldn't sign on to another cherished Reagan fantasy: Star Wars.

And now, Burt has switched sides dramatically. Though he wouldn't say his principles have changed; rather the facts of the new nuclear age have. In his new incarnation as a hardheaded prophet of Zero, Burt, along with Blair, came up with an action plan for the summit that was meant not to scare the diplomats: the goal of Zero would be incremental, to be achieved between now and 2030. There would be intervals of sharp reductions and then . . . The only place where the Global Zero action plan becomes a bit wish-fulfillment dreamy is in its final phase, where the two superpowers will have to relinquish their last nukes and, in primitive zoological terms, bare their bellies to one another, displaying their no nukes naked vulnerability—and trusting to some unspecified international authority to provide continuous international "intrusive" inspections and an enforcement power to make sure nobody "reconstitutes" their nukes or pulls a "break-out scenario," in which a small group of nuke assemblers suddenly tells the denuclearized world they're now the only nuclear power, and presents everyone with a list of demands.

This leads to the obvious question: wouldn't the inspection regime require explosive weapons powerful enough to blow open sealed underground bunkers where prohibited nuclear mischief might be going on? Wouldn't that regime require large sums of money for the most sophisticated nuclear detection devices, all to be supplied by the nations they're supposed to be strict with? In fact, the inspection regime would somehow have to be the most powerful political entity on earth, perhaps relying on a monopoly of nuclear weapons itself, and thus deterrence, and we're back where we started, only it may never happen because the superpowers are going to treat any version of that idea like kryptonite.

The problem with the John Lennon strategy—"Envision Zero" as the Zeroistas were in effect saying at that first press conference—is that the more you envision Zero the more like a mirage it seems.

Burt admits the final stage will be the hardest to conceive much less execute, but he argues that the cumulative trust-building effects of the arms reduction to near-Zero will encourage confidence in the final step across the final line.

When Burt said "I'm just a tool of Bruce Blair" he said it jocularly, but it turned out Blair had been the key to Burt's conversion. He'd known Blair for three decades since they were both at London's elite think tank, the International Institute for Strategic Studies. And they'd remained in touch even as their career paths diverged and their attitude toward nuclear weapons did as well. Blair's bringing Burt over helped confirm something I'd begun to feel about Blair.

He had had some remarkable, almost uncanny powers of persuasion, a kind of low-key charisma, even perhaps a mesmeric effect on people. It had something to do with the fact that he wasn't just another policy wonk or just another wide-eyed peacenik. He was a deep student of the strategic and technical aspects of nuclear weapons. More importantly, it had something to do with having had his hands on the keys. He was like those figures who visit the Underground in Homeric and Virgilian mythology and then return to life aboveground having gained—and being known for—some kind of near-mystical authority. He had had the power in his hands to murder 20 million people with a twist of a key. Somehow this kind of power had an effect that worked unconsciously on those who listened long enough. He was the Ancient Mariner who's been on the death ship so long that an aura of dread clung to his words.

Burt would not say he had been won over by the force of Blair's personality but rather that he was being entirely consistent in his own basic principles, though their application had evolved with changing circumstances in the post–Cold War second nuclear age. In the twentieth century he believed nuclear weapons were a stabilizing factor. "In the twenty-first century," he said, "they're destabilizing."

Having been so close to the risks of instability—he confirmed for me the close-call moments surrounding Operation Able Archer in the early 1980s, for instance, when the Soviets mistook a realistic NATO, nuke-simulated war game for the run-up to a surprise attack on the Soviet Union and prepared to preempt—he was now passionate about the threat nukes posed to creating order in the international system.

Burt told me that three factors led him to the conclusion that it was time to shift the arms control paradigm from reductionism to Zero—and to find a practical, verifiable, enforceable way to get there. First, "the international environment had shifted" radically. He felt "there was no longer a realistic chance of conflict between the U.S. and the Russian Federation"—not the kind of "ideological death struggle" as he put it that led to the Mutually Assured

Destruction standoff with forty thousand nuclear warheads on high-alert pointed at each other.

The second historical change hospitable to Zero in Burt's view was technological. "In the twentieth century nuclear weapons were Great Power weapons. Proliferation was mainly vertical—the arms race between the superpowers reaching greater and greater heights." But now, he says, in the twenty-first century, nuclear weapons are weak-state weapons. "The technology has become widespread . . . and the proliferation has been horizontal."

And, finally, the third post–Cold War change, according to Burt, is the advent of post-9/11 suicidal martyrdom by nonstate actors. This threat has undermined deterrence to the point that the only way back to stability is not to perpetuate another precarious locked-in, launch on warning, superpower bipolar deterrence system, but to take that system down completely: to use deep cuts by big powers as a way of getting medium-size nuclear powers such as China and India to agree to move toward Zero (the incentive: if they don't make cuts the big powers won't proceed with theirs) and cumulatively use that momentum to persuade weak states to agree to the verification and enforcement that would ensure no one else, no rogue state or substate, could possess them.

Burt is nothing if not thorough in addressing the difficulties on every step of the step-by-step blueprint for Zero. "You have to remember," he told me at one point, "that when I was negotiating the START treaty [the 1991 Strategic Arms Reduction Treaty] we spent four years producing an eight-hundred-page annex on inspection and verification. And it's held up." He also understands the real-world power of rhetoric. First get Zero into people's heads as a possibility—get it out of the realm of cloud-cuckoo-land and ground it in specifics. Get people discussing it and realizing there are sane non-"Kumbaya" types who think it's possible. Force the people with the power to do something about it to contend with Zero, even if it's to marshal objections to it.

In order to do this, Burt, Blair, and the Global Zero experts have framed their abolition program as an extension of the post–Cold War arms reduction model that resulted in lowering the peak number of up to forty thousand nuclear warheads deployed by the two superpowers during the Cold War to the approximately twenty thousand in existence now, although only about five thousand are on active alert.

The Global Zero action plan offers a PowerPoint-ready chart extrapolating the same rate of diminishment: from forty thousand to twenty thousand in twenty years, making it seem like getting from twenty thousand to Zero in another twenty years would not be radical or impossible so long as mutually agreed on inspection, verification, and enforcement could be achieved. One problem, though, is that the lower the numbers get, the more difficult it is to lower them further. The Pentagon gets nervous that we won't have enough for every contingency. Speakers at the Pentagon's Strategic Deterrence Symposium in Omaha singled out this difficulty: they argued that nations such as Japan, South Korea, and Taiwan have been convinced not to go nuclear themselves in return for the U.S. offering them the nuclear umbrella, more formally called a PSA, a positive security assurance, which is meant to assure them that U.S. nuclear deterrence will be extended to deter attacks on them. As the number of U.S. nukes is reduced radically, such nations may well be inclined to believe they need to develop their own nuclear deterrent, and thus, paradoxically, some argue and Burt acknowledges, big cuts in our arsenal may result in increases in international nuclear proliferation totals.

Another potential weakness in the roll-out of the Global Zero action plan was the absence of what has been one of Bruce Blair's urgent concerns: defusing the possibility for accidental nuclear war by de-alerting the current arsenals as they are being reduced. This means doing things like detaching warheads from missiles so they can't be fired on impulse or because of mistaken warnings. It's nice to think of abolishing nuclear weapons by 2030, but isn't it at least as important to make sure World War III doesn't break out by 11:30 tonight?

That's too "near-term," Burt told me. He was wary of distracting from the big-picture vision of Zero at this point with alerting questions—what he called "wholesale revamping" of the current nuclear structure. He just wanted to diminish, miniaturize it until it vanished.

But I would argue there is no practical reason that the alerting issue can't be addressed in tandem with the reduction in numbers and that Blair's de-alerting steps (outlined in chapter 6) should be adopted now, before it's too late.

The action plan proposed by Blair and Burt's Global Zero also presupposes a world in which conflicts like those between Israel and Palestine and Iran, Russia and Georgia, India and Pakistan, Taiwan and China, North and South Korea would have been resolved. Otherwise, the withdrawal of the nuclear umbrellas could cause the breakout of conventional wars, conventional arms races, or even the breakout of hidden nuclear weapons.

But would there ever be such a world and, if so, could it evolve by 2030, when the last nuclear weapons would be handed over to some international authority for destruction? At first glance the Global Zero plan had seemed somewhat conservative: reduction to about a thousand warheads each for the U.S. and Russia would take till 2018. If the Obama-Medvedev announced goal of 1,500 each by 2012 were then met, getting down to a thousand in six more years doesn't seem impossible. But getting rid of that final thousand in twelve more years envisions an entirely transformed, conflict-free world, ready to accept a kind of global super-government to police the no nukes agreement.

It envisions not only a new political order but a new human character. And what will prompt an almost genetic deep change of that sort? In the short term, meaning in less than several million years, I have a terrible feeling that it will take a catastrophic event like a regional nuclear war to jump-start a change in human nature. Zero is a nice dream, but with a tragic if not fatal flaw, at least it seems that way to me.

The Zero advocates adopt this no nukes posture because they say deterrence has failed and yet depend at the end of it for some unnamed international body to have the deterrent force to prevent de-nuked superpowers from renuking, restocking their arsenals, or preventing smaller powers from renuking their deterrent stock.

What are you going to threaten them with? The nukes you took away from them? Then assuming they'd ever do it—you've created a nuclear-powered world government that derives its legitimacy from . . . the nuclear threats of a nuclear monopoly.

## MEANWHILE THE END IS BEGINNING

But to return from a neverland future. Right now, there is Pakistan. When our conversation turned to Pakistan as a potential failed state, Burt said something that indicated he had not lost his hard edge. With a rather peremptory tone he said, "If I were president I would want to see a plan on my desk about what are we gonna do if these weapons go out of stable control? What are we going to do to secure these weapons, take them into custody?"

Whoa: take them into custody! I see a regional, potentially global, nuclear war growing out of that scenario. For us to take custody would require us to know exactly where every nuclear weapon was. We would presumably take custody from a disintegrating Pakistani military, or an Al Qaeda–Taliban faction that has overthrown the government. And talk of taking custody in the press had made some wonder whether elements of the Pakistani army, in nominal control of all nukes, and supposedly working closely with the U.S. to secure them, might find this a potential usurpation of their sovereignty and seek to conceal them from custody, leaving them vulnerable to falling into the hands of extremists hostile to the U.S.

I'd heard of top secret war games in which special ops teams descend on Pakistan to take command of their nukes, seize them, and take them into custody. I had a sense Burt either participated in them or war games came naturally to his mind. And somehow the intrusion of Pakistan, now, made 2030 seem even further away. Made Pakistani-generated nuclear war scenarios look closer even than Israel–Iran. The fuse is lit and burning toward Islamabad. The end could well begin there.

And so something is needed to jump-start Zero. And here is where I think a discovery I made in the nuclear vault might play a role.

# THE NUCLEAR TABOO AND NUKE PORN
# IN THE NUCLEAR VAULT

A rainy, cold spring morning on H Street in Washington: I recall with great clarity the circumstances of my first encounter in "the nuclear vault," with the so-called Burke documents, the ones that laid out a road not taken in the development of our nuclear strategy a half-century ago. A road that yet might take us back from the still all too dangerous default hair-trigger posture we remain in today. Take us back if not all the way to Zero, then a giant step in that direction, a giant step away from "world holocaust," a chilling phrase I first came upon in the Burke documents.

The "nuclear vault" is the informal name given to a division of the privately funded National Security Archives, now housed in the library of George Washington University on H Street. The archives, founded two decades ago, has devoted itself to getting millions of pages of top secret, classified national security documents declassified, primarily through the Freedom of Information Act. The nuclear vault, the repository for an astonishing compilation of confidential declassified discussions about the bomb, has been presided over for two decades by Dr. William Burr, another Yoda of FOIA, using that legislative tool like a light-saber to cut through the fog of secrecy that surrounds nuclear weapons and nuclear war strategy. The conference room of the nuclear vault is a Dickensian jumble, an Old Curiosity Shop of the nuclear age, filled to bursting point with documents; file folders were piled to the ceiling for archiving and digitizing into the nuclear vault's "Electronic Briefing Books."

Dr. Burr is a youthful-looking though slightly gnomish gentleman, a Californian who did his doctorate in pre-nuke American history and whose mind is a marvel of memory for the documents he's been pursuing so relentlessly for so long and for the themes and subtexts that connect them. Maybe Yoda isn't so much the right name for him, perhaps he might better be thought of as a nuclear Talmudist. You can hear the deep satisfaction in his voice when he learns that he's got some document re-declassified, which didn't declassify enough the first time Burr filed suit. Sometimes he will go back to litigate several times over declassifying a single paragraph. I once met a Pentagon contactor hired to redact, black out, passages in declassified documents, who, when I mentioned Burr's name, visibly shrank with a look of dread like Dracula reacting to a bulb of garlic. Burr is as relentless as a buzz saw to the paper empire of secrecy the Pentagon has built.

The feeling of a Strangelovian Old Curiosity Shop was reinforced when I first sat down across a conference table from Burr and noticed the rather bizarre backdrop: a semicircular wall of brown cardboard packing boxes that had all been Magic Markered "NUCLEAR WEAPONS SECRETS."

"They're from the Hansen Collection," Burr said, noticing me staring at the boxes. It turns out Hansen was some California techie who had devoted his life to FOIA and other private investigations into the design, engineering, and deployment of nuclear warheads, and it seems after his recent death he'd willed his wall of storage cartons to the nuclear vault where Burr has only begun to plumb them.

They looked like props from a bad thriller or a *parody* of a bad thriller (like *Strangelove* was). But setting aside the Strangelovian edge to it, a visit to the nuclear vault either in person or even virtually on their Web site is cumulatively awe-inspiring. The real thing. The target-planning documents. Heavily redacted parts of the sacred SIOP. Revelations of once above-top-secret struggles over whose finger was on what triggers.

When I first coined the term "nuke porn" I was mostly disparaging this genre of nuclear thriller, caricaturing it as "the finger on the trigger, bringing the trembling world to the brink of a shattering climax." I was disparaging exploitative fiction. But the factual reality of it can be even more luridly alluring. And the nuclear vault is ground zero for all the lurid allure.

I've always found those blacked-out redacted passages the most teasing and seductive. They let you see so much that is disturbing. What can be behind the many Xeroxed layers of blackness that betray no hints of coherent words?

It's the forbiddenness of it. Getting to listen in to the secretive talk about the deadly embrace that was Mutually Assured Destruction, getting to listen in to the debates over first use, first strike, preemptive war, preventive war, and the subtle distinctions between launch on warning and launch on alert and the strategic thinking behind the distinctions—it has the perverse attraction of letting you envision your own death.

I don't want to aestheticize it, after all we are dealing with the record of humanity's ongoing flirtation with self-destruction. But being present in an archive of the most intimate conversations of White House and Pentagon officials, generals and admirals, all speaking about the unspeakable with the candor that comes from not thinking that—thanks to a few obsessed archivists like the nuclear vault's Burr and the Federation of American Scientists' Kristensen—they would ever be overheard. The pillow talk of the war planners.

Thanks to Burr, I came across in my vault research the chilling phrase "world holocaust." All the more chilling since it was uttered by a member of the Joint Chiefs of Staff, Admiral Arleigh A. Burke, a half-century ago during a heated and ultimately tragic debate over our nuclear strategy. It was a debate Burke lost then, but which offers what is now an even more powerful argument for his "finite deterrence" nuclear strategy.

Having read thousands upon thousands of pages of declassified documents, I can say that by the time you get to be one of the gods of the nuclear realm, one of the Joint Chiefs of Staff—at the very peak of the military and nuclear pyramid, you don't hear or read phrases like "world holocaust." You hear euphemisms like "maximum damage expectancy." It was genuinely shocking to find a four-star admiral using such inflammatory language in a classified communiqué, which led me to pay closer attention than I might have otherwise, to the cache of secret, top secret, confidential, and classified-stamped documents that made up the just declassified series of Admiral Burke papers in the Nuclear Vault Electronic Briefing Book #275. They turned out to be the Dead Sea Scrolls of nuclear history, an alternate vision that casts light on why we are still shackled to those thousands of missiles in silos on hair-trigger alert.

The Burke documents, I've come to believe, are not just a historical footnote to nuclear strategy history but could serve as evidence of the still urgent need for debate over whether a civilization-destroying nuclear war, a world holocaust, is avoidable or inevitable. Electronic Briefing Book #275—the digital collection of the Burke documents, whose publication coincided with my visit—seemed to me a sensational recovery of a lost past, a lost path in nuclear history.

In Burke, I came across a plan. Not for Zero, which I still believe is probably unattainable. But for ten. Or less than a hundred. One that sacrifices the perfection of Zero for the attainability of minimum numbers.

At the very least the Burke papers offer a contribution to the debate—something I refrained from offering the first time I immersed myself in the mechanics and the morals of nuclear war at the height of the Cold War in part because I couldn't imagine the experts would have failed to find a fail-safe solution, but they did fail. They were only saved by the bell, by the fall of the Wall from the Armageddon we were heading for.

As it turns out, the late Admiral Arleigh Burke—the unexpected theoretician—first called the worst-case scenario a "world holocaust" more than half a century ago at a decisive turning point in nuclear arms deployment. According to Jesse Sheidlower, the American editor of the *Oxford English Dictionary*, the word "holocaust" as in "nuclear holocaust" had first been used in 1954.

"Nuclear holocaust" took a while to catch on; it's a powerful phrase conflating as it does Hitler and Hirsohima, Hitlerizing the nuclear cataclysm. But "world holocaust" seems to have been Burke's own coinage.

The context was a classified memorandum dated March 4, 1959, I found in the Nuclear Vault's briefing book on the Burke documents, a memorandum that laid out a blueprint for an alternative to what would be the balance of terror, the Mutually Assured Destruction deterrence based on each side having thousands of highly vulnerable land-based warheads on a hair-trigger alert that would characterize the remaining three decades of the Cold War.

Burke argued for the advantages of submarine-based "finite deterrence." You needed far fewer submarine-based missiles because submarines would run silent and were thus virtually undetectable, making their deterrent far more reliably survivable than the Air Force's silo-based missiles. He said stationing our main nuclear force on the American continental landmass automatically made the U.S. and its population the chief target of Soviet nuclear missiles. He said relying on the submarine-launched nuclear missiles just then coming into production under the name Polaris could remove the U.S. landmass as an inevitable first strike target and virtually make a first strike incapable of degrading our retaliatory deterrent capacity.

It was an argument he ultimately lost to the Air Force missleheads. But it could have gone the other way. It would not have been impossible. It was 1959, the U.S. had not yet committed itself to the entire land-based, silo-buried force that would come to be the centerpiece of our nuclear arsenal at its peak.

Who was this Burke fellow and why should his fifty-year-old conception of nuclear war posture matter to us now?

Burke was not known as a nuclear strategist or a defense intellectual. He got to his post of chief of naval operations, highest-ranking naval officer and navy representative on the Joint Chiefs of Staff because of his distinguished World War II record as destroyer captain and because his blunt temperament appealed to both Presidents Harry Truman and Dwight Eisenhower, the latter of whom promoted him over hundreds of other higher-ranking officers to the top Navy job. And he was not a battle-shy type: he'd earned his Navy nickname "31 Knots Burke" because of his aggressive conduct during a Pacific sea battle.

Destroyer boilers were built to pressurize steam so that it powered a top speed of 36 knots. Putting on more speed, and thus pressure, was known to blow out the boilers. Apparently this happened with Burke in the midst of a Pacific battle, when his tin can was charging a Japanese battleship. The boiler blew out, was patched up, but the bandaged version slowed his ship. Still Burke wanted to get in on the action. He thundered down the radio line to the rest of the fleet, "This is Commander Burke coming through at 31 knots."

Maybe you had to be there.

Burke was there for the birth of the so-called triad, the three-sided nuclear force—missiles, manned bombers, and submarines—the U.S. was embarked upon building. He had a remarkably clear-sighted view of the drawbacks of the land-based elements of the architecture—one that transcended Navy parochialism.

The Burke documents date from internal Navy and interservice memoranda arguing the merits of each leg of the triad. The documents from Burke's side are notable for their terse but devastating dismissal of assumptions and estimates of the other sides of the triad.

He was confident that—if the Pentagon and the Joint Chiefs could only see the advantages of making submarine-based deterrence the centerpiece of our nuclear arsenal—we could not only save billions of dollars but billions of lives. The alternative—the first strike capability of land-based missiles "hidden" in plain-sight silos—would incite an arms race by each side to destroy the other's first strike capacity first and increase the chance of nuclear war and world holocaust. Instead, Burke argued, invulnerable submarine-based retaliatory deterrence was the best way to a peaceful stalemate. Let there be competition in the economic and political spheres. Just rule out striving for a first strike capacity by allowing (through negotiation) each side just enough sub-based nuclear missiles for a devastating retaliatory capacity that would make a first strike suicidal.

It's there in his March 4, 1959, "Confidential Memorandum for All Flag officers. Subject: 'Views on Adequacy of US Deterrent/Retaliatory Forces as Related to General and Limited War Capabilities'. . . . This document should be held closely." He begins by thoroughly demolishing what would soon be enshrined literally in concrete, in the so-called silo farms for generations of land-based missiles. Basing our missiles on the U.S. continent, he argued, made the U.S. continent a target for a hailstorm of missiles seeking silos to blast in a first strike. And even if they were in the badlands of Dakota the cumulative impact would be devastating. Attacking silos requires up to four missiles targeted on each hardened silo now designed theoretically to withstand direct hits by two standard-size Russian ICBMs. "There is nothing we can do to prevent major destruction of an unpredictable but appreciable amount on our land-based forces," Admiral Burke wrote. "The problem is to build sufficient invulnerable forces—forces whose survival is insured." Submarines in other words.

Burke's "world holocaust" paragraph—the one that caught my attention—compresses the argument more powerfully than I'd seen elsewhere, certainly anywhere that early in the Cold War. He argued his Polaris submarine—launched ICBMs would require dozens rather than thousands of missiles and bombs to threaten certain retaliation. Submarines were then—and are now—sufficiently undetectable. On the one hand, his was a purely defensive deterrent strategy (sub-based missles lacked first-strike accuracy) that virtually guaranteed we would never be the first to use nuclear weapons. On other hand, the submarines and their Polaris missiles can only be successful as a deterrent if the few of them threaten to murder millions of civilians.

Robert McNamara famously opined that to ensure deterrence a nation needed the capacity to kill 25 percent of a foe's population. No problem: with a few dozen Polaris missiles targeted on population centers we could kill the requisite 75 to 100 million Russians. The second act of a world holocaust. Of course the point of it all, the point Admiral Burke was making, was that this was the best way to deter a world holocaust. It was the Air Force's necessarily hair-trigger missiles that would be more likely to precipitate a world holocaust.

Or as Burke put it in that powerful paragraph: "To be effective at all, a United States strategy based on destroying the enemy's retaliatory capability [i.e., founded on the more accurate silo-based ICBMs] would require preventive war—in essence a surprise attack. Unless ICBMs were used to strike first they were at the mercy of a surprise attack with less than 15 minutes warning. Also it would require correct intelligence on the location of all significant enemy targets." This is deceptively mild. "Correct intelligence" means that in order to ensure no retaliation from a foe, the whereabouts of whose weapons, including subs we were unaware of, we would have to blanket their land with nuclear detonations.

Then he delivers the rhetorical coup de grâce: "The decision to launch a world holocaust would be the most drastic and desperate decision made since civilization began—and it might very well end civilization."

Words count in the world of virtual nuclear warfare and war planning. That's why the actual words are so often euphemisms— "economic infrastructure" for killing urban civilian populations. "Damage Limitation" for a nuclear first strike against the foe's nukes.

But for a veteran chief of naval operations like Burke to use the phrase "world holocaust" had to count for something. It meant being unafraid to sail at full steam into the fog of euphemism.

Burke's proposal brought down upon him, as the documents in the electronic briefing book attest, the wrath of the Air Force, which was deeply attached to its land-based missiles because they were Air Force missiles and because land-based missiles were more accurate and could be used not just for retaliation but for a first strike. But what if Burke had won the debate? Would it have changed history? I'd argue that if Burke's submarine-based, finite deterrence strategy had been adopted it might have been possible to avert the constant danger of hair-trigger launch on warning, launch on attack, launch on attack assessment—the whole spectrum of postures that led to our near-disasters. Of course it would have had to have been adopted by both sides in the Cold War, but there's no reason why the negotiations couldn't have gone down that road to a far less costly and less dangerous objective than the shaky stability of SALT.

Even more saliently it became apparent to me, from reading the Burke documents, that the Burke strategy could still offer a path back from the brink we still perch on, a giant step toward the possibility of reaching Zero—or at least ten, a hundred even. But before offering that possibility, permit me an important digression—one suggested to me by Dr. Burr himself: the so-called nuclear taboo.

## HIROSHIMA AND NUCLEAR CULTURE

The question that had been bothering Dr. Burr lately, he told me, was: why have nuclear weapons never been used in the sixty-four years since Nagasaki? Is there a nuclear taboo, and, if so, what kind of power does it have? Can we rely on this taboo to prevent the outbreak of nuclear war?

It doesn't make sense that we escaped nuclear war when you read of the twenty thousand warheads each side had on high alert, the recurrent close calls and the spoon-and-string command and control apparatus designed to keep them in line, the flaws, the holes, the sketchy lines of communication and succession from the very top of the national chain of command to the very bottom of the silos. I've read the congressional testimony. It's not reassuring. Was it, as Robert McNamara told director Errol Morris during the filming of *The Fog of War*, the documentary on McNamara, just "luck"? It seems improbable.

So the question then is this: what worked, despite all the flaws, the holes, the errors, and false alarms? For forty years we were minutes away from an annihilating nuclear holocaust. That's a very long lucky streak. If we knew what worked it would give us an edge in the future, right?

Dr. Burr reaches into one of the interstices of the stacks of boxes marked "NUCLEAR SECRETS" for a hardcover book and drops it with a thud on the conference table. *The Nuclear Taboo: The United States and the Non-Use of Nuclear Weapons Since 1945*, by Nina Tannenwald, a Cambridge University Press book, part of the "Cambridge Studies in International Relations" series. It was a book that addressed another why-the-dog-didn't-bark type mystery.

I got my own copy of *The Nuclear Taboo* as soon as I returned from Washington and found it fascinating because the answer to the question is far from obvious. Tannenwald argues that the prevailing explanation—which she attributes to the realist school of foreign policy, which tends to see the behavior of nations as the pure product of self-interest—is wrong. It doesn't explain why the U.S. refrained from using nukes against the Chinese in Korea or even against the Soviets during the period from 1945 to 1949 when America had a nuclear monopoly.

Tannewald covers three possible factors that might explain non-use. First, that, to some degree deterrence worked: fear of physical immolation in retaliation intimidated both Cold War superpowers into not launching first strikes.

But she argues for a second explanation for nuclear non-use, something from the realm of ideas and ideals that nonetheless acquired real-world power: the development of a "nuclear taboo" that evolved from an abstract ethical norm into something more than a norm, something more numinous and yet with more effectual force, something genuinely, historically consequential. A taboo.

She finds the origins of the taboo developing early on, citing for instance Paul Nitze, who would later become one of the foremost nuclear hawks of the late Cold War period, declaring during our nuclear monopoly period that "initiating a [nuclear] first strike went against our culture and our self-image as a nation."

(I have a memorable image of Nitze, no shrinking violet when it came to the use of force. We happened to be riding up in the same Senate elevator as Nitze was going to testify against his former friend and colleague Paul Warnke, who had been nominated by Jimmy Carter to be our nuclear arms negotiator but was regarded by nuclear hawks as too dovish. Nitze, then in his sixties, yet fit and sleekly garbed in an expensive investment banker's suit, started throwing punches in the air, barely missing those of us in the elevator. He turned to an associate accompanying him and said, "Gotta keep knocking 'em off balance." His pumped-up testimony succeeded in defeating Warnke. And yet even Nitze knew there was a taboo against first use as far back as the late 1940s.)

Tannenwald finds instance after instance of American leaders thinking that first use of nuclear weapons, as in preventive or preemptive war, was wrong—not strategically or tactically necessarily, but wrong morally and ethically, "inconsistent with American values," which call for "discrimination and proportionality in use of force."

She traces the way the norm was tested as it evolved, with mixed results. At first in Korea. General Douglas MacArthur wanted Truman to use nukes against the Chinese pouring over the border and almost driving the American army into the sea, but Truman and his advisers, including Nitze, decided against it, at least in part because they thought it would be morally wrong. But in the Taiwan Straits crises in the 1950s, Eisenhower (we learn—through documents declassified by the good Dr. Burr) authorized the use of nukes if necessary to stop an invasion of Taiwan by the Beijing regime; the Chinese didn't provide the occasion to test this determination, but obviously the taboo had not yet become entrenched.

She takes us through the trauma of the Cuban Missile Crisis, the greatest challenge to the taboo, with generals such as Curtis LeMay eager for an excuse for a definitive nuclear war he was sure his Air Force could "win," while the Kennedy brothers by all accounts had internalized the taboo to the extent of secretly giving Khrushchev what he wanted—withdrawal of U.S. missiles from Turkey and a no-invasion pledge on Cuba. (The heroic Kennedy victory in the affair has been downsized by subsequent revelations summarized in Michael Dobbs's 2009 book, *One Minute to Midnight*.)

The next test of the taboo was Vietnam where both Lyndon Johnson and even Richard Nixon at his maddest decided to forgo using nukes. Though Nixon liked to pose as a "madman" who threatened to do it, the very fact that the act was, by then, considered only the last resort of a madman was indicative that the ethical norm against nuclear use had attained the status of a taboo. She takes us up beyond the Cold War to the two Gulf Wars—by which time the taboo, she says, had virtually taken nukes off the table. The taboo has worked in part, she says, because by now everyone seems to think there's a taboo, and she quotes nuclear strategist Bernard Brodie to the effect that "what is perceived to be real is real."

But she also supports her explanation of nuclear non-use by citing an important study of the period by the nuclear historian and analyst George Quester. Quester's was also a name I knew well—not merely for its metaphoric resonance—since it was largely Professor Quester's testimony before a congressional committee investigating the flaws and dilemmas of nuclear command and control in the late 1970s that had first inspired me to look into the mechanics of it.

After reviewing nearly two dozen alternative hypotheses for why the U.S. leaders did not carry out preventive war before 1949 when the Soviets first tested an atomic bomb, Quester concluded that "the failure to even threaten [it] has to be explained more by moral absolutes than by the rational calculations of the American government." It's a daring argument—that morality and ethics counted against, perhaps even outweighed, the sheer power of multi-megaton nuclear warheads on alert. It asks us to believe that abstractions, "values," fear of moral opprobrium, "stigmatization," "shaming"—the punishments for breaking taboos—became real-world factors as decisive as warhead throw-weight. It's also an attractive argument, because it suggests that military and political leaders have a conscience that evolved in the face of a possible world holocaust. It suggests human nature itself may have evolved or adapted to the radical threat to our survival. Darwin has saved us from Einstein. (I know: not literally.)

It would be nice to believe. But that taboo certainly did not filter down to the missile crewmen I interviewed, who were mainly concerned, as the spoon-and-string episode shows, with making sure they could carry out the genocidal threat of deterrence. Instead, it was almost taboo—as Major Hering found out—to talk about reasons for not committing retaliatory genocide, such as questioning the sanity of whoever gave the order.

Still, I should say, Tannenwald has been scrupulous enough to include a third explanation for non-use: luck. She means the kind of luck that had Colonel Petrov on duty in 1983 instead of someone more rule-bound. And that luck shows up regularly today, including as recently as February 2009 when two friendly nuclear subs—one British, one French—collided in the middle of the Atlantic despite both having state-of-the-art sonar, in an accident the BBC reported as a "one in a million" happenstance. And though the *Daily Mail* described the subs as "likely loaded with nuclear missiles," there was little damage except to the sense of complacency about nuclear accidents not being much to worry about.

As *Time* reported the incident in its March 1, 2009, issue: "The seemingly impossible collision of two subs in a large ocean should remind us of the fallacy by which we assume nuclear weapons will never be used. Because the threat of global nuclear war is not zero, even a small chance of war each year, multiplied over a number of years, adds up to the likelihood that the weapons will be used. Like those two subs stalking through the Atlantic, the odds will begin to align. Mathematically, they are destined to."

There are two further problems with Tannenwald's taboo analysis aside from downplaying luck. She doesn't go into detail about what makes the bright line so bright between conventional and nuclear weapons. Does the taboo extend down to even the smallest battlefield nuclear-tipped artillery, less powerful than many conventional weapons? Or does it apply only to major nuclear weapons with genocidal potential? What is the threshold of the taboo? In fact, the nuclear community has been divided from the beginning on the question of whether nuclear weapons are built mainly to threaten and deter, not to use, because use would inevitably be subject to catastrophic escalation.

The nonexceptionalists like Herman Kahn saw nukes as usable parts of an arsenal, weapons that could deter through threat but could and should be designed for war fighting. This term might include limited nuclear combat with tactical shorter range battlefield nuclear weapons and bunker-buster mini-nukes to blow open buried nuclear weapons-making facilities. Or we could launch precise strikes on military targets in a deliberate escalation from conventional conflict, taboo be damned. The case for nuclear war fighting—sometimes called "counterforce" strategy—did not die with Herman Kahn. It survives in the nuclear strategy community and was put forth forcefully recently by Georgetown University's Keir Lieber and Dartmouth's Daryl Press in a widely noticed polemic in *Foreign Affairs* in its Winter 2009 issue. The authors again raised the specter that nobody believed we'd carry out the indiscriminate genocidal threat of nuclear deterrence—that such horrendous over-kill was either just a bluff or looked like just a bluff—so we had to provide for the use of smaller, more accurate, less genocidal nukes to maintain the credibility of any use at all. They argued that a bright line, a taboo, was a delusion and envisioned nuclear first strikes with precisely guided weapons that could take out oppos-ing weapons and cause as few as seven hundred immediate deaths!

So is there really a bright line? Is it more than merely an expo-nentially higher degree of explosiveness per kiloton that distin-guishes nuclear from nonnuclear weapons that has given rise to a taboo? Or is there something more malign about nuclear weap-ons? Tannewald doesn't really answer why nuclear weapons are more malign by an order of moral, as well as explosive, magnitude. She briefly alludes to the development of a post–World War I taboo against the use of poison gas, and makes a comparison to the way some radiation and radiation poisoning was initially at least seen as analogous to poison gas, the psychological wedge by which the norm and then the taboo entered the culture. I think there's some-thing to that.

But the dimension Tannenwald tends to neglect in constructing her thesis about a taboo is culture. It's understandable: it's hard to measure, no brain scan yet to gauge its residual effects. And yet if one believes in the power of a taboo, that power depends on how the tabooed phenomenon is construed by the culture. She writes repeatedly about this or that leader thinking it's "wrong," that it goes "against our national character" to contemplate using nukes, and she gives the impression that abstract ethical thinking alone was responsible for something as powerful as this taboo. But was it all high-minded abstract ethics or was there something prior, deeper, an element of terror and grief over deaths foretold in the taboo? She neglects two things: Hiroshima and the way it's been portrayed and virtually sacralized, and the power of popular cul-ture, even, indeed, especially nuke porn.

If the Hiroshima bomb is merely conceived of as the most efficient way of ending a war and avoiding an invasion that could have cost a million deaths on both sides, that's one thing. But if Hiroshima is viewed through the prism of John Hersey's very personal and immensely moving accounts of the civilian victims of the blast, their lives before and after the blast, the years of radiation sickness that follow . . . that is something different.

It could be argued that the reason so many leaders thought it was "wrong"—not that winning the war was wrong, but using the bomb to do it—was Hersey's *New Yorker* reportage and then the best-selling book that came from it. That, and the memorable *Life* magazine photographs that showed the horrifically burned and scarred victims of Hiroshima.

There is still a running argument over whether Hiroshima was in some respects more humane, in that, again using brute numbers, it spared a million lives on each side that would have been lost in an American invasion if Hiroshima and Nagasaki had not forced Japan to surrender.

But the power of Hersey's spare but unsparing prose was the foundation stone, the rock on which the taboo was founded, and it may be one instance in which the pen has proven mightier than the sword. As much admired as he is for his literary talent, he deserves even more credit for the geopolitical effect of his slender but horrifying book on the dormant consciences of the word's leaders.

Since it was published, film and literature have taken Hersey's Conradian subtext—"the horror, the horror"—and built a vast edifice of work from the highbrow (*Hiroshima, Mon Amour*) to the low (*Them*, one of the 1950's science fiction films about giant radiation-mutated ants, and of course the Godzilla series). There have been tart knife-edged satires like *Dr. Strangelove* and weepy but powerful melodramas like *On the Beach*. Cumulatively culture has had a powerful effect in creating the norm and contributing to the taboo. I would even go so far as to say that popular culture more than politics was responsible for the peace movement becoming—in its nuclear freeze phase—a mass phenomenon. I've said that my life was forever changed by holding the key to a Minuteman launch key, but without the mental and emotional framing of that moment by the ambient culture, by a junior high school viewing of *On the Beach*, I'm not sure that key would have the transformative taboo power it did.

(I'd even add to the cultural sources of the taboo, especially in Washington, the cartoon Bomb character drawn and used incessantly by the *Washington Post*'s Herblock, a personified Bomb that was bloated, grotesque, and malign, grinning in triumph over the tiny bureaucrats attempting to contain it.)

And twenty years after *On the Beach*, the fictional 1983 TV film *The Day After* had a devastating effect on millions of Americans who watched an exchange between NATO and the Warsaw Pact escalate to full-scale nuclear war between the United States and the Soviet Union. This wasn't about Japan or Australia, this was here, it wasn't in some hazy future, it was now.

Credit for keeping doom alive during the "holiday from history" must also be given to the two *Terminator* films, especially the explicit nuclear blast imagery of *Terminator 2*. The catchphrase from the first *Terminator* had an eerie resonance as well: "I'll be back." And now it—nuclear dread—is back. The torch was passed, you might say, in 2006 to Cormac McCarthy's *The Road*, which Oprah Winfrey selected for her book club, a curious choice for a book so unrelievedly grim and offering but a glimmer of false hope in the end in a landscape of ashes and atavistic, cannibalistic, human self-consumption. One thing I found interesting about the book was the not uncommon wish to deny it was a post-nuclear landscape. One person insisted it was really just a father-son story. *Just?* True, it was not a typical learn-how-to-feel-good-about-yourself Oprah book. But Oprah was acting as a kind of cultural seismograph for the return of that dread. Beyond the denialism of "just a father-son story."

These cartoons, movies, photographs, and magazine stories had their moralizing moments, yes, but they fed into the power of the taboo by means of terror and grief rather than ethics. Perhaps the best way to characterize their effect is to say they buttressed the exceptionalist case for nuclear weapons use. Acts on the continuum of conventional war did not produce these grotesque cartoonishly nightmarish horror movie aftereffects. The gore of Tom Hanks war movies on HBO didn't do it, awful as it was. Conventional war, conventional weapons killed the body, but didn't distort the soul in the sense of calling forth the grotesque and unnatural beasts within.

Thinking about the nuclear taboo and its sources made me rethink my own experience of Hiroshima, the trip I took there before I began researching this book, a kind of penitent pilgrimage.

At the time I was deeply—and I thought strangely—unmoved. Or not as profoundly moved as I thought I should be. I was unimpressed by the "Peace This" and "Peace That" memorials in Hiroshima's "Peace Park," the country club lawns that had been built up over the blast's ground zero, the proliferation of what I described in print as "peace kitsch" and "peace tchotchkes." It seemed they couldn't do justice to what they were covering up.

The city itself, blandly modern, seamlessly covered up the blast site; at the time of my visit it seemed a hysterically anodyne cover-up of the raw truth. A truth that could be seen, yes, in photographs and radiation-burned relics in the museums that sold "Peace" T-shirts, all of which made it seem like it happened far away. A distant galaxy of grief.

But it seemed to me that nothing could do justice to what had happened there. I had the same feeling about the plans for the site of New York City's 9/11 Ground Zero. Stop with the endless memorials and "Freedom Towers" and leave the raw wound, the bloody hole in the city visible as the most effective memorial to what had happened. At first my inclination was to feel a visit to Hiroshima was about as admonitory as visiting Phoenix (if I may choose a metaphorically named city). The devastation has been all built over just like the desert had in Arizona, the guilt metaphorically air-conditioned, the message—at least at first—seemed to be that recovery from nuclear attack was eminently possible. Nuclear attack was a tragedy of war you remembered and built memorials to and then forgot.

But over time something subtle happened. Perhaps it had

some distant relation to what the World Court was getting at in its unusual language about the dominion of nukes over space and time. Perhaps it was impossible to assimilate at once in a visit, but the effects seemed to persist over time, and grow more powerful.

Having been there was important. But the meaning of the experience continued to change over time. There was a growing realization that, yes, the museums and the T-shirts with the doves, and "Peace Park" and the peace kitsch were inadequate to the occasion, but the very inadequacy or the realization of their inadequacy provoked a recognition of the enormity of what the souvenir shops could not convey. That enormity is what had caused leaders to say that what happened there was antithetical to "our national character." That we should never use nuclear arms again, whatever we threaten. I'll never forget a spooky trip I made to an all-night copy shop through the deserted wind-whipped streets of Hiroshima at about four in the morning to fax a story for a U.S. deadline. I know it was my overheated imagination but in the wind of the empty streets I felt I could hear the whisper of a hundred thousand ghosts. It was a whisper that I will never forget.

But—it is often forgotten—we did use nuclear arms again after Hiroshima. At Nagasaki. Three days later. The significance of Nagasaki, coming after the horror of Hiroshima, is hard to assess. There was little time for second thoughts or full realization of the effects of the first strike. But it suggests that in a wartime situation commanders don't err on the side of restraint, or second thoughts, even with nuclear weapons.

The nuclear taboo can be seen as a coalescing of post-Nagasaki second thoughts at least in the beginning. But eventually a passive culture of nuclear dread and opprobrium grew into a feeling among a majority of civilian and military leaders that nukes were the untouchables among weapons whatever the war fighters said, the shameful skeletons in the closet, the zombies among weapons that scared us from ever opening the door.

They were weapons designed to terrify but not to be used. And paradoxically antinuclear culture, nuke porn played a role in deterring their use by graphically subjecting the entire population to nightmarish enactments of nuclear terror. We terrorized others, but we also terrorized ourselves. In that terror was the beginning of the taboo.

## BACK TO THE KEYS

But is the taboo enough? There's a section in Nina Tannenwald's book in which she discusses the most explicit, weighty formulation of the nuclear taboo: the 1982 statement by the National Conference of Catholic Bishops. This was the one that not only declared nuclear use immoral, but said even threatening the use of nuclear weapons, as in deterrence, is unequivocally evil.

Here the taboo could undo the taboo. If there is no certainty of retaliatory response, because tabooed, a foe would be more likely to use or threaten to use nuclear weapons for a first strike regardless of the taboo since they would have reason to believe retaliation was taboo.

I dwell on the taboo, because it seems to me to embody the tragic paradox that efforts to prevent the outbreak of nuclear war since 1945 have devolved into: the development of a taboo that undermines itself, undermines itself by subverting deterrence, convincing a foe that it might not suffer nuclear reprisal or face premeditated nuclear attack for its own aggressive nuclear or conventional attacks, because of the force of the nuclear taboo, thus increasing the likelihood of a nuclear outbreak by those for whom the taboo is less powerful than some other imperative.

And there's the one-sidedness of tabooed nuclear intentions—we have no indication that such a taboo has been inculcated into the Russian, much less the newer nuclear powers', way of thinking. It doesn't feature much in whatever internal discussions we know of that go on in North Korea for instance. The taboo may have grown stronger, but taboos are made to be broken. In a sense they are only defined when they're broken.

It has become clear to me through decades of study of nuclear strategists devising all sorts of chess games with their missile and missile-alert postures and sending each other cryptic messages in footnotes that the one step that can be taken now is for the two superpowers to listen to the long ago advice of Admiral Arleigh Burke, who warned against their instability—and yank those land-based missiles out of their silos so that they don't present a threat of accidental war, or a reason to believe either side is imperiled by a surprise first strike capability.

The terrible wrong turn in nuclear policy that was signaled by the Air Force land-based missile triumph over Burke's sub-based "finite deterrence" can and must be reversed. It is far more important than reducing the number of land-based missiles to 1,000 or 1,500 by 2018. It must be done now.

It is abundantly clear that we have no need to maintain a "strategic triad"—missiles, bombers, and submarines—and an army of nuclear strategists to worship at the triune perfection of the "nuclear triad." There is nothing sacred about the triad although it has become the object of Trinity-like worship by the Pentagon and its paid civilian strategist-enablers. Of the three legs of the triad, the land-based silo-embedded missiles are the least subject to human control in a crisis; they represent the turning over of the Armageddon decision in great part to automation, to "dual phenomenology" and PERIMETR. If you want to put more distance between ourselves and Armageddon now, then pull those missiles out of the ground and pour quick-drying cement into the silos. That doesn't mean disarm. It means going to a subs-only deterrent posture (assuming a diminished role for aging bombers).

"In the coming years," Burke wrote in his confidential memo, "the ability to consider and weigh such decisions [to launch or not to launch] will increase in importance. When both sides have quantities of ballistic missiles there may be periods of tension in which there are some indications that missiles might be launched by the enemy but these indications are not positive. Our political leaders will then be in a quandary as to whether or not to launch which missiles before they are sure the enemy has launched its attack. If they wait, our ballistic missiles in known locations may be destroyed. If they launch on mistake, we will have started a devastating war."

One development in favor of a neo-Burkean finite deterrence plan is that the Russians are already on their way to modernizing their submarine fleet. They should have no qualms about the reliability of their sub force at whatever level it's frozen. The nuclear missiles on the new Yasen-class Russian subs have been reported by the Moscow news service Novosti to have a range of three thousand miles.

That's enough deterrent power, don't you think?

It's remarkable how the thinking behind Burke's half-century-old "finite deterrence" has emerged again in the state-of-the-art "minimum deterrence" and "minimal deterrence" plans advanced almost simultaneously in 2008 respectively by Hans Kristensen of the Federation of American Scientists and Dr. Jeffrey Lewis of the New America Foundation.

Still the sanest solution to an insane, obscene problem seems to me a submarine-only Burkean "finite deterrent" configuration with enough subs for devastating deterrent retaliation (but not enough for a first strike "war-fighting" capability). And yet even the sanest solution is likely to involve or escalate to genocide if it fails, even if it is the least likely to fail, and the most likely to prevent genocide. It too must be weighed in an awful calculus that balances the diminished likelihood but nonetheless indubitably possible outcome that a system that was designed to reduce the chance of genocide commits us to genocide if the threat fails.

It can sometimes seem astonishing to anyone who seriously considers the continual, indeed rising, level of risk of nuclear war in this second nuclear age to witness the continuing denial, the inexplicable ability of much of the world to ignore a fate hurtling toward us. The mechanisms of denial have become so sophisticated by now, we don't notice them, the way we scarcely notice the millions of tons of nuclear warheads hidden beneath the surface of the Great Plains.

This was the virtue of Obama articulating his dream of Zero whatever fate it ultimately has. It makes denial of the reality more difficult.

What I hoped to be able to say at the close of this book is "At least you can't say you haven't been warned."

So let me say it for emphasis: At least you can't say you haven't been warned.

But just to focus the attention of those who have gotten this far: the three most likely sources of nuclear war right now are an accidental war between the United States and the former U.S.S.R. triggered by tension and error. And a second Holocaust–driven nuclear war in the Middle East. The latter may be impossible to forestall. And then there is Pakistan.

If a Middle East nuclear war is unlikely to be avoided the other chief danger—accidental or deliberate nuclear war between the superpowers—can be diminished at least. If those malevolent silo-based missiles on hair-trigger alert were destroyed on both sides, Admiral Burke's plan might be a way of convincing the military establishments of the nuclear powers that they were not engaging in disarmament, so much as a more certain deterrence by shifting from land-based to sea-based minimal deterrence.

And I would look upon it as the best we could do in a hopeless situation, where our only choice may be how totally devastating the next nuclear war will be. Maybe the neo-Burkean minimalist plans are a way to some small less-than-world-holocaust number of nukes. I'm not hopeful but it seems to me that if there's a way to reduce the chance of a "world holocaust" we would be derelict in not trying it.

The remaining question is that of rogue nations such as North Korea, Syria, or ones like Iran that proclaim that they cannot be deterred by massive population losses because of their suicidal martyrdom/Hidden Imam ideology/theology. That is one reason I focused on the Israeli raid on the Syrian reactor in 2007. And that chilling quote, "If people had known how close we came to world war three that day there'd have been mass panic."

The world didn't know, the raid didn't result in a Third World War, but the next raid, or one like it, or one initiated by another nation could be the one to go global. Perhaps mass panic would have been salutary. Mass complacency is not.

Here is the last limited role for the nuclear-armed bomber fleet, perhaps. Getting rid of the lethal and destabilizing rogue nation warheads is the fastest, best way to make a world holocaust less likely. Bombers at least are under human control up till the last minute, and unlike ballistic missiles they can be called back. If preemption of a rogue state is required, a small bomber force might be necessary and bombers have the advantage of being able to convey menace, to deter without dropping a single bomb.

Personally, I can't get enough of listening to the nuke pros on the armscontrolwonk.com blog talk shop. Following the release of the Burke papers in the electronic briefing book, there was an epic discussion in the comments section about what aspect of the triad was dispensable and what weapons and warheads should be retained. Military, ex-military, and military wonks and strategists chimed in. It was fascinating but it's clear there's no consensus as to what to do with all the nukes, how to base them, how to reduce them, who should operate them. And these are mainly Americans arguing with mainly Americans. Imagine the exponential difficulty of carrying out a negotiation with the Russians when they have their own crowd of rowdy military theorists and competitors cat-calling from the stands.

There is no consensus, there may never be, it's probably too late for that, it's probably too late to reduce the role nukes will play in the future—or lack of future—of civilization. It's beyond our ingenuity or goodwill. It's all about luck now. I'm a pessimist. I think only luck has saved us regardless of the configuration of nukes we deploy and our luck is bound to run out before we find a way to eliminate nukes. We cannot escape from the Faustian bargain we made.

But to give up and to give in is not like us. For all we know our American obsession with solutionism might someday produce a solution. It hasn't yet, there may be no way to succeed but there are many ways to try that have yet to be tested. I'm proposing one: Arleigh Burke's minimal subbased deterrence + de-alerting + destroying land-based missiles now. You have a better one? Write me. Maybe we'll save the world. There's still time, brother.

And who am I to advocate a nuclear weapons plan? An obsessed outsider, an amateur student. But the pros have failed! The pros have gotten us into this jam. The pros, the so-called wizards of Armageddon, pro- and anti-nuke, can't agree on a thing. Look where it's led to: defending "minimal" nuclear war, which is about the same as defending "minimal" genocide. Zero may be the only answer, but Zero seems out of the question.

And so this desparing message is for everybody, not just for those who have access to the keys. I'll never forget a lovely white-haired woman at a Hiroshima Day anti-nuke protest in Boston back in the 1970s who explained her refusal to pay taxes, because part of her money was going to support nuclear weapons. She was not saying the Cold War was one of moral equivalence. She was making an exceptionalist argument: she was just saying she didn't want to feel she'd contributed in however slight a way to a nuclear holocaust, or more likely then, a "world holocaust."

So we can't stand above the battle if we pay our taxes. We're all responsible for what's done in our name.

All I can say is—if this were my letter of last resort:

If you're in a position to launch, whoever you are, now or in the future, if you're in a position to send the targeting codes, if it's up to you, whoever you are, my plea is: Nothing justifies following orders for genocide. Don't send those codes, don't twist those keys.

# NOTES

## 1. WE CAME SO CLOSE

PAGE

1 Spectator *is the oldest:* Founded in 1711 by Richard Addison.

1 *holiday from history:* George Will, "The End of Our Holiday from History," *Washington Post,* September 12, 2001, Opinion Section, p. A31.

2 *"SO CLOSE TO WAR":* James Forsyth and Douglas Davis, "We Came So Close to War," *The Spectator,* September 20, 2007, online edition; October 6, 2007, print edition.

2 *"meticulously planned, brilliantly executed":* Ibid.

2 *as was later confirmed:* "Background Briefing with Senior U.S. Officials on Syria's Covert Nuclear Reactor and North Korea's Involvement," Office of the Director of National Intelligence, April 24, 2008, www.dni .gov/interviews/20080424_interview.pdf.

3 *electronic countermeasures:* David A. Fulghum, "Why Syria's Air Defenses Failed to Detect Israelis," *Aviation Week,* October 3, 2007, www.aviationweek.com/aw/blogs/defense/index.jsp?plckCon troller=Blog&plckBlogPage=BlogViewPost&newspaperUserId= 27ec4a53-dcc8-42d0-bd3a-01329aef79a7&plckPostId= Blog:27ec4a53-dcc8-42d0-bd3a-01329aef79a7Post:2710d024-5eda-416c-b117-ae6d649146cd&plckScript=blogScript&plckElementId= blogDest (accessed 4/15/10).

3 *Their target, later identified:* Background Briefing, with Senior U.S. Officials.

3 *The Soviets, for instance:* Georgetown University Library National Security Archives, www.gwu.edu/~nsarchiv/NSAEBB/NSAEBB98/press .htm (accessed 4/15/10).

3 *Israel . . . is a substantial nuclear power:* Jane's Defence Weekly, April 10, 2010, www.janes.com: Israel estimated to have "100 to 300 nuclear warheads and has a power similar to that of Britain."

3 *Seymour Hersh reported:* Seymour Hersh, *The Samson Option: Israel's Nuclear Arsenal and American Foreign Policy* (New York: Random House, 1991).

4 *"obliterate" Iran:* "In an interview on ABC's *Good Morning America* today, Hillary Clinton pledged that if Iran launches a nuclear attack against Israel, the United States would retaliate against Iran. 'I want the Iranians to know that if I'm the president, we will attack Iran,' Clinton said. 'In the next 10 years, during which they might foolishly consider launching an attack on Israel, we would be able to totally obliterate them.'": www .guardian.co.uk/commentisfree/2008/apr/22/clintonandiran.

4 *sixty to one hundred warheads:* David E. Sanger, "Pakistan Strife Raises U .S. Doubt on Nuclear Arms," *New York Times*, May 4, 2009, p. A1, www .nytimes.com/2009/05/04/world/asia/04nuke.html.

5 *Nuclear proliferation scholar Benjamin Frankel:* Benjamin Frankel, "Assessing Nuclear Threats," *International Security* 34, no. 3 (Winter 2009): 10.

5 *"The world has arrived":* Rob Edwards, "The A-bomb: 60 Years on, Is the World Any Safer?," *New Scientist*, No. 2508 (2005), www.newscientist .com/article/mg18725083.800-the-abomb-60-years-on-is-the-world- any-safer.html?page=3.

5 *"We are at the tipping point":* Michael Crowley, "The Stuff Sam Nunn's Nightmares Are Made Of," *New York Times Magazine*, February 25, 2007, www.nytimes.com/2007/02/25/magazine/25Nunn.t.html?scp= 2&sq=Sam%20Nunn&st=cse.

5 *"The current global nuclear order":* Graham Allison, "Nuclear Disorder: Surveying Atomic Threats," *Foreign Affairs* 1, no. 89 (January/February 2010), www.foreignaffairs.com/articles/65732/graham-allison/ nuclear-disorder.

5 *India and Pakistan nearly used: Online NewsHour:* "Nuclear Nightmare," May 31, 2002, www.pbs.org/newshour/bb/asia/jan.../nuclear_5-31 .html; Alan Sipress and Thomas Ricks, "Report: India, Pakistan Were Near Nuclear War in '99," *Washington Post*, May 15, 2002, www.cdi .org/nuclear/nuclearshadow.cfm.

6 *revelation by Michael Dobbs:* Michael Dobbs, *One Minute to Midnight* (New York: Alfred A. Knopf, 2009), p. 209.

6 *captain of the Soviet submarine:* Ibid., p. 317.

6 *flock of geese:* Dr. Martin Hellman, quoted in *Breakthrough: Emerging New Thinking: Soviet and Western Scholars Issue a Challenge to Build a World*

*Beyond War* (New York: Walker, 1988), www-ee.stanford.edu/~hell man/Breakthrough/book/pdfs/breakthrough.pdf.

6  *Brzezinski was awakened:* cited by Stansfield Turner, CIA director under President Carter, in his book *Caging the Nuclear Genie: An American Challenge for Global Security* (Boulder: Westview, 1997).

7  *And then there was Colonel Petrov:* David Hoffman, *The Dead Hand* (New York: Doubleday, 2009), p. 6–11.

7  *A British mole in the KGB:* Oleg Gordievsky, Book review of *War Scare: Russia and America on the Nuclear Brink,* by Peter Vincent Pry, *The Spectator,* November 20, 1999.

9  *August 17, 2007, announcement by Vladimir Putin:* Full text of Putin's statement: www.acronym.org.uk/docs/0708/doc04.htm.

10  *a small-circulation military magazine:* Alexander Mladenov, "Back on the Beat," *AirForces Monthly,* April 2008, pp. 31–48.

10  *Yes, the NORAD major confirmed:* Author telephone interview with Major Bryan Martin, April 2008.

11  *two of those interactions:* Mladenov, "Back on the Beat," p. 48.

11  *Rice eventually condemned:* Jonathan S. Landay, "Rice Warns Moscow About Its Bomber Runs off Alaska," McClatchy Newspapers, August 19, 2008, www.mcclatchydc.com/2008/08/18/49125/rice-warns-moscow-about-its-bomber.html.

11  *strategic flights would be landing:* Alex Nicholson, "Russia May Send Strategic Bombers to Cuba, Venezuela," Bloomberg News, March 14, 2009.

13  *the Russian government has kept:* International Environmental Law blog, April 10, 2010.

13  *Victor Mizin, the director:* Victor Mizin, "Russia's Nuclear Renaissance," *Journal of International Security Affairs* 14 (Spring 2008): 61–69.

14  *The Minot Mistake:* The fullest account of the affair is now available due to a Freedom of Information Act declassification of the "Commander's Investigation," a PDF of which can be found linked on the armscontrol wonk blog: www.armscontrolwonk.com/2693/minot-afb-investigation-meet-foia#comment.

14  *nuclear fuses had been shipped:* Josh White, "Nuclear Parts Sent to Taiwan in Error," *Washington Post,* March 25, 2008, www.washington post.com/wp=dyn/content/article/2008/03/25/AR2008032501309 .html.

15  *frenzied blogospheric speculations:* Here's an example: www.newsfollowup .com/aipac-cheney.htm.

16  *"When Bill Clinton briefed":* Raymond Bonner, book review of *Descent into Chaos,* by Ahmed Rashid, *New York Times,* August 5, 2008.

16 *A. Q. Khan, who has been called:* Douglas Frantz and Catherine Collins, *The Nuclear Jihadist* (New York: Twelve Books, 2007).

17 *very sophisticated war gaming:* For an example of profoundly confusing but, alas, not utterly implausible regional to global nuclear war scenario, see this obsessive amateur's six nuclear war scenarios: www.carolmoore.net/nuclearwar/alternatescenarios.html.

18 *Pakistan's Inter-Services Intelligence agency:* "Pakistan's ISI Still Linked to Militants, U.S. Says," Reuters, March 28, 2009.

19 *But nearly simultaneous reports: Wall Street Journal,* November 29, 2007, p. 1; www.nytimes.com/2007/11/18/washington/18nuke.html.

19 *More than one nuclear strategist:* Author interview's with war gamer Colonel Sam Gardiner and an anonymous Israeli source.

19 *North Korea is estimated:* North Korea Advisory Group, final report, www.fas.org/nuke/guide/dprk/nkag-report.htm.

19 *"The bad news about North Korea":* David E. Sanger, "We May Miss Kim Jong-il (and Maybe Musharraf)," *New York Times,* Week in Review, September 13, 2008.

20 *the 2007 National Intelligence Estimate:* See Background Briefing with Senior U.S. Officials, Chapter 8.

20 *independently discovered facts:* A summary of the November 19, 2008, IAEA report can be found here: Ephraim Asculai, "So It Really Was a Reactor in Syria," *Institute for National Security Studies Insight* no. 81, November 23, 2008, www.inss.org.il/publications.php?cat=25&incat=&read=2352.

21 *The Israeli historian Benny Morris:* www.nytimes.com/2008/07/18/opinion/18morris.html?pagewanted=all.

21 *published a seventy-seven page war game:* Anthony H. Cordesman, "Iran, Israel and Nuclear War," Arleigh A. Burke Chair in Strategy, Center for Strategic and International Studies, revised November 19, 2007, http://csis.org/publication/iran-israel-and-nuclear-war.

21 *Samson Option:* Hersh, *The Samson Option.*

22 *Threatening China with nukes:* See Ralph N. Clough, *East Asia and U.S. Security,* Brookings Institution, Washington, D.C., 1974.

23 *One Chinese general, apparently going:* Joseph Kahn, "Chinese General Threatens Use of A-Bombs if U.S. Intrudes," *New York Times,* International Section, July 15, 2005, www.nytimes.com/2005/07/15/international/asia/15china.html.

23 *report in the* National Journal: "The Weapons of World War III," July 8, 2008.

23 *Two years later a front-page report:* Staff writers, "China Proves to Be an

Aggressive Foe in Cyberspace," *Washington Post*, November 11, 2009, www.washingtonpost.com›World›Asia/Pacific.

23 *2001 Nuclear Posture Review:* Greg Granger, "The Paradox of Unilateralism," analysis in section "Strategic Nuclear Weapons in George Bush's National Security Policy," May 20, 2003, www.unc.edu/depts/diplo mat/archives_roll/2003_04-06/granger_paradox/granger_paradox2 .html.

24 *But one part of it has been declassified:* The document can be viewed at www.fas.org/programs/ssp/nukes/.../WarPlanIssueBrief2010.pdf.

24 *According to Kristensen:* Author interview.

26 *"The first use of nuclear weapons":* Ian Traynor, "Pre-emptive Nuclear Strike a Key Option, Nato Told," *The Guardian*, January 22, 2008, www .guardian.co.uk/world/2008/jan/22/nato.nuclear.

27 *Suddenly, as Elbridge Colby:* Author interview.

29 *it's hard to disagree with Joseph Cirincione:* Joe Cirincione, "It's About the Bomb, Not Obama," *Huffington Post*, October 9, 2009, www.huffington post.com/joe-cirincione/its-about-the-bomb-not-ob_b_315446.html.

30 *site of the nuclear command post:* See chapter 3.


## 2. MAJOR HERING'S FORBIDDEN QUESTION

PAGE

32 *He also wanted to know:* "Case of the Dubious Missileman," *Washington Post*, January 20, 1975.

33 *"I have to say I feel":* *Detroit Free Press*, November 2, 1975.

33 *"It is inherent":* Ibid.

33 *"I have always stated":* Ibid.

34 *George W. Bush's vice president:* Transcript of Vice President Dick Cheney on *Fox News Sunday*, Fox News, December 22, 2008.

34 *frenzy among constitutional scholars:* The Volokh Conspiracy (blog), www .volokh.com/archives/archive_2008_12_21-2008_12_27.shtml; "24 hours a day, by a military aide carrying a football that . . .": Orin Kerr, "A President's Lawful Authority to Respond to a Nuclear Attack:", The Volokh Conspiracy, December 23, 2008, http://volokh.com/2008/ 12/23/a-presidents-lawful-authority-to-respond-to-a-nuclear-attack/ (accessed 4/19/10).

34 *Defenders of Cheney argued:* The Prize Cases, 67 U.S. 635 (1863).

35 *"I could leave this room":* Austin Darat and Thomas R. Keanis, *Law's Violence* (Ann Arbor: University of Michigan Press, 1992), p. 25.

35 *What Schlesinger did:* " 'Erratic' Nixon Might Set Off Nuclear Cri-

sis, Officials Feared," *Montreal Gazette*, August 28, 1974, http://
news.google.com/newspapers?nid=1946&dat=19740828&id=
BokxAAAAIBAJ&sjid=1KEFAAAAIBAJ&pg=988,3742207.

36 *After his dismissal from the Air Force:* Author interview
37 *Akhil Reed Amar has called:* Akhil Reed Amar testimony at Hearing
before the Subcommittee on the Constitution of the Committee of the
Judiciary House of Representatives, October 6, 2004.
37 *its "bumping" provision:* Suzanne Nelson, "Continuity Commission
Weighs Presidential Succession," *Roll Call*, October 28, 2003, www
.continuityofgovernment.org/pdfs/102803RollCall.pdf (accessed 4/
19/10).
37 *George Quester as its main witness:* See for instance George Quester, "Cultural Barriers to an Acceptance of Deterrence," in Roman Kolkowicz,
ed., *The Logic of Nuclear Terror* (London: Allen & Unwin, 1987).
38 *Blair told the committee:* Statement of Dr. Bruce Blair to Hearing of House
Government Operations Committee, September 26, 1985.
38 *commission to consider continuity of government:* "The Continuity of the
Presidency: The Second Report of the Continuity of Government Commission, June 2009," Preface: "The Continuity of Government," www
.continuityofgovernment.org/SecondReport.pdf.
39 *To compound the confusion:* Text of National Security Presidential Direc-
tive/NSPD 51, available at www.democraticunderground.com.
40 *Mel Halbach:* Author interview.
40 *the Letter of Last Resort:* "The Human Button," BBC Radio 4 FM, December 2, 2008.
41 *London's* Daily Mail *reported:* Peter Hennessy and Richard Knight,
"HMS Apocalypse: Deep in the Atlantic, a Submarine Waits on Alert,"
*Daily Mail*, November 30, 2008, www.dailymail.co.uk/news/article-
1090400/HMS-Apocalypse-Deep-Atlantic-submarine-waits-alert-
nuclear-missiles-end-world--.html.
41 *"The U.K. MOD":* E-mail from David Murtagh.
43 *Azar Gat argues:* Azar Gat, *War in Human Civilization* (New York: Oxford
University Press, 2006).
43 *Peter Berkowitz argues:* Author interview.

## 3. THE FORBIDDEN QUESTION AT THE QWEST CENTER

PAGE
44 *"They're scared":* Author interview.
44 *co-author of an important new treatise:* Hans M. Kristensen, Robert S. Nor-

ris, and Ivan Oelrich, "From Counterforce to Minimal Deterrence: A New Nuclear Policy on the Path Toward Eliminating Nuclear Weapons," Occasional Paper No. 7 (Washington, D.C.: Federation of American Scientists and the Natural Resources Defense Council, April 2009), p. 2, www.fas.org/pubs/_docs/OccasionalPaper7.pdf.

47 *They let me take a seat:* Ron Rosenbaum, "The Subterranean World of the Bomb," *Harper's*, March 1978.

48 *Fred Kaplan memorably called them:* Fred Kaplan, *The Wizards of Armageddon* (New York: Simon & Schuster, 1983).

48 *such stuff as Herman Kahn's* On Escalation: Herman Kahn, *On Escalation* (New York, Basic Books, 1965).

50 *General Chilton's career:* United States Strategic Command First Annual Strategic Deterrence Symposium, program, "Keynote Speakers," p. 3, www.stratcom.mil/search/?q=chilton.

50 *encomium to nuclear deterrence:* Tape-recorded by author.

51 *General Chilton had already clashed:* Elaine M. Grossman, "Top U.S. General Spurns Obama Pledge to Reduce Nuclear Alert Posture," Global Security Newswire, January 27, 2009.

51 *"It is misleading to us the term:* Ibid.

52 *At her confirmation hearing:* Walter Pincus, "Clinton's Goals Detailed," *Washington Post*, Politics Section, January 19, 2009, www.washington post.com/wp-dyn/content/article/2009/01/18/AR2009011802268 .html.

53 *the Moscow-specific GPS codes:* Nathan Hodge, "Nuke Review: Deploying, De-MIRVing, and De-Targeting," Wired, Danger Room, April 6, 2010, www.wired.com/dangerroom/2010/04/the-nuclear-posture-review-deploying-de-mirving-and-de-targeting.

53 *"dual phenomenology":* Military Periscope, "Dual Phenomenology," www .periscope.ucg.com/terms/t0000114.html.

54 *officially the head:* "The National Institute for Public Policy is a nonprofit public education organization that focuses on a wide spectrum of rapidly evolving foreign policy and international issues," www.nipp.org.

54 *Many of these ideas were criticized:* Robert S. Norris, Hans M. Kristensen, and Christopher E. Paine, "Nuclear Insecurity: A Critique of the Bush Administration's Nuclear Weapons Policy," Natural Resources Defense Council, September 2004, www.nrdc.org/nuclear/insecurity/critique.pdf.

54 *He took the lead in advocating junking:* Prepared Statement, Dr. Keith B. Payne, President, National Institute for Public Policy, Faculty, Georgetown University, School of Foreign Service, National Security Studies Program, http://74.125.45.132/search?q=cache:hR9zDUI19G8J:www

.globalsecurity.org/space/library/congress/1999_h/99-10-13payne .htm+%22Keith+Payne%22+%22ABM+Treaty%22&cd=2&hl= en&ct=clnk&gl=us.

55 *a tireless advocate of nuclear "bunker busters":* Josiane Gabel, "The Role of U.S. Nuclear Weapons After September 11," *Washington Quarterly* 28, no. 1 (Winter 2004–2005): 181–95, http://muse.jhu.edu/login?uri=/ journals/washington_quarterly/v028/28.1gabel.html.

55 *Max Singer:* Author interview, July 2008.

55 *350-pound author:* Jeremy J. Stone, "Every Man Should Try: Adventures of a Public Interest Advocate" (New York: Public Affairs, 1999), p. 5, http://catalytic-diplomacy.org/everymanPDFs/Ch1.pdf.

55 *notorious mid-1960s books:* Herman Kahn, *Thinking About the Unthinkable* (New York: Horizon, 1962); *On Thermonuclear War* (Princeton: Princeton University Press, 1960).

55 *In the closing section:* Keith Payne, "Examination of U.S. Strategic Forces Policy," *Strategic Studies Quarterly* 3, no. 1 (Spring 2009), www.au.af .mil/au/ssq/2009/Spring/payne.pdf.

56 *more technically advanced nukes:* Jonathan Medalia, Congressional Research Service, "Nuclear Warheads: The Reliable Replacement Warhead Program and the Life Extension Program," RL33748, updated December 3, 2007, www.fas.org/sgp/crs/nuke/RL33748.pdf.

56 *so-called Life Extension Program:* Jonathan Medalia, Congressional Research Service, "The Reliable Replacement Warhead Program," RL32929, July 27, 2009, www.fas.org/sgp/crs/nuke/RL32929.pdf.

56 *mysterious FOGBANK controversy:* The most comprehensive and informed speculation about the highly classified issue can be found here: www .armscontrolwonk.com/1814/fogbank.

57 *"I don't know how it developed":* "Navy Never Received Refurbished W-76 Warhead," Global Security Newswire, May 29, 2009, http://gsn.nti .org/gsn/nw_20090529_9664.php.

57 *That encounter had occurred:* Rosenbaum, "The Subterranean World of the Bomb," pp. 92–98.

60 *In 1958 Congress had actually passed:* James E. King, Jr., "Strategic Surrender: The Senate Debate and the Book," review of *Strategic Surrender: The Politics of Victory and Defeat* by Paul Kecskemeti (Stanford: Stanford University Press, 1958), www.jstor.org/pss/2009201.

60 *a RAND Corporation analyst had done:* Paul Kecskemeti *Strategic Surrender: The Politics of Victory and Defeat* (Stanford: Stanford University Press, 1958), pp ix, 287, http://journals.cambridge.org/action/display Abstract?fromPage=online&aid=5341716.

60  *"That's the thing you know"*: Rosenbaum, "The Subterranean World of the Bomb."

60  *My source on Cold War nuclear subculture:* Author interview.

61  *The way the system worked:* Author interview with SAC escort.

61  *But the missile crewmen:* Author interview.

62  *I later learned from Bruce Blair:* Author interview.

62  *Major General C. Donald Alston:* First Annual Strategic Deterrence Symposium, p. 8.

63  *The chief of staff of the Air Force was fired:* "Air Force Leaders Fired over Nuke Handling," *Arms Control Today*, July/August 2008, www.armscontrol.org/act/2008_07-08/AirForce.

63  *"Say deterrence fails":* Author interview.

67  *Our official policy had been the ride-out:* "U.S. to Ride Out Any Big Attack," *Herald-Journal*, May 4, 1961, http://news.google.com/news papers?nid=1876&dat=19610304&id=8m8sAAAAIBAJ&sjid= rcsEAAAAIBAJ&pg=5721,822315.

68  *Senior Colonel Yao Yunzhu:* First Annual Strategic Deterrence Symposium, program, p. 16.

68  *"Deterrence will not fail":* Author interview.

69  *"That's a very interesting question":* Author interview.

## 4. THE NUMBER

PAGE

71  *Daniel Ellsberg, then an attaché:* Author interview, September 2009.

71  *the words Henry Kissinger spoke:* Daniel Ellsberg, *Secrets: A Memoir of Vietnam and the Pentagon Papers* (New York: Penguin, 2002), pp. 434–44.

72  *Few aside from Nixon and Kissinger knew:* National Security Archive: "New Evidence on the Origins of Overkill," November 21, 2007; William Burr, "The Nixon Administration, the SIOP, and the Search for Limited Nuclear Options, 1969–1974," National Security Archive Electronic Briefing Book 173, posted November 23, 2005, www.gwu.edu/ ~nsarchiv/NSAEBB/NSAEBB173/index.htm.

73  *the Yoda of nuclear strategists, Thomas Schelling:* Schelling was Ellsberg's Harvard Ph.D. thesis adviser on "uncertainty," later to be called "ambiguities of warning" in nuclear game theory strategy: Ellsberg, *Secrets*, pp. 233–34.

73  *so-called Wizards of Armageddon:* Coined by Fred M. Kaplan in his book with that title: http://books.google.com/books?id=yJXu7kMSc44C&dq= wizards+of+armageddon&printsec=frontcover&source=bn&hl=

en&ei=rXDVS8nWOpXs9gSo_pXIDw&sa=X&oi=book_result&ct=
result&resnum=4&ved=0CCUQ6AEwAw#v=onepage&q&f=false.

73 *Schelling is credited:* Jeffrey Kimball, "Did Thomas C. Schelling Invent
the Madman Theory?," History News Network, October 24, 2005;
Tyler Cowen, "Thomas Schelling: New Nobel Laureate," February 28,
2005, History News Network, http://hnn.us/articles/17183.html.

74 *give the Air Force's nukes:* See Burke papers discussion, chapter 9.

74 *his studies in the art of nuclear blackmail:* Daniel Ellsberg, "The Theory
and Practice of Blackmail" (Santa Monica: RAND Corporation, 1968;
reprint), www.rand.org/pubs/papers/P3883/.

74 *junior member of the Ex-comm:* Ellsberg, *Secrets,* p. 33.

75 *I too had a close encounter:* Ron Rosenbaum, "The Subterranean World of
the Bomb," *Harper's,* March 1978, p. 99.

75 *Initially there was only one targeting plan:* Author interview.

77 *"Blowtorch" Komer:* Defense.gov News transcript: "Amb. Edelman's
Remarks," www.defense.gov/Transcripts/Transcript.aspx?TranscriptID
=3739.

77 Whole World on Fire: Lynn Eden, "The Physics and Politics of Mass
Fire," in *Whole World on Fire: Organizations, Knowledge, and Nuclear Weapons Devastation* (Ithaca: Cornell University Press, 2004), pp. 221–52,
www.fas.harvard.edu/~hsdept/bios/jasanoff.html.

79 *"Most everyone [over there] is thinking":* Author interview.

80 *National Conference of Catholic Bishops declared:* "The Challenge of Peace:
God's Promise and Our Response," pastoral letter reprinted as appen-
dix to *The Bishops and the Bomb: Waging Peace in a Nuclear Age* (Garden
City: Doubleday, 1983).

80 *"Just war" theorists of conventional war talk:* John Forge, "Proportionality, Just War Theory and Weapons Innovation," *Science and Engineering Ethics 15,* no. 1 (Spring 2009), www.springerlink.com/content/
x5n36t2500384727/.

80 *"distinction" refers to the ability:* Mark R. Amstutz, *International Ethics:
Concepts, Theories, and Cases in Global Politics,* 3rd ed. (Lanham, Maryland: Rowman & Littlefield, 2008), http://books.google.com/books?
id=_V6f8j9pgDoC&printsec=frontcover&source=gbs_v2_summary_
r&cad=0#v=onepage&q&f=false.

81 *In another one of its euphemisms:* Transcript, "The Language of War," Center for Defense Information, www.cdi.org/adm/Transcripts/345/.

83 *He too had been inspired by the major:* Author interview.

83 *Ellsberg also knew that the system:* Author interview.

83 *assigned to make a tour:* Author interview.

83 *among other recently declassified:* "Ike Delegated Approval for Nuclear Strike, Files Show," *Los Angeles Times,* March 21, 1998, http://articles .latimes.com/1998/mar/21/news/mn-31132.

84 *The International Court of Justice in The Hague: International Review of the Red Cross* 316, February 28, 1997, pp. 92–102, www.icrc.org/web/eng/ siteeng0.nsf/html/57JNFS.

84 *Paul Ramsey sought to defend:* Barry Penn Hollar, "U.S. Methodism Deals with War and Peace," article from project "The Theology of Peace and War," www.mupwj.org/methodism.htm.

85 *at the heart of the World Court's 1996 opinion:* Eric David, "The Opinion of the International Court of Justice on the Legality of the Use of Nuclear Weapons," *International Review of the Red Cross* 316 (February 28, 1997): 21–34, www.icrc.org/web/eng/siteeng0.nsf/htmlall/57JNFL.

85 *The words the court used:* Ibid.

86 *a conversation I had with George Steiner:* Author interview; Ron Rosenbaum, *Explaining Hitler* (Random House: New York, 1998), pp. 300–18.

86 *"breaks the reinsurance on human hope":* Ibid., p. 314.

87 *a real doomsday machine buried:* See chapter 5.

## 5. BRUCE BLAIR: THE DOOMSDAY DISCOVERY
### AND THE REAL DANGER

PAGE

88 *P. D. Smith, a British Cold War historian:* P. D. Smith, *Doomsday Men: The Real Dr. Strangelove and the Dream of the Superweapon* (London: Penguin, 2007).

88 *a 1993 piece:* William J. Broad, "Russia Has 'Doomsday' Machine, U.S. Expert Says," *New York Times,* October 8, 1993, www.nytimes.com/ 1993/10/08/world/russia-has-doomsday-machine-us-expert-says .html.

88 *my 2007* Slate *essay:* Ron Rosenbaum, "The Return of the Doomsday Machine?," *Slate,* August 31, 2007, www.slate.com/id/2173108.

88 *David Hoffman's scrupulous 2009 chronicle:* David E. Hoffman, *The Dead Hand* (New York: Doubleday, 2009).

89 *In Peter George's Novelization of the Film:* Quoted in Smith, *Doomsday Men,* p. 434.

89 *Leo Szilard, the Nobel Prize–winning:* Edward R. Landa and John R. Nimmo, "Soil History: The Life and Scientific Contributions of Lyman J. Briggs," *Soil Science Society of American Journal* 67, no. 3 (May/June 2003): 681–93, http://soil.scijournals.org/cgi/reprint/67/3/681.

89 *Szilard came up with the notion:* Smith, *Doomsday Men,* p. 21.

90 *he had a unique career arc:* Author interview.

90 *what Blair had told Smith:* Smith, *Doomsday Men,* p. 434.

91 *In his 1993* New York Times *piece:* "Russia's Doomsday Machine," *New York Times,* Oct. 8, 1993.

93 *After studying and critiquing the flaws:* Michael R. Gordon "Tug of War, with a Twist, on Secrets," *New York Times,* May 15, 1986, p. B14, www .nytimes.com/1986/05/15/us/tug-of-war-with-a-twist-on-secrets .html. See also "Our Nation's Nuclear Warning System: Will It Work if We Need It?", Testimony of Bruce G. Blair before the House Committee on Government Operations, 99th Congress, September 26, 1985, http://armedservices.house.gov/comdocs/testimony/105thcongress/ 97-3-13Blair.htm.

93 *"I had a design bureau":* Author interview.

94 *Anna Politkovskaya, whose book* Putin's Russia: www.annapolitkovskaya .com/putinsrussia001.htm.

94 *Soviet style of jailing:* For jailings, Ellen Barry, "Investigation of Jail Death Is Criticized in Russia," *New York Times,* April 23, 2010, p. A4, www.nytimes.com/2010/04/23/world/europe/23moscow.html?scp= 2&sq=Ellen%20Barry&st=cse.

96 *"The main problem with command and control":* Statement of Bruce Blair to Government Operations Subcommittee.

99 *Rivet Joint:* www.fas.org/irp/program/collect/rivet_joint.htm.

99 *He cites the Chinese interception:* James Hasik, "The Crash of the Aerial Common Sensor," January 23, 2006, www.slideshare.net/jhasik/the-crash-of-the-acs.

100 *Except we did, at least once:* Jeremi Suri, "The Nukes of October: Richard Nixon's Secret Plan to Bring Peace to Vietnam, *Wired,* February 25, 2008, www.wired.com/politics/security/magazine/16-03/ff_nuclearwar.

101 *"You cited the spoon-and-string":* Ron Rosenbaum, "The Subterranean World of the Bomb," *Harper's,* March 1978, p. 98.

103 *Blair brought to my attention:* Unedited draft of letter provided to author by Bruce Blair.

106 *Blair was the first: Bulletin of the Atomic Scientists* 53, no. 6 (November 1997): 23, http://books.google.com/books?id=vgwAAAAAMBAJ&printsec= frontcover&source=gbs_v2_summary_r&cad=0#v=onepage&q&f= false.

106 *electromagnetic pulses:* The problem of a high-altitude, nuclear airburst–generated electromagnetic pulse (EMP) continues to plague defense planners, particularly those concerned with nuclear command, control,

and communications. A July 22, 2004, report of the congressionally established Committee to Assess the Threat to the United States from Electromagnetic Pulse Attack concluded gloomily that there was no way to assess the degree of damage a high-altitude blast—which creates a sudden shock wave of highly charged electronic particles that impact on all metallic (and, obviously, electronic) devices on the surface of the planet beneath it. And that protective measures could only be tested by exploding a high-altitude nuclear weapon—thus in effect must go untested. The problem was first recognized in the 1960s and made widely public in a series by *New York Times* science reporter William Broad in a 1980 issue of *Science* magazine. The implications for this continuing unknown factor on all the highly calibrated targeting plans of every nuclear power are obvious: nobody knows whether any given pattern of launches will be disabled completely or to what extent by EMP: Dr. William R. Graham, Chairman, Commission to Assess the Threat to the United States from Electromagnetic Pulse Attack, www .iwar.org.uk/iwar/resources/emp/07-22-2004-emp-hearing.htm.

107  *"Spelled NEACP":* Walter J. Boyne, *Beyond the Wild Blue: A History of the U.S. Air Force, 1947–1997,* 2nd ed. (New York: St. Martin's, 2007), p. 299.

109  *in 1998 the Navy came across:* Joe St. Saveur, "Cyber War, Cyber Terrorism and Cyber Espionage, v1.2," PowerPoint presentation at IT Security Conference, Fargo North Dakota, October 21–22, 2008, slide 15, www.uoregon.edu/~joe/cyberwar/cyberwar.ppt.

## 6. COLONEL YARYNICH'S "100 NUCLEAR WARS" AND THE APOCALYPSE EQUATION

PAGE

111  *author of a remarkable book:* Valery E. Yarynich, *C3: Nuclear Command, Control, Cooperation* (Washington, D.C.: Center for Defense Information, 2003), www.cdi.org/program/document.cfm?documentid=1503&pro gramID=32&from_page=../friendlyversion/printversion.cfm.

112  *the sort of secrets that spies:* See for instance the diagram and description of the Russian nuclear command structure on pp. 151–58.

112  *the details about PERIMETR: C3,* "fig.37 PERIMETR system," p. 158.

112  *His intent at the time:* Author interview, December 9, 2009.

112  *That fear of decapitation:* David E. Hoffman, *The Dead Hand* (New York: Doubleday, 2009), pp. 61–63.

113  *Operation Able Archer 83:* William Bennett Jones, "Operation RYAN, Able Archer 83, and Miscalculation: The War Scare of 1983," for the Univer-

sity of California, Santa Barbara, International Graduate Student Conference on the Cold War, April 2008, www.wilsoncenter.org/topics/docs/08%2004%2001%20Nathan%20Jones%20Operation%20RYAN%20Able% 20Archer%2083%20and%20Miscalculation%20IGSCCW.pdf.

113 *David Hoffman asserts:* Hoffman, *The Dead Hand*, p. 95.

113 *Here is where Colonel Yarynich:* Author interview.

113 *How do you estimate the probability:* F. S. Nyland, "Some Potential Risks at Lower Levels of Strategic Nuclear Weapon Arsenals," June 1998, U.S. Arms Control and Disarmament Agency, Washington, D.C., www.dtic.mil/cgi-bin/GetTRDoc?AD=ADA348992&Location=U2&doc=GetTRDoc.pdf; Bruce G. Blair, *The Logic of Accidental Nuclear War* (Washington, D.C.: Brookings Institution, 1993).

116 *This new plan:* "100 Nuclear Wars," unpublished draft given to author.

118 *the greater issue is de-alerting:* Ron Rosenbaum, "A Real Nuclear Option for the Nominees: Averting Accidental Nuclear War in Two Easy Steps," *Slate*, April 9, 2008, www.slate.com/id/2191104.

119 *In Phase 1 of Blair's approach, he recommends:* Blair quoted in ibid.

119 *In addition, Blair suggests:* Ibid.

120 *In Phase 2 of Blair's de-alerting proposals:* Ibid.

120 *Blair's third and fourth phase proposals:* Bruce G. Blair, *De-Alerting Strategic Forces* (Washington, D.C.: Brookings Institution Press, 2004).

121 *The first echelon would be:* Yarynich, "100 Nuclear Wars," p. 2.

125 *he became famous in tech circles:* Michael Graham Richard, "The Risks of Failure of Nuclear Deterrence," online post, November 26, 2008, http://michaelgr.com/2008/11/26/risks-failure-nuclear-deterrence.

125 *He constructed his mathematical model:* Dr. Martin E. Hellman, "Risk Analysis of Nuclear Deterrence," in *The Bent of Tau Beta Pi* (Stanford University, Spring 2008), p. 15, http://nuclearrisk.org/paper.pdf.

126 *"During the next century that failure rate":* www.nuclearrisk.org/email 26explained.php.

127 *"well above the level":* Ibid.

128 Scientific American's *recent estimate: Scientific American*, "Laying Odds on the Apocalypse," August 20, 2010.

128 *Jonathan Tepperman:* Jonathan Tepperman, "Why Obama Should Learn to Love the Bomb," *Newsweek*, September 7, 2009, www.newsweek.com/id/214248.

128 *How Confident Should a Nuclear Optimist Be?:* Martin Hellman, "How Confident Should a Nuclear Optimist Be?," Nuclear Age Peace Foundation, September 9, 2009, www.wagingpeace.org/articles/2009/09/09_hellman_nuclear_optimism.php.

130 *a citation from a Russian scientist:* Yuri Zamoskin quoted in "Defusing the Nuclear Threat: A Primer, http://nuclearrisk.org/4change.php.

131 *Harvard's Graham Allison:* Graham Allison, "Nuclear Disorder: Surveying Atomic Threats," *Foreign Affairs* 89, no. 1 (January/February 2010), www.foreignaffairs.com/articles/65732/graham-allison/nuclear-disorder; http://belfercenter.ksg.harvard.edu/experts/199/graham_allison.html.

## 7. "THE ASHES ARE STILL WARM": THE SECOND HOLOCAUST, ISRAEL, AND THE MORALITY OF NUCLEAR RETALIATION

PAGE

132 *"History teaches us":* Shimon Peres to Jeffrey Goldberg, "Shimon Peres on Iran: Overreaction Is Better than Under-Reaction," *The Atlantic*, May 6, 2009, www.theatlantic.com/international/archive/2009/05/shimon-peres-on-iran-overreaction-is-better-than-underreaction/17191/.

134 *2012–2013 being the most mentioned:* See Jeffrey Lewis, "Iran's Centrifuge Operations," April 6, 2007, www.armscontrolwonk.com, www.armscontrolwonk.com/1452/irans-centrifuge-operations.

134 *Iran's Ayatollah Ali Akbar Hashemi Rafsanjani has talked:* Alan Dershowitz, "Why the U.S. and Israel Can't Attack Iran," *The Spectator*, April 22, 2006, http://israel-palestina.info/modules.php?name=News&file=print&sid=145.

135 *from Karl Marx's* Eighteenth Brumaire of Louis Bonaparte: www.gutenberg.org/etext/1346.

135 *book by the historian Jeffrey Herf:* Jeffrey Herf, *Nazi Propaganda for the Arab World* (New Haven: Yale University Press, 2009), http://yalepress.yale.edu/yupbooks/book.asp?isbn=9780300145793.

135 *Herf had discovered:* Paul Berman, *The Flight of the Intellectuals* (New York: Melville House, 2010), pp. 67–71, www.mhpbooks.com/book.php?id=233.

136 *When I asked the co-author:* Author interview.

136 *Historians such as Michael Oren:* www.zionism-israel.com/dic/6daywar.htm.

136 *In 2007, Benny Morris published:* Benny Morris: "This Holocaust Will Be Different," *Jerusalem Post*, January 18, 2007.

137 *Another key difference:* www.thememriblog.org/blog_personal/en/14018.htm.

138 *Yusef al-Qaradawi, praying to Allah:* "Sheik Yusuf al-Qaradawi: Theologian of Terror," Anti-Defamation League, posted February 2, 2009, updated

August 4, 2009, www.adl.org/main_Arab_World/al_Qaradawi_report_20041110.

138 *the founding charter of Hamas:* "The Day of Judgement will not come about until Muslims fight the Jews (killing the Jews), when the Jew will hide behind stones and trees. The stones and trees will say O Muslims, O Abdulla, there is a Jew behind me, come and kill him. Only the Gharkad tree would not do that because it is one of the trees of the Jews": www .bigpicweblog.com/exp/index.php/weblog/comments/an_examination_ of_the_hamas_charter_by_two_un_non_governmen tal_organization/.

138 *Ayatollah Ali Khamenei is also clear:* American Israel Public Affairs Committee, "Words of Hate: Iran's Escalating Threats," March 16, 2009, www.aipac.org/Publications/AIPACAnalysesMemos/AIPAC_Memo_ Words_of_Hate_Iran.pdf.

139 *Its key personnel were prosecuted:* Michael Bazyler, in course syllabus, Fall 2008, Whittier Law School, Costa Mesa, California, p. 71; www .michaelbazyler.com/downloads/HGAL-Reader-Spring-2008.doc.

139 *Rome Treaty on Preventing Genocide:* Treaty of the International Criminal Court, the U.N; Dr. Gregory Stanton, "Preventing Genocide" (PowerPoint presentation, slide 46), www.unitar.org/ny/sites/default/ files/Preventing%20Genocide%20by%20Greg%20Stanton,%20Geno cide%20Watch(1).pdf.

140 *"A Referral of Iranian President Ahmadinejad":* www.icejcanada.org/index .asp?pid=50&spid=view&linkid=7.

140 *"who had escaped the Nazi":* Anshel Pfeffer "Comparing Iran to Nazis Harms Israel," *Ha'aretz,* June 12, 2009, http://haaretz.com/jewish-world/news/ anshel-pfeffer-comparing-iran-to-nazis-harms-israel-1.277792.

141 *he likened PLO leader Yasser Arafat:* Tom Segev, translated by Haim Watzman, *The Seventh Million: The Israelis and the Holocaust* (New York: Henry Holt, 1991), www.jstor.org/stable/2624603.

141 *Twenty-five years later, Prime Minister Benjamin Netanyahu:* "Netanyahu's '1938' Speech," *Jewish Current Issues,* posted November 16, 2006, http://jpundit.typepad.com/jci/2006/11/netanyahus_1938.html.

142 *study of a possible nonnuclear Israeli attack:* Anthony Cordesman, "Study on a Possible Israeli Strike on Iran's Nuclear Development Facilities," Center for Strategic and International Studies, March 14, 2009, http:// csis.org/files/media/csis/pubs/090316_israelistrikeiran.pdf.

143 *nuclear affairs that Thomas Powers:* Thomas Powers, *Heisenberg's War: The Secret History of the German Bomb* (New York: Alfred A. Knopf, 1993).

143 *Philip Roth's 1993 novel:* Philip Roth, *Operation Shylock: A Confession* (New York: Simon & Schuster, 1993).

144 *when I quoted it:* Ron Rosenbaum, "Second Holocaust: Roth's Invention Isn't Novelistic," *New York Observer,* April 4, 2002; reprinted in Ron Rosenbaum, ed., *Those Who Forget the Past: The Question of Anti-Semitism* (New York: Random House, 2004), pp. 170–77.

144 *"The meanings of the Holocaust":* Roth's speech quoted in Rosenbaum, ed., *Those Who Forget the Past,* p. 171.

145 *Thus on the talk show* Charlie Rose: A panel discussion about global anti-Semitism with guest host David Remnick, broadcast July 12, 2002, www.charlierose.com/view/interview/2461; www.charlierose.com/guest/view/663.

145 *a columnist for the* New York Times: Clyde Haberman, "NYC; Among Jews, Urge to Panic Is Premature," *New York Times,* June 18, 2002, www.nytimes.com/2002/06/18/nyregion/nyc-among-jews-urge-to-panic-is-premature.html?scp=1&sq=among%20jews%20urge%20to%20panic&st=cse. Haberman's geographic mischaracterization was initially repeated then corrected in subsequent editions, by the authors of *The Israel Lobby* (John Mearsheimer and Stephen Walt, New York: Farrar, Straus & Giroux, 2007).

145 *Cynthia Ozick takes up the story:* Quoted in the Afterword to Rosenbaum, ed., *Those Who Forget the Past,* pp. 606–7.

146 *"In a [2003]* New York Times Magazine *piece:* Ian Buruma, "How to Talk About Israel," *New York Times Magazine,* August 31, 2003.

146 *philosopher Berel Lang was thinking:* Explaining Hitler, 220.

147 *The Supreme Court just reaffirmed:* David G. Savage, "Justices Leave Voting Rights Act Intact," *Seattle Times,* June 23, 2009, http://seattletimes.nwsource.com/html/nationworld/2009370902_scotus23.html.

147 *Leon Wieseltier, who called concern:* Wieseltier, "Against Ethnic Panic," reprinted from *The New Republic* in Rosenbaum, ed. *Those Who Forget The Past,* pp. 178–88.

148 *2006 Tehran Holocaust deniers conference:* "Israel Assailed at Holocaust Conference," CBS News, Tehran, Iran, December 12, 2006, www.cbsnews.com/stories/2006/12/12/world/main2250002.shtm.

148 *David Perlmutter in an op ed piece:* "The Samson Option," *Los Angeles Times,* April 7, 2002.

149 *"You're asking something new":* E-mail to author.

150 *Berel Lang, one of the few academics:* In Berel Lang, *Post-Holocaust: Interpretation, Misinterpretation, and the Claims of History* (Bloomington: Indiana University Press, 2004).

150 *Some Jews did attempt: Newsweek,* book excerpt, *The Avengers* by Rich Cohen, September 2, 2000, www.accessmylibrary.com/coms2/summary_0286-28241758_ITM.

150 *I gave a talk to:* Yale Interdisciplinary Initiative for the Study of Anti-Semitism, newsletter 1, no. 9.

151 *the* Jerusalem Post *printed:* Yaakov Katz, "In Possible Signal to Iran, Israel Sends Subs Through Suez Canal," *Jerusalem Post,* July 3, 2009.

152 *Michael Walzer, the author:* Michael Walzer, *Just and Unjust Wars: A Moral Argument with Historical Illustrations,* 4th ed. (New York: Basic Books, 2006). *Just and Unjust Wars* examines the moral issues surrounding military theory, war crimes, and the spoils of war, http://books.google.com/books?id=kZnx7WVJbeUC&printsec=frontcover&source=gbs_v2_summary_r&cad=0#v=onepage&q&f=false.

152 *he felt he was entering:* Author interview.

153 *his book on idolatry:* Moshe Halbertal and Avishai Margalit, *Idolatry* (Cambridge: Harvard University Press, 1998), www.hup.harvard.edu/catalog/HALIDO.html.

154 *the following report appeared on a Web site:* "Israel's German-Made Dolphin Submarines Have Been Heavily Modified," October 4, 2009, DEBKA-file, http://worldnewsandpolitics.wordpress.com/2009/10/04/sraels-german-made-dolphin-submarines-have-been-heavily-modified/.

155 *"Here was a supreme emergency":* Walzer, *Just and Unjust Wars,* pp. 259–60.

156 *"Should I wager this determinate crime":* Ibid., p. 260.

157 *"such an experiment was a double crime":* Ibid., 268.

158 *The entire notion of an "esoteric strategy":* Henry Kissinger, *Diplomacy* (New York: Simon & Schuster, 1994).

161 *"Israel would not be the first":* Michael I. Karpin, *The Bomb in the Basement: How Israel Went Nuclear and What That Means for the World* (New York: Simon & Schuster, 2006).

161 *Project Daniel:* www.middleeastexplorer.com/Israel/Project-Daniel.

163 *quite real in 1973:* Michael Broyden, "The Third Temple's Holy of Holies: Israel's Nuclear Weapons," The Counterproliferation Papers, Future Warfare Series No. 2, USAF Counterproliferation Center, Air War College, Air University, Maxwell Air Force Base, Alabama, September 1999, www.fas.org/nuke/guide/israel/nuke/farr.htm.

## 8. IRAN: "THE ENIGMATIC BOX" AND THE NIE

PAGE

166 *the three elements of a nuclear weapon:* "Nuclear Weapon Design," www.fas.org/nuke/intro/nuke/design.htm.

166 *Leon Panetta reported: This Week* transcript, ABC News, June 28, 2010.

166 *"notional journey of the phantom flotilla": London Sunday Times,* May 30, 2010, www.timesonline.co.uk/world/middleeast/article7148555.ece.

167 *those who believed or misread:* David E. Sanger and William J. Broad, "U.S. Sees an Opportunity to Press Iran on Nuclear Fuel, *New York Times,* January 3, 2010, p. A1. See also http://washingtontimes.com/news/ 2010/jan/19/review-says-iran-never-halted-nuke-work-in-2003/; and Background Briefing with Senior U.S. Officials on Syria's Nuclear Reactor and North Korea's Involvement, April 24, 2008; Officer of the Director of National Intelligence, www.dni-gov/interviews/20080424_ interview.pdf; author e-mail exchange with Siobahn Gorman, national security correspondent for the *Wall Street Journal.*

168 *have been quietly pursuing:* www.tabletmag.com/news-and-politics/30847/ war-games/.

168 Red Cloud at Dawn: Michael D. Gordin, *Red Cloud at Dawn: Truman, Stalin, and the End of the Atomic Monopoly* (New York: Farrar, Straus & Giroux, 2009).

169 *Syria first denied:* Hugh Naylor, "Syria Tells Journalists Israeli Raid Did Not Occur," *New York Times,* October 11, 2007, www.nytimes.com/2007/ 10/11/world/middleeast/11syria.html?em&ex=1192248000&en= 5a807a1973909288&ei=5087%0A; found at www.globalsecurity.org/ military/world/war/070906-airstrike.htm.

169 *an informal Israeli-Syrian deal:* "Syrian Air Defenses Fire on IAF Planes," CBS News, September 6, 2007, http://israel.indymedia.org/he/arti cle/2007/9/syrian-air-defenses-fire-iaf-planes.

169 *out of the blue, North Korea: Jerusalem Post,* "Bolton: Why Would North Korea Protest Syria Raid?," September 17, 2007.

169 *a North Korean freighter docking:* "That Israeli Raid on Syria: A 'Clear Message for Iran'?," September 17, 2007, www.hyscience.com/archives/ 2007/09/that_israeli_ra.php.

170 *Hersh wrote a* New Yorker *piece:* Seymour Hersh, "A Strike in the Dark," *The New Yorker,* February 11, 2008.

170 *Everyone in the know went silent until April 2008:* See "Background Briefing with Senior U.S. Officials on Syria's Covert Nuclear Reactor and North Korea's Involvement," April 24, 2008, www.dni.gov/interviews/ 20080424_interview.pdf.

171 *a "Calder-Hall" model:* Office of the Director of National Intelligence, briefing.

171 *"PSYCHO CABBIE": The News of the World,* June 6, 2010, p. 1.

173 *found evidence in soil samples:* Syria Not Answering IAEA's Questions," Institute for Science and International Security, June 5, 2009, http:// isis-online.org/uploads/isis-reports/documents/Syria_IAEA_Report_ Analysis_5June2009.pdf.

174 *I was reminded of something:* Phone conversation with author, 1978.

174 *The emphasis on the North Korean partnership:* David E. Sanger and Peter
    Baker, "Obama Limits When U.S. Would Use Nuclear Arms," *New York
    Times,* April 6, 2010, p. A1, www.nytimes.com/2010/04/06/world/
    06arms.html.

181 *The whole "green light" rhetoric:* Jon Taplin, "Did Bush Greenlight an
    Israeli Attack on Iran?," June 7, 2008, http://jontaplin.com/2008/06/
    07/did-bush-greenlight-an-israeli-attack-on-iran/.

183 *Two years later the degree of cooperation:* "Iran's Nuclear Program: What
    Is Known and Unknown," The Heritage Foundation, www.heritage
    .org/.../Iran-s-Nuclear-Program-What-Is-Known-and-Unknown.

185 *"estimative language":* "Build New or Buy Old?," November 24, 2008,
    www.armscontrolwonk.com/2109/build-new-or-buy-old. See also
    "Saying One Thing and Doing Another: A Look Back at Nearly 60
    Years of Estimative Language (Original Research)," May 19, 2008,
    http://sourcesandmethods.blogspot.com/2008/05/saying-one-thing-
    and-doing-another-look.html.

197 *I had to check my perceptions:* Author interview.

197 *The* New York Times *has reported that Israel's:* David E. Sanger, "U.S.
    Rejected Aid for Israeli Raid on Iranian Nuclear Site," *New York Times,*
    January 11, 2009, p. A1, www.nytimes.com/2009/01/11/washington/
    11iran.html.

198 *in January 2009, the* Wall Street Journal *reported:* Peter Fritsch, "Chi-
    nese Evade U.S. Sanctions on Iran," *Wall Street Journal,* January 4,
    2010, Asia Business Section, p. A1, http://online.wsj.com/article/
    SB126256626983914249.html.

198 *Robert Gates, who was Bush's secretary of defense:* Sanger, "U.S. Rejected
    Israeli Request to Aid Attack on Iran," p. A1.

199 *a professional war gamer:* www.sourcewatch.org/index.php?title=Sam_
    Gardiner.

199 *The number of nuclear warheads:* www.globalsecuritynewswire.org/gsn/
    nw_2408php.

200 *What he found was a tangled web:* Author interview.

200 *First the system of shared control:* "Key Issues: Nuclear Weapons: Issues:
    NATO Nuclear Policies," Project of the Nuclear Age Peace Foundation,
    www.nuclearfiles.org/menu/key-issues/nuclear-weapons/issues/
    nato-nuclear-policies/index.htm.

201 *NATO had a "first use" policy:* R. Jeffrey Smith, "NATO Again Rejects 'No
    First Use' Policy," *Washington Post,* June 28, 1990.

202 *in the midst of the fighting in Georgia:* Ronald Asmus, *A Little War That
    Shook the World"* (New York: Palgrave Macmillan, 2010).

202 *SS-26, he explained, is the NATO designation:* http://defense-update.com/products/i/iskander.htm.

203 *James Baker handed a letter to Tariq Aziz:* Frontline: "The Gulf War: Oral History: James Baker," www.pbs.org/wgbh/pages/frontline/gulf/oral/baker/1.html.

204 *This was his reply:* E-mail to author from Elbridge Colby.

205 *The SS-26s have surfaced more than once:* Martin Sieff, "Russian Iskander Missiles Ready to Roll," UPI, November 24, 2008, www.spacewar.com/reports/Russian_Iskander_Missiles_Ready_To_Roll_999.html.

206 *The Bush plan was thankfully revoked:* Lars Olberg, "European Missile Defense Tour," March 7, 2010, http://missilemonitor.wordpress.com/.

206 *"the SS-26 movement to Kaliningrad":* Associated Press, in post on blog, https://dogbrothers.com/phpBB2/index.php?topic=1677.0.

207 *war game Gardiner ran for* The Atlantic: "*The Atlantic* Revisits an Iran War Game," www.safehaven.com/forums-17700.htm; James Fallows, "The Nuclear Power Beside Iraq," *The Atlantic,* May 2006, www.theatlantic.com/magazine/archive/2006/05/the-nuclear-power-beside-iraq/4819/2/?.

207 *In that war game, the conclusion:* Author interview with Colonel Sam Gardiner.

## 9. ENDGAME

PAGE

209 *the first Obama administration Nuclear Posture Review:* http://docs.google.com/viewer?a=v&q=cache:ar_fnmF38QoJ:www.defense.gov/npr/docs/2010%2520nuclear%2520posture%2520review%2520report.pdf+nuclear+posture+review+report+February+18,+2010&hl=en&gl=us&pid=bl&srcid=ADGEEShJRFLbdkd8RqYF4U2hHxMtyOQkWJ50PcfK_47YrRvKljlrteN4EbHslWwvcYq4MYKfekL5TUc82cj6O1B_BQut64HQLhsK6mfyHxE2n26SVjLCcXR4J10GHwULGHWdfOEPV9e&sig=AHIEtbTPKU6-aDJveX5RzNYj3s8_BrSfbA.

209 *"A status quo document," Bruce Blair told:* Jonathan Weisman and Peter Spiegel, "U.S. Keeps First-Strike Nuclear Strategy," *Wall Street Journal,* April 6, 2010, http://online.wsj.com/article/SB10001424052702304620304575166263632513790.html.

209 *"Because of quirks in counting":* Jonathan Weisman and Peter Spiegel, "After Arms Pact, a Push to Ratify," *Wall Street Journal,* Europe News, April 9, 2010, http://online.wsj.com/article/SB10001424052702304198004575171203223830386.html.

210 *nothing at all was done to change:* Press release, Union of Concerned Scientists, "NPR Will Test President Obama on Transforming Nuclear Policy," April 5, 2010, www.ucsusa.org/news/press_release/npr-will-test-president-obama-on-nuclear-policy-0368.html.

210 *In the Introduction to the NPR:* Introduction, "Maximizing Presidential Decision Time," p. x.

210 *"The NPR concluded that the current alert posture":* Ibid.

210 *"efforts should continue to further diminish":* Ibid.

211 *The Obama defenders have argued:* Julian Borger, "START Signed, Sealed, Not Yet Delivered," guardian.co.uk, April 7, 2010, www.guardian.co .uk/world/julian-borger-global-security-blog/2010/apr/08/start-treaty-prague.

211 *And there were those who said:* William J. Perry and George P. Shultz, "How to Build on the Start Treaty," *New York Times*, op-ed, April 11, 2010, www.nytimes.com/2010/04/11/opinion/11shultz.htm.

211 *On the other hand there were those:* The Heritage Foundation, "The START Treaty: Undermining National Security," April 5, 2010, www.heritage .org/Research/Factsheets/The-START-Treaty-Undermining-National-Security.

211 *Iran was boasting of a new generation:* "Iran Builds New Generation of Centrifuges—Nuclear Chief," RIA Novosti, Moscow, April 9, 2010, http://en.rian.ru/world/20100409/158502207.html.

211 *Israel announced a stepped-up program:* "Deputy Defense Minister: Tel Aviv Will Be Enemy's Main Target," Arutz Sheva, April 7, 2010, www .israelnationalnews.com/News/News.aspx/136891.

212 *Barack Obama, wrote an essay:* William J. Broad and David E. Sanger, "Obama's Youth Shaped His Nuclear-Free Vision," *New York Times*, July 5, 2009, p. A1, www.nytimes.com/2009/07/05/world/05nuclear.html.

212 *that ol' peacenik Henry Kissinger:* George P. Shultz, William J. Perry, Henry A. Kissinger, and Sum Nunn, "A World Free of Nuclear Weapons," *Wall Street Journal*, January 4, 2007, p. A15; reprinted, Friends Committee on National Legislation, www.fcnl.org/issues/item.php?item_id= 2252&issue_id.

214 *I had a brief exchange with him:* Author interview.

214 Nuclear Tipping Point: Film produced by National Security Project, www.nationalsecurityproject.org.

218 *an agonized recantation:* Peregrine Worsthorne, "The Unanswered Question About the Cold War," *The Spectator*, September 4, 1996.

219 *"I felt important," he said:* Author interview.

219 *"When I wrote the article [in 1997] with [Sam] Nunn":* Bruce Blair and

Sam Nunn, "From Nuclear Deterrence to Mutual Safety: As Russia's Arsenal Crumbles, It's Time to Act," *Washington Post*, June 22, 1997, www.cdi.org/aboutcdi/bblair_publications.html.

220 *referring to Strategic Command and Control:* Bruce Blair, *Strategic Command and Control* (Washington, D.C.: Brookings Institution, 1985).

220 *Nixon was drunk during the Yom Kippur whirlwind:* "A Conversation with Author Alistair Horne," *Charlie Rose*, July 7, 2009, www.charlierose.com/view/interview/10457.

221 *Blair portrays McNamara as shocked:* Confirmed by exchange with Robert McNamara relayed to author by Errol Morris, director of *The Fog of War: Eleven Lessons from the Life of Robert McNamara*, from interview.

227 Abolishing Nuclear Weapons, *a 130-page study:* George Perkovich and James M. Acton, *Abolishing Nuclear Weapons* (London: Routledge/International Institute for Strategic Studies, 2008).

227 *Bruce Blair's Global Zero Initiative:* "Presidents Obama and Medvedev, U.N. Secretary General Ban Among Leaders to Announce Support for the Global Zero Summit, www.globalzero.org/.

228 *In a review of the Acton-Perkovich pro-abolition book:* Review essay by Elbridge Colby of George Perkovich and James Acton, *Abolishing Nuclear Weapons*, Adelphi Paper No. 396, International Institute for Strategic Studies, London, www.docstoc.com/docs/25708946/A-Response-to-Elbridge-Colby.

228 *Reagan-Bush–era nuclear arms negotiator:* R. Jeffrey Smith, "Ambassador Chosen as Arms Negotiator," *Washington Post*, February 4, 1989, http://news.google.com/newspapers?nid=1755&dat=19890204&id=vjEcAAAAIBAJ&sjid=1nkEAAAAIBAJ&pg=5155,4028365.

229 *"I'm just a tool of Bruce Blair:* Author interview.

229 *Global Zero's four-step blueprint:* "Global Zero Action Plan," Global Zero Commission, February 2010, http://static.globalzero.org/files/docs/GZAP_6.0.pdf.

229 *one of Medvedev's top nuclear advisers:* "Political, Military Leaders from China, India, Pakistan, and Britain Respond to Obama Prague Speech: All Nuclear Powers Should Commit to Multi-Lateral Negotiations for Elimination of All Nuclear Weapons," Global Zero Commission press release, April 6, www.globalzero.org/en/global-zero-press-release-april-6.

229 *an anti-Zero op-ed:* John Hughes, "A Nuclear-Free World? Not Yet," *Christian Science Monitor*, June 18, 2009, www.csmonitor.com/Commentary/Opinion/2009/0618/p09s01-coop.html.

234 *nuclear umbrella, more formally called:* NTI: Nuclear Threat Initiative: Non

Proliferation Treaty, tutorial, www.nti.org/h_learnmore/npttutorial/glossary.html.

237 *Burke Documents: National Security Archives:* "How Much Is Enough?: The U.S. Navy and 'Finite Deterrence,'" William Burr, ed., National Security Archive Electronic Briefing Book #275, May 1, 2009, www.gwu.edu/~nsarchiv/nukevault/ebb275/index.htm.

238 *Heavily redacted parts of the sacred SIOP:* "Released SIOP Histories Point to Nuclear Overkill Plans," National Security Archive Electronic Briefing Book #236, www.hsdl.org/hslog/?=node/3784.

238 *"the finger on the trigger":* Ron Rosenbaum, "The Subterranean World of the Bomb," *Harper's,* March 1978, p. 87.

239 *the chilling phrase "world holocaust":* National Security Archive Electronic Briefing Book #275.

239 *euphemisms like "maximum damage expectancy":* Janne E. Nolan, *An Elusive Consensus: Nuclear Weapons and American Security After the Cold War* (Washington, D.C.: Brookings Institution, 1999), http://books.google.com/books?id=aXdI14wY-RUC&printsec=frontcover#v=onepage&q&f=false.

239 *Nuclear Vault Electronic Briefing Book #275:* National Security Archive Electronic Briefing Book #275.

240 *the word "holocaust" as in "nuclear holocaust":* Author e-mail exchange with Jesse Sheidlower.

241 *his Navy nickname "31 Knots Burke":* David M. Abshire Lecture, "The Inimitable Admiral Arleigh '31 Knots' Burke: Lessons for Leadership and Strategy Today," Washington, D.C., January 29, 2010, http://csis.org/event/inimitable-admiral-arleigh-31-knots-burke-lessons-leadership-and-strategy-today.

242 *"Confidential Memorandum for All Flag officers":* National Security Electronic Briefing Book #275.

243 *Robert McNamara famously opined:* Excerpt on moving towards discriminate deterrence from Wohlstetter's book, March 14, 2009, www.albertwohlstetter.com/archives/excerpt_on_moving_towards_discriminate_deterrence_from_wohlstetter_books_introduction.html.

243 *Or as Burke put it in that powerful paragraph:* "Confidential Memo to all Flag Officers." National Security Archive Electronic Briefing Book, #275.

245 The Nuclear Taboo: The United States and the Non-Use of Nuclear Weapons Since 1945: Nina Tannenwald, *The Nuclear Taboo: The United States and the Non-Use of Nuclear Weapons Since 1945,* Cambridge Studies in International Relations, no. 87 (New York: Cambridge Univer-

sity Press, 1987, www.cambridge.org/catalogue/catalogue.asp?isbn= 9780521524285.

249 *As* Time *reported the incident:* "An Amazing Article in *Time* Magazine," *Defusing the Nuclear Threat,* March 1, 2009, http://nuclearrisk.org/ email11.php.

249 *was put forth forcefully recently:* Keir Lieber and Daryl Press, "The Nukes We Need: Preserving the American Deterrent," *Foreign Affairs* 88, no. 6 (November/December 2009), pp. 39–51.

251 *But if Hiroshima is viewed through the prism:* http://herseyhiroshima.com/ hiro.php; www.librarything.com/work/45205/editions/.

251 *Hersey's* New Yorker *reportage:* John Hersey in an article filling the entire August 31, 1946, issue of *the New Yorker,* presented his account of the bombing of Hiroshima, http://herseyhiroshima.com/hiro.php.

252 The Day After: "Fallout from *The Day After:* The Impact of a TV Film on Attitudes," *Journal of Applied Social Psychology* 19 (1989): 433–48, www .lrdc.pitt.edu/people/person-detail.php?id=43.

253 *made me rethink my own experience of Hiroshima:* Ron Rosenbaum, "Welcome to the Hotel Hiroshima: Has the Ground Zero of the Nuclear Age Become Too 'Normal'?," www.slate.com/id/2187282/.

256 *"In the coming years,"* Burke *wrote:* "Confidential Memo to All Flag Officers."

257 *the new Yasen-class Russian subs:* http://dutchintell.wordpress.com/2010/ 03/29/rfs-sarov-b-90-will-be-upgraded/.

257 *Hans Kristensen of the Federation of American Scientists:* Hans M. Kristensen, "From Counterforce to Minimal Deterrence: A New Nuclear Policy on the Path Toward Eliminating Nuclear Weapons," Occasional Paper No. 7, April 2009, Federation of American Scientists and the Natural Resources Defense Council, www.fas.org/pubs/_docs/occa sionalpaper7.pdf.

257 *Dr. Jeffrey Lewis of the New America Foundation:* Jeffrey Lewis, "Minimum Deterrence," *Bulletin of the Atomic Scientists* 64, no. 3 (July/August 2008), http://thebulletin.metapress.com/content/gj678n525m044026/.

# INDEX

Able Archer, Operation, 7, 113, 127, 232

*Abolishing Nuclear Weapons* (Acton and Perkovich), 227–28

Acton, James, 227–28

Ahmadinejad, Mahmoud, 137, 140

Allison, Graham, 5, 131

Al Qaeda, 16, 18, 29, 236

Alston, C. Donald, 63–67

Amar, Akhil Reed, 37

Andropov, Yuri, 7, 112–13

anti-ballistic missile (ABM) treaty, 55

Assad, Hafez al, 174

Aziz, Tariq, 203

Baker, James, 203

Ballistic Missile Defense (BMD), 12–13, 24, 27

Begin, Menachem, 140–41, 145–46

Belgium, 206–7

Bennett, Tim, 23

Beres, Louis René, 161–62

Berkowitz, Peter, 43, 79

Bhutto, Benazir, 17–18

bin Laden, Osama, 18

Blair, Bruce, 88–110, 218–32
    Burt's relationship with, 231–32
    on conventional weapons, 221–22
    on eliminating nuclear weapons,

    90, 95, 98, 218–22, 226–32
    on EMPs, 106–7
    letter to *Bulletin of the Atomic Scientists* of, 103–5
    on Looking Glass plane, 95, 100, 106–7
    on morality, 222–23
    NPRs and, 209
    on nuclear weapons command and control, 38, 53, 62, 90–98, 100–110, 119–20, 215–16, 218–26, 232, 234–35
    on PERIMETR, 88–92, 107
    on preventing accidental use of nuclear weapons, 119–21, 123
    on reconnaissance of Russia, 98–100
    SIOP and, 93, 97, 99, 222
    work in Russia of, 90, 93–94
    Yarynich's relationship with, 93–94, 110, 119
    on Yom Kippur War, 220–21

Bonner, Raymond, 16

Brookings Institution, 38, 90, 94, 96, 218

Brzezinski, Zbigniew, 6–7, 127

*Bulletin of the Atomic Scientists*, 103–5

Burke, Arleigh A., 239–44, 256–59

Burke documents, 237, 239–45, 259
    nuclear submarines and, 241–44, 256–57

Burke documents (*continued*)
  on nuclear weapons reduction,
     240, 256
  on retaliatory deterrence, 242–43
Burr, William, 237–39, 245, 247
Burt, Richard R., 228–36
  Blair's relationship with, 231–32
  Cold War and, 228, 232–33
  on eliminating nuclear weapons,
     228–35
  on reducing number of nuclear
     weapons, 231, 233–35
Buruma, Ian, 145–46
Bush, George H. W., 50, 120, 228
Bush, George W., 29, 119, 121, 198
  on conventional weapons, 14–15
  Georgia crisis and, 202–3
  Iran and, 9, 181
  missile defense systems and, 8–9,
     206
  normalizing nuclear weapons use
     and, 23–25
  NPR of, 23, 55, 209
  on nuclear weapons command
     and control, 34, 39
  Pakistan and, 16
  Syrian nuclear facility and, 182,
     185, 187, 191

Calder Hall nuclear reactors, 171,
     184, 190
Canada, 10
*Canterbury Tales* (Chaucer), 45
Carnegie Endowment for Interna-
     tional Peace, 5, 90, 218, 227
Carter, Jimmy, 6–7, 60, 246
Castro, Fidel, 6
Center for Strategic and Interna-
     tional Studies (CSIS), 21, 142
Central Intelligence Agency (CIA),
     6, 166, 173–74, 176, 204
  Syrian nuclear facility and, 170–
     71, 173, 182, 185

*Challenger* tragedy, 129–30
*Charlie Rose*, 145
Chaucer, Geoffrey, 45
Cheney, Dick, 16, 34
Chilton, Kevin P.:
  on eliminating nuclear weapons,
     51–52
  NPR and, 210–11
  on nuclear retaliation, 69–70, 210
  and nuclear weapons command
     and control, 44, 50, 52, 54,
     215
  at Qwest Center deterrence sym-
     posium, 50–52, 54, 69–70
China, 17, 24, 69, 77, 202–3
  cyber-warfare of, 23, 32–33
  eliminating nuclear weapons and,
     233, 235
  Iranian nuclear weapons program
     and, 198
  nuclear taboo and, 246–47
  nuclear weapons of, 14, 22–23,
     222
  Taiwan's relations with, 22, 227,
     235
  U.S. secret reconnaissance on, 99
Chon Chibu, 182
Churchill, Winston, 56, 155–56
Cirincione, Joseph, 29
Clinton, Bill, 16, 29, 212
Clinton, Hillary, 4, 53, 207, 266*n*
Colby, Elbridge "Bridge," 27
  on eliminating nuclear weapons,
     228
  on Georgia crisis, 204–5
Cold War, 1, 5–12, 45, 55, 131, 203,
     212–13, 222–23, 243–44, 260
  Burke documents and, 240–41
  Burt and, 228, 232–33
  close calls in, 5–8, 12, 74, 76,
     100, 113, 117–18, 127–28,
     130, 164, 220–21, 225–26,
     232, 247–48

eliminating nuclear weapons and, 213, 218, 233–34
end of, 24, 28, 30, 42, 94, 212, 215, 222
NATO's preemptive strike option and, 26–27
nuclear de-escalation after, 118
nuclear deterrence in, 24–27, 84
nuclear freeze movement and, 212
nuclear retaliation and, 49
nuclear taboo and, 246–47
nuclear war casualties and, 86
nuclear war games in, 199–202, 206–7
and nuclear weapons command and control, 32, 34, 42, 52, 57, 61, 65, 90, 96–97, 100, 103–4, 106, 120
"100 Nuclear Wars" plan and, 116, 123
PERIMETR and, 88
Russian strategic flights and, 9, 11
U.S. nuclear ambiguity and, 25
U.S. secret reconnaissance and, 99
Comprehensive Nuclear Test Ban treaty, 57, 214
Congress, U.S., 197, 205, 246, 277*n*
and nuclear weapons command and control, 34–35, 37–38, 46, 62, 90, 93, 96–98, 110, 216, 248
nuclear weapons treaties and, 13, 57, 211, 214
on surrender, 60–61
Syrian nuclear facility and, 170, 172, 182
Constitution, U.S., 33–34, 36–37, 39, 220
Cordesman, Anthony, 21
*Countdown to Zero*, 49

Cowen, Tyler, 73
*C3: Nuclear Command, Control, Cooperation* (Yarynich), 111–12, 118–19
Cuba, 11–12
Cuban Missile Crisis, 6, 12, 74, 76, 117–18, 164, 247
in Hellman's analysis, 127–28, 130
cyber-warfare, 23, 32–33, 110, 170

Daniel, Project, 161–62
*Day After, The*, 252
Dayan, Moshe, 163–64
de-alerting, 201, 219, 259
eliminating nuclear weapons and, 234–35
Nunn on, 215–17
"100 Nuclear Wars" plan and, 120–21
in preventing accidental use of nuclear weapons, 118–21
DEBKAfile, 154–55
Defence Ministry, British, 41–42
Defense Department, U.S., 21, 73–74, 171, 199, 238–39, 256
Alston and, 63, 66–67
Burke documents and, 242
Chinese cyber-warfare and, 23, 32–33
on conventional weapons, 14–15
eliminating nuclear weapons and, 29, 234
and invasions of Iraq, 203
on LEP, 57
on missile defense systems, 206
NPRs and, 209–11, 216
nuclear vault and, 239
on nuclear war casualties, 71, 76–77, 79–80
and nuclear weapons command and control, 32–33, 42, 46, 50, 53–54, 74, 84, 97–98, 103–6

Defense Department, U.S. (*continued*)
  nuclear weapons reductions and, 121
  Pakistani nuclear weapons and, 18
  Russian strategic flights and, 10
Defense Intelligence Agency (DIA), 23, 171
*Defense Week*, 97–98
Dobbs, Michael, 6, 247
doomsday devices:
  in *Dr. Strangelove*, 88–90, 92
  of Russia, *see* PERIMETR
*Doomsday Men* (Smith), 88, 90
*Dr. Strangelove*, 27, 36, 39, 48, 55, 59, 238, 251
  doomsday device in, 73, 88–90, 92
dual phenomenology, 54, 67–68, 112, 127, 256
Dulles, John Foster, 22

Eden, Lynn, 77
Egypt, 3, 21, 136, 163, 220
Einstein, Albert, 89, 143
Eisenhower, Dwight, 22, 84, 241, 247
electromagnetic pulses (EMPs), 106–7, 276n–77n
Ellsberg, Daniel, 71–84, 90, 164
  Hering and, 83–84
  on nuclear war casualties, 71–73, 75–81, 86–87
  on nuclear weapons command and control, 71, 74, 83–84
  Pentagon Papers leaked by, 71–72, 74–76
  at RAND, 73–74
  SIOP and, 74–76, 82
Energy Department, U.S., 56–57
estimative language, 184–86, 195
Europe, 22, 216, 230
  and fear of decapitation and surprise attack, 112–13

Holocaust and, 144–45, 149–50
Iranian nuclear weapons program and, 9, 192
missile defense systems in, 112, 116, 127, 205–6
nuclear war games and, 200–202, 207
nuclear weapons treaties and, 13
Russian strategic flights and, 10
U.S. nuclear ambiguity and, 25

fail-safe, 99–100, 240
  and nuclear weapons command and control, 31–32, 49, 61–63, 83
*Failsafe*, 48
FOGBANK Controversy, 57
France, 60, 78, 123, 130
  collision of nuclear submarine of, 248–49
  supreme emergencies and, 155–56
Frankel, Benjamin, 5

Gardiner, Sam, 199–204
  on Georgia crisis, 202–4
  nuclear war gaming of, 199–201, 206–7
Gat, Azar, 43
Gates, Robert, 29, 198, 210–11
George, Peter, 89
Georgia, 11, 27, 202–5, 235
Germany, 60, 89, 117, 130, 141, 146
  and extermination of Jews, 135–37
  Israeli nuclear submarines and, 21–22, 154–55
  NATO's preemptive strike option and, 26
  in nuclear war games, 201–2
  supreme emergencies and, 155–56
Giant Lance, Operation, 100

global warming, 81
Global Zero Initiative, 90, 227–31,
  233–35
Gordievsky, Oleg, 7, 113
Gordin, Michael, 168
*grenzsituation*, 130–31
*Guardian, The*, 25–26, 198

Hadley, Stephen, 202–5
hair-trigger alert, 52–54, 67–68, 74,
  110, 209, 215–17, 258
  Burke documents and, 240–41,
    243–44
  eliminating nuclear weapons and,
    216, 237
  NPR and, 210–11
  Nunn on, 215–16
  preventing accidents and, 118,
    120
Halbach, Mel, 40, 61
Halbertal, Moshe, 152–65
  on human nature, 164–65
  on IDF's ethics, 152, 158, 160,
    162
  nuclear deterrence and, 152–53,
    158
  on nuclear retaliation, 152, 155–
    56, 158–60, 162, 165
  on preemptive nuclear strikes,
    152, 155–56, 159–62, 164
  on second Holocaust, 136, 163
  on supreme emergencies, 152,
    155–57, 159–60, 163
  on Yom Kippur War, 163–64
Hamas, 134, 138–40
Hansen Collection, 238
Hayden, Michael:
  on Iran, 195
  Syrian nuclear facility and, 171,
    173–78, 181–91
Heidegger, Martin, 146
Hellman, Martin:
  on nuclear optimism, 128–30

in quantifying nuclear war risk,
    125–31
Herf, Jeffrey, 135–36
Hering, Harold I.:
  Blair on, 104, 110, 226
  nuclear taboo and, 248
  on nuclear weapons command
    and control, 31–39, 42, 46,
    83–84, 104, 110, 226, 248
Hersey, John, 251
Hersh, Seymour, 3–4, 21, 170, 172
Hezbollah, 134, 160
Hiroshima, 8, 49, 56, 77, 125, 128,
  157, 161, 227, 240
  nuclear taboo and, 250–51, 253–
    54
Hitler, Adolf, 80, 84, 132–47, 164,
  202, 218, 240
  and extermination of Jews, 136,
    138–41, 143
  Holocaust of, 20, 22, 77, 86,
    134–39, 141–42, 144–47, 150
  and invention of nuclear weap-
    ons, 143
  supreme emergencies and, 155–
    56
Hodge, Nathan, 103
Hoffman, David, 88, 113
Holocausts, 133–50, 163–64
  denial of, 148, 163
  feelings toward perpetrators of,
    133, 143–44
  geographic displacement variety
    of, 145
  of Hitler, 20, 22, 77, 86, 134–39,
    141–42, 144–47, 150
  inconsequentialism of, 145–48
  Roth on, 143–44
  second, 20–22, 133, 135–50, 152,
    163, 258
"How Confident Should a Nuclear
    Optimist Be?" (Hellman),
    128–30

"How to Talk About Israel"
    (Buruma), 146
Hughes, John, 229
Husseni, Haj-al-Amin, 135–36

India, 30
    eliminating nuclear weapons and,
        233, 235
    nuclear war casualties and, 77
    nuclear weapons of, 5, 16–17
    Pakistani relations with, 5,
        16–18, 227, 235
Inman, Robert, 128
Intermediate-Range Nuclear Forces
    Treaty, 13, 211
International Atomic Energy Agency
    (IAEA), 173, 188, 214
International Court of Justice,
    84–86, 254
International Criminal Court, 139
International Institute for Strategic
    Studies, 227, 231
Inter-Services Intelligence (ISI), 18
Iran, 166–71, 175, 206, 258
    Israel and, 3–4, 15, 17, 19–21,
        26, 79, 134, 137–39, 141–43,
        148, 153–55, 160–61, 163,
        166–70, 179, 181, 197–98,
        207, 211, 235–36, 266n
    Minot mistake and, 16
    NIEs on, 20, 167, 170, 192–95,
        197–98
    nuclear deterrence and, 167,
        208
    nuclear preemption and, 160–61,
        169
    nuclear retaliation and, 155, 179
    nuclear war casualties and, 79
    in nuclear war games, 199–200,
        207–8
    nuclear weapons program of,
        3–4, 9, 15, 17, 19–21, 26, 29,
        134, 137–38, 141–43, 160,

        166–68, 170–71, 179–81, 183,
        192–98, 207, 211, 266n
    Pakistani nuclear weapons and,
        4, 17
    sanctions against, 166, 180, 192
    Syrian nuclear facility and, 171,
        179–80, 184, 186, 194, 208
Iraq, 135, 173
    alleged weapons of mass destruc-
        tion of, 176, 179, 187, 194
    Israel and, 179
    U.S. invasions of, 176, 194, 203,
        247
irrational-behavior theory, 73
Isaiah scroll, 150–51
Islam:
    and extermination of Jews,
        280n
    Israel and, 134–36, 138–39, 155
Israel, 132–55, 160–64, 227
    Iran and, 3–4, 15, 17, 19–21, 26,
        79, 134, 137–39, 141–43, 148,
        153–55, 160–61, 163, 166–70,
        179, 181, 197–98, 207, 211,
        235–36, 266n
    nuclear ambiguity of, 158–59,
        161–62
    nuclear deterrence and, 167, 198
    nuclear preemption and, 133–34,
        140, 142, 152, 160–62, 164,
        169
    nuclear retaliation and, 133, 141–
        42, 149–52, 154–55, 158, 160,
        162, 179
    in nuclear war games, 199–200,
        207
    nuclear weapons of, 17, 21–22,
        123, 133–34, 137–38, 140–42,
        149–52, 154, 158, 161–64,
        167, 179, 182, 208, 211
    Pakistan and, 17–18, 134, 179
    Samson Option and, 21–22,
        141–42

second Holocaust and, 20–22, 133, 135–50, 152, 163
in start of nuclear war, 132–33, 140, 142–43, 151–52
Syrian nuclear facilities and, 2–5, 8, 11, 15–16, 113, 134, 140, 145–46, 168–73, 177–83, 186–89, 197, 199, 208, 258
wars between Arabs and, 3, 127, 136, 163–64, 220–21
*see also* Jews
Israel Defense Forces (IDF), 152–53, 158, 160, 162

Japan, 8, 11, 234, 242, 251–52
Jews, 164
extermination of, 135–41, 143, 146–48, 150, 280*n*
and morality of retaliation, 149–52
Roth on, 143–45
in U.S., 143, 147
*see also* Israel

Kahn, Herman, 48, 55, 249
Kennedy, John F., 6, 118, 247
Ellsberg and, 71, 76
nuclear war casualties and, 76–77
Khamenei, Ayatollah Ali, 138
Khan, A. Q., 16, 20, 193
Kim Jong-il, 19, 66
Kissinger, Henry, 61, 220
on eliminating nuclear weapons, 212, 214–15, 218
Ellsberg and, 71–72, 74
Madman theory of, 100
Knoll, Erwin, 49–50
Komer, Robert, 77
Korea, North, 66, 235, 258
Iran and, 168, 183, 194–95
nuclear taboo and, 255
nuclear weapons of, 16, 19–20, 123, 177–80, 182–83, 195–96

South Korean relations with, 19, 25
Syrian nuclear facilities and, 3, 169–70, 172, 174–78, 181–90, 194–96
U.S. nuclear targeting plan on, 24–25
Korea, South, 19, 25, 170, 234–35
Korean Air Lines (KAL) shootdown, 100
Korean War, 246–47
Kristensen, Hans M., 24–25, 44, 199, 203, 257
Kubrick, Stanley, 39, 73, 90

Lang, Berel, 146, 150
Lasker, Larry, 47
launch on alert, 52, 122, 239
launch on attack, 54, 67–68
launch on warning, 52, 54, 68, 83, 96, 118–20, 122, 220, 233, 239
launch voting, 101–2, 105
Letters of Last Resort, 40–41, 91, 108, 149, 152
Lewis, Jeffrey, 197, 257
Lieber, Keir, 249–50
Life Extension Program (LEP), 56–57
Looking Glass plane, 95, 100, 106–7
Lugar, Richard, 215, 219

MacArthur, Douglas, 247
McCarthy, Cormac, 81–82, 252
McConnell, Mike, 197
Syrian nuclear facility and, 171–74, 181–82, 184–92
McNamara, Robert, 221, 243, 245
Ellsberg and, 74, 76, 83
Madman theory, 100
Manhattan Project, 89, 143
Martin, Bryan, 10–11

Medvedev, Dmitri:
   eliminating nuclear weapons and,
      29, 229, 235
   Georgia crisis and, 205
   missile defense systems and,
      206
   nuclear weapons treaties and, 12,
      209, 229
Minot mistake, 14–16, 63
Mizin, Victor, 13–14
Monte Carlo runs:
   invention of, 115
   "100 Nuclear Wars" plan and,
      123
   on probability of success of
      nuclear attack, 113–16, 125–
      26, 131
   value of, 123–24
   Yarynich and, 111, 113, 115–16,
      123, 125, 131
Morris, Benny, 21, 136–37, 164
Morris, Errol, 245
*Most Dangerous Man in America, The,*
      71–72
Murtagh, David, 41
Mutually Assured Destruction
      (MAD), 24, 26–27, 30, 108,
      116, 169, 213, 222, 232–33,
      239–41

Nagasaki, 125, 157, 161
   nuclear taboo and, 245, 251, 254
National Conference of Catholic
      Bishops, 80, 84–85, 255
National Emergency Airborne
      Command Post (NEACP),
      107
National Intelligence Estimates
      (NIEs), 20, 167, 170, 192–95,
      197–98
National Security Agency (NSA), 5,
      99, 128, 171, 185

National Security Archives, 237
near earth object (NEO) extinction
      events, 126
Netanyahu, Benjamin, 141
*New York Times,* 31, 71, 97, 145–46,
      197, 228, 277n
   Pakistan and, 16, 19
   PERIMETR and, 88, 91
Nitze, Paul, 246–47
Nixon, Richard:
   Cold War close calls and, 100,
      127
   Ellsberg and, 71–72, 75
   nuclear taboo and, 247
   nuclear war casualties and, 86
   and nuclear weapons command
      and control, 35–36
   Yom Kippur War and, 220
North American Aerospace Defense
      Command (NORAD), 6–7
   Russian strategic flights and,
      10–11, 100
North Atlantic Treaty Organization
      (NATO), 200–202
   in Cold War close calls, 7, 113,
      232
   and fear of decapitation and
      surprise attack, 7, 112–13
   first use option of, 25–27, 201
   Georgia crisis and, 205
   nuclear taboo and, 252
   in nuclear war games, 200–201,
      206, 232
   and nuclear weapons command
      and control, 201, 216
   Russian strategic flights and,
      10–11, 100
nuclear ambiguity, 22, 25, 217
   in Georgia crisis, 203
   of Israel, 158–59, 161–62
*Nuclear Family Vacation, A* (Hodge
      and Weinberger), 103

nuclear optimism, 128–30
Nuclear Posture Reviews (NPRs), 23–24, 216–17
  of Bush, 23, 55, 209
  of Obama, 175, 183, 209–11, 216
nuclear submarines, 61, 114, 199
  Blair on, 108–9
  Burke documents and, 241–44, 256–57
  Cold War close calls and, 118
  collision of, 248–49
  of Israel, 21–22, 142, 149–52, 154–55, 160–62, 166–67, 211
  in nuclear weapons command and control, 108–9
  in "100 Nuclear Wars" plan, 122
  and preventing accidental use of nuclear weapons, 120
  of U.K., 40–41, 158, 248–49
*Nuclear Taboo, The* (Tannenwald), 245–50, 255
*Nuclear Tipping Point,* 215–16
nuclear vault, 236–41
nuclear war:
  aftermath of, 28, 49, 78, 82, 148
  casualties in, 8, 21, 28, 33, 35, 41–42, 46, 50, 56, 58–60, 65, 68, 71–73, 75–81, 84–87, 89–90, 95, 122, 128–31, 133–35, 137, 157, 159, 161, 165, 201–2, 217, 219–20, 222–23, 228, 232, 243–44, 250, 257
  close calls and, 5–8, 12, 74, 76, 100, 113, 117–18, 127–28, 130, 164, 168–69, 171–72, 199, 208, 220–21, 225–26, 232, 244–45, 247–48, 258
  firestorms in, 77–78, 134
  gaming of, 66, 73, 81, 199–202, 206–8, 232
  morality of, 8, 63–71, 76, 79–80, 82, 84–86, 124–25, 133, 149–

50, 152, 155–60, 165, 210, 217–18, 222–23, 240, 247–48, 250, 255
  quantifying risk of, 113–16, 123–31, 200
  regional, 21–22, 131–32, 179, 194, 199, 236
  simulations of, 224–25
  start of, 47, 132–33, 140, 142–43, 151–52, 179, 199, 203, 216, 236
  surrender in, 60–61
  taboo associated with, 85, 245–55
  winning in, 114–15
nuclear weapons:
  accidental use of, 12, 93–94, 116, 118–21, 123, 201, 210, 213, 225, 234, 256, 258
  command and control of, 18–19, 31–42, 46–54, 56–68, 71, 74, 82–84, 90–98, 100–112, 117–21, 132, 142, 149–52, 158–59, 162, 201–2, 207, 210–11, 215–26, 230, 232, 234–36, 238, 240, 245, 248, 251–52, 256, 260, 276n–77n
  conventional vs., 8, 14–15, 21, 51, 85, 112, 125, 129, 221–22, 227, 230, 235, 249–50, 253, 255
  defenses against, 8–9, 12–13, 24, 27, 55, 112, 116, 127, 137, 198, 205–6, 211, 230
  destruction of, 122–23, 215, 219, 226, 228, 235, 259
  in deterrence, 3, 5–8, 16, 22–27, 30, 36, 40–42, 44–45, 48–52, 54–58, 63, 65–66, 68–70, 73, 80, 82, 84–87, 96–97, 106, 108, 112, 116, 121–22, 124–25, 127, 148–49, 151–

nuclear weapons (*continued*)
54, 158, 162, 167, 169, 198,
200–205, 208–9, 213, 217–
19, 222–23, 230–35, 239–43,
246, 248–50, 255–59
elimination of, 28–30, 44–45, 48,
51–52, 54, 56, 81, 85, 90, 95,
98, 127, 211–22, 226–35, 237,
240, 245, 257, 259–60
exceptionalism of, 80, 85, 252
false positive alerts on, 6, 67–68,
83
first strike preemptive use of, 7,
9, 17, 21, 24–27, 41, 55, 60,
63–68, 76, 80–81, 90–91, 95,
106, 108, 112–18, 120–22,
132–34, 140–42, 149, 152,
154–56, 159–64, 169, 199,
201, 216, 220, 232, 239,
241–44, 246–48, 250,
255–57
forensics of, 64
high-altitude explosions of, 106,
276n–77n
invention of, 89, 143
legality of, 84–85, 222
mini-nukes, 24, 249
missile delivery of, 14–15, 19,
21, 23, 46–48, 52–55, 58–63,
67–68, 74, 82–83, 90–91,
93–96, 101–5, 108–10, 112–
14, 116–22, 133, 137, 158–59,
166, 172, 179, 192–95, 198,
201–5, 207, 210–11, 222–
25, 240–45, 248–49, 251–52,
255–56, 258–59
modernization of, 13–14, 56–57
of nonstate actors, 51, 233
normalizing use of, 23–25
opposition to, 25, 47–50, 80, 89,
254–55, 260
production of, 49–50, 56–57,
226, 249

proliferation of, 5, 16, 20, 24, 26,
56, 180, 183, 192–93, 196,
233
public relations on, 64, 67, 103
race for, 30, 233, 242
reducing number of, 12–13, 27,
44, 116, 118, 121, 123, 204,
209–13, 215, 218, 227–29, 231,
233–35, 240, 244, 256, 258
retaliatory use of, 21–22, 40–42,
44, 48–50, 54, 58–61, 63–70,
73, 76–80, 87–93, 96–98,
106–8, 110–12, 114, 116–19,
122, 133, 141–42, 149–52,
154–56, 158–60, 162–65, 179,
199, 207, 210, 217–18, 241–
44, 246, 248, 255–56
of rogue states, 26, 110, 123,
206, 233, 259
tactical, 24, 85–86, 249
total number of, 131, 199
treaties on, 12–13, 27, 55, 57,
116, 121–23, 204, 209–12,
214, 228–29, 233, 244
*Nuclear Weapons and Foreign Policy*
(Kissinger), 212
nuclear winter, 78, 82, 148
Nunn, Sam, 5
on eliminating nuclear weapons,
212, 214–18, 221
on nuclear demolition, 215, 219
on nuclear weapons command
and control, 215–17

Obama, Barack, 174–75, 198–99,
204–6
Chilton's clashes with, 52, 54
on conventional weapons, 14–15
on eliminating nuclear weapons,
28–30, 44, 51–52, 54, 81, 212,
214, 229, 235, 257
missile defense systems and, 9,
12–13, 206

Nobel Prize of, 28–29
NPR of, 175, 183, 209–11, 216
nuclear optimism and, 128
on nuclear retaliation, 70
nuclear war casualties and, 81
on nuclear weapons command
 and control, 52–54
nuclear weapons treaties and, 12,
 209, 211, 229
Qwest Center deterrence symposium and, 30, 44, 50–52,
 54, 57
Office of the Director of National
 Intelligence (ODNI), 27, 197
on Syrian nuclear facility, 172–
 92, 194–96
Offutt Air Force Base, 30, 45–46, 95
"100 Nuclear Wars" plan, 116, 120–
 24
*One Minute to Midnight* (Dobbs), 6,
 247
*On Escalation* (Kahn), 48, 55
*On Nuclear War* (Kissinger), 61
*On the Beach*, 30, 48, 251–52
*Operation Shylock* (Roth), 143–45
Ottinger Committee, 37–38
Ozick, Cynthia, 145–46

Pakistan, 24, 30
 Indian relations with, 5, 16–18,
  227, 235
 Israel and, 17–18, 134, 179
 nuclear war casualties and, 77
 nuclear weapons of, 4–5, 16–19,
  29, 123, 134, 179, 207, 236,
  258
Panetta, Leon, 166
Payne, Keith, 54–57
Pentagon Papers, 71–72, 74–76
Peres, Shimon, 132, 141
PERIMETR, 87–93, 107, 119, 256
 how it works, 89, 91–92, 112
 Yarynich and, 111–12, 116

Perkovich, George, 227–28
Perlmutter, David, 148
Permissive Action Links (PALs), 221
Petrov, Colonel, 7, 225–26, 248
Pipes, Richard, 113–14
Poland, 9, 12–13, 27, 140, 205–6
Politkovskaya, Anna, 94–95
Pollack, Jonathan, 19
Powell, Colin, 175–76, 215
Powell, Robert, 200
Powers, Thomas, 143
pre-delegation, 39–40, 104
 Ellsberg on, 71, 83–84
Presidential Succession Act, 37
Press, Daryl, 249–50
Prompt Global Strike plan, 14–15
Putin, Vladimir, 13, 27, 205–6
 Georgia crisis and, 205
 Minot mistake and, 14–15
 missile defense systems and, 206
 purges of, 94–95
 strategic flights and, 9–11,
  14–15, 100
*Putin's Russia* (Politkovskaya), 94–95

Qaradawi, Yusuf al-, 138
Quester, George, 37, 46, 248
Qwest Center deterrence symposium, 30, 44–45, 49–52,
 54–57, 63–70

Rafsanjani, Ayatollah Ali Akbar
 Hashemi, 134, 138
RAND Corporation, 60, 73–74, 83
Reagan, Ronald, 212, 228–30
 Burt and, 228–29
 in Cold War close calls, 7, 127
 on eliminating nuclear weapons,
  229–30
 and fear of decapitation and surprise attack, 7, 112–13
 on nuclear retaliation, 218
 PERIMETR and, 92

*Red Cloud at Dawn* (Gordin), 168
Reliable Replacement Warhead
    (RRW), 56–57
Rice, Condoleezza, 11
ride-out doctrine, 67–68
Rivet Joint, 98–100
*Road, The* (McCarthy), 81–82, 252
Romania, 13, 206
Rome Treaty on Preventing Geno-
    cide, 139
Roosevelt, Franklin D., 89, 143
Rosenbergs, 74–76
Roth, Philip, 143–45
Russia, 17–18, 22, 24–25, 130, 243,
    255–59
  atmosphere of fear in, 94–95
  Blair's work in, 90, 93–94
  Burke documents and, 241
  in Cold War close calls, 6–7, 12,
    113, 117–18, 225, 232
  and collapse of Soviet Union, 215
  doomsday machine of, 87–93,
    107, 112
  eliminating nuclear weapons and,
    29, 211, 213, 229–35
  Ellsberg and, 75
  on EMPs, 107
  in encounters with U.S. bombers,
    99–100
  and fear of decapitation and sur-
    prise attack, 7, 112–16
  Georgia invaded by, 11, 27, 202–
    5, 235
  Iran and, 3, 167, 170
  Israel and, 3–4, 220
  lowered nuclear threshold of,
    204
  Minot mistake and, 14–15
  missile defense systems and, 9,
    12–13, 27, 205–6, 211
  Monte Carlo runs and, 113–15,
    124
  nuclear optimism and, 128

  nuclear submarines of, 257
  nuclear taboo and, 246, 252, 255
  nuclear war casualties and,
    76–77, 79, 81
  in nuclear war games, 199–201,
    207
  nuclear weapons acquired by,
    168, 248
  and nuclear weapons command
    and control, 52–53, 59–60,
    82, 90–94, 98, 100, 104, 107,
    110–11, 120, 216
  nuclear weapons modernization
    and buildup of, 13–14
  nuclear weapons treaties and,
    209, 211
  in "100 Nuclear Wars" plan,
    121–23
  in preventing accidental use of
    nuclear weapons, 118–20, 123
  and reducing number of nuclear
    weapons, 12–13, 44
  strategic flights of, 9–12, 14–15,
    27, 100
  Syrian nuclear facilities and, 3–4
  U.S. cooperation with, 93–94,
    111–12, 116–18
  U.S. secret reconnaissance on,
    98–100
"Russia's Nuclear Renaissance"
    (Mizin), 13–14
Rwandan genocide, 139, 148

Samson Option, 21–22, 141–42, 148
Schell, Jonathan, 49
Schelling, Thomas, 73, 158
Schlesinger, James, 35–36, 220
*Scientific American*, 77–78, 128
"Second Holocaust Will Not Be
    Like the First, The" (Morris),
    136–37
Sheidlower, Jesse, 240
Shultz, George, 212, 215, 229–30

Single Integrated Operational Plan
(SIOP), 22, 92–93, 222, 238
Blair and, 93, 97, 99
Ellsberg and, 74–76, 82
Six Day War, 127, 136
Smith, P. D., 88–90, 92
*Spectator, The,* 1–2, 4, 113, 179
Spiegel, Peter, 209–10
spoon-and-string maneuver, 62–63,
71, 83, 101, 158–59, 245, 248
Star Wars system, 55, 230
State Department, U.S., 135, 171,
194, 204, 228–29
Steiner, George, 86
Strategic Air Command, *see* Strategic
Command
Strategic Arms Reduction Treaties
(START), 12–13, 27, 116, 121,
123, 209–12, 228–29, 233, 244
Strategic Command (STRATCOM),
10, 44, 54, 69, 210, 220
and nuclear weapons command
and control, 36, 38, 46, 50,
57–63, 103–4
Qwest Center deterrence symposium and, 30, 45, 50
Rosenbaum's visits to, 45–50,
57–63, 75
secret Russian reconnaissance of,
99–100
war room of, 46–47
*Strategic Command and Control* (Blair),
96, 220
"Subterranean World of the Bomb,
The" (Rosenbaum), 48–50
Supreme Court, U.S., 34–35, 37,
147
supreme emergencies, 152, 155–57,
159–60, 163
Suri, Jeremi, 100
Syria, 21
nuclear facilities of, 2–5, 8, 11,
15–16, 113, 134, 140, 145–46,

168–92, 194–97, 199, 202,
208, 258
Pakistani nuclear weapons and,
4, 17
in wars with Israel, 136, 163
Szilard, Leo, 89–90, 143

Taiwan, 14, 22, 227, 234–35
Taiwan Straits crises, 247
Tannenwald, Nina, 245–50, 255
Tepperman, Jonathan, 128–29
terrorism, 34, 110, 116, 212, 221
and collapse of Soviet Union, 215
cyber-, 23, 32–33
India-Pakistan relations and, 16–18
NATO's preemptive strike option
and, 26–27
on 9/11, 24, 47, 233, 253
nuclear, 51, 78, 81, 131, 233
nuclear forensics and, 64
of nuclear weapons, 1, 5, 8, 16,
18, 26, 51
and nuclear weapons command
and control, 63–64, 103, 105
Traynor, Ian, 26
Truman, Harry, 241, 247
Turner, Stansfield, 6–7

Ulam, Stanislaw, 115
United Kingdom, 1–2, 10, 25–26,
88, 123, 171
in Cold War close calls, 7, 113
collision of nuclear submarine of,
248–49
and nuclear weapons command
and control, 40–42, 158
supreme emergencies and, 156
Syrian nuclear facilities and, 2,
4–5, 179
United Nations, 29
Iran and, 20, 166, 180
and morality of retaliation, 67
and U.S. invasion of Iraq, 176

Vietnam War, 36, 71, 74–77, 98,
        100, 247

Walker, Lucy, 49
*Wall Street Journal,* 19, 198, 209–10,
        212
Waltz, Kenneth, 128
Walzer, Michael, 152–53, 155–57,
        159
*WarGames,* 47
*War in Human Civilization* (Gat), 43
Warnke, Paul, 246
Warsaw Pact, 25, 112, 201, 252
        in nuclear war games, 206–7
*Washington Post, The,* 23, 53, 219, 252
Weinberger, Sharon, 103
Weisman, Jonathan, 209–10
*Whole World on Fire* (Eden), 77
"Why No Retaliation?" (Lang), 150
"Why the Soviet Union Thinks It
        Could Fight & Win a Nuclear
        War" (Pipes), 113–14
Winfrey, Oprah, 252
"World Free of Nuclear Weapons,
        A," 212
world holocaust, 258–60
        Burke on, 239–40, 242–44
World War II, 117, 135, 140, 148

Burke in, 241–42
casualties in, 78
nuclear taboo and, 251, 254
nuclear weapons in, *see* Hiro-
        shima; Nagasaki
supreme emergencies in, 155–56
Worsthorne, Sir Peregrine, 218

Yao Yunzhu, 69
Yarynich, Valery E., 110–23
        Blair's relationship with, 93–94,
                110, 119
        and fear of decapitation and sur-
                prise attack, 112–16
        Monte Carlo runs and, 111, 113,
                115–16, 123, 125, 131
        and nuclear weapons command
                and control, 94, 111–12, 117–
                21
        "100 Nuclear Wars" plan of,
                116, 120–23
        PERIMETR and, 111–12, 116
        on preventing accidental use of
                nuclear weapons, 118–21, 123
Yom Kippur War, 127, 163–64,
        220–21

Zamoshkin, Yuri, 130–31

# ACKNOWLEDGMENTS

I've dedicated the book to ex-Major Harold I. Hering (Ret.), whose courage in asking a Forbidden Question about the efficacy and sanity of our nuclear command and control system first led me to begin reporting on these questions at the height of the Cold War.

I'd like to thank Lewis Lapham, legendary *Harper's* editor, for supporting my two-year foray into "the subterranean world of the bomb" initiated by Major Hering's question.

I would like to thank all those, such as Bruce Blair, who sought to reawaken the world to the danger of the second age of nuclear war we were entering and shook me out of my complacency sufficiently to make it my mission to try to map out the terra incognita (terror incognita?) of the new nuclear landscape.

Among them I'd include Cormac McCarthy, someone I've never met, but whose novel *The Road*, which came to my attention when reviewed in the same issue of the *New York Times Book Review* as my Shakespeare book, sensitized me to the continued potential for annihilation we faced. And recalled to me the exchange at the close of *King Lear*:

"Is this the promised end?"

"Or image of that horror."

I'm grateful as well to those four signers of the *Wall Street Journal* nuclear abolition manifesto who demonstrated that the case for Zero was not some peeling peacenik bumper sticker, but a strategic goal worthy of debate. And to the president, who put nuclear abolition at the forefront of our foreign policy at a time when it had largely been forsaken or forgotten.

I'm indebted to researchers, writers, thinkers, and activists such as Hans Kristensen of the Federation of American Scientists and William Burr of George Washington University's National Security Archive for uncovering shocking deficiencies of nuclear command and control in the first nuclear age that, they've demonstrated, persist into the second. To Dr. Jeffrey Lewis and his extremely well-informed cohorts at the armscontrolwonk.com blog, for penetrating the scrim of PR and euphemism that often masks the truth about our nuclear posture. And to intelligent skeptics of abolitionism such as Elbridge Colby, Anne Applebaum, Peter Berkowitz, and Bret Stephens, whose arguments challenged the Zeroistas and forced me to sharpen my thinking on the question. To authors such as Michael Dobbs and David Hoffman, who revealed just how precarious the supposed stability of the first nuclear age was.

And to independent—and seemingly omniscient—researchers such as my longtime friend Craig S. Karpel whose acuity and sources were invaluable.

My long-running conversations with my friend Errol Morris, who dealt with many of these issues in *The Fog of War*, have always been thought-provoking as has his infallible sense of the absurd.

And having an attorney like Dan Kornstein who is also an excellent Shakespearean is a lucky break for me.

And I would alike to thank all those others I talked to, quoted here or not, who acknowledged the seriousness of my questions even if they differed in their answers.

At Simon & Schuster I would like to thank then-publisher David Rosenthal and editor-in-chief Priscilla Painton for seeing the merits of the book from the beginning and for unflagging enthusiasm and thoughtful support throughout the writing process. The early enthusiasm of Mike Jones, editor at Simon & Schuster U.K., meant a lot to me. And new publisher Jon Karp, who'd been a terrific editor for *Explaining Hitler*, made valuable suggestions.

I would like to take special note of the contribution of Priscilla's omnicompetent assistant, Michael Szczerban, who helped me on many levels with his cheerful intelligence.

Special thanks also to the sharp-eyed copy editor, Fred Chase.

I will always be profoundly grateful to Kathy Robbins, literary agent extraordinaire, who helped me think through how to refine the vast landscape I had taken on and gave me her unvarnished assessments of early versions. Her always astonishingly acute judgment and empathic toleration of my frequent nuclear stress has meant the world to me.

She always attracts a crew of the best and brightest to her employ, led by the calm and reassuring presence of David Halpern. I'm especially grateful for the almost daily support of Kathy's assistant, Mike Gillespie, and couldn't have done without Katie Hut, Ian King, Rachelle Bergstein, Rebecca Anders, Robert Simpson, and Kate Rizzo Munson.

Jacob Weisberg, David Plotz, head honchos at *Slate*, and my super-smart editor, Julia Turner, deserve my thanks for encouraging the reporting I did on various aspects of nuclear contentions as I was writing the book. Fred Kaplan, my colleague there and author of the superb study of the first age of nuclear strategy, *The Wizards of Armageddon*, was especially generous with his encouragement and suggestions. As was his wife, Brooke Gladstone, host of NPR's *On the Media*, who made me feel I had something to say. Speaking of NPR, I was impressed by the way Ira Glass saw the larger dimensions of my "Letter of Last Resort" *Slate* column for his *This American Life* interview, which you can hear on a podcast.

My research assistant, Liz Groden, has made an extremely valuable contribution to the book, tracking down the arcane and inaccessible with remarkable skill. I couldn't have put this book together without her help.

I'll never be able to thank my sister, Ruth Rosenbaum, enough. A talented psychotherapist, her calm and belief in me has made all the difference, not just in this book but in my life.

I have so many friends and colleagues to thank that I know I will be waking up in the middle of the night slapping my forehead and saying, How could I have left him or her out. Please forgive me if you're one of those.

But to begin there is Betsy Carter and her husband, Gary Hoenig, Stanley Mieses, Steve Weisman, Jonathan Rosen, Susan Kamil, David Samuels, Virginia Heffernan, Peter Kaplan, Jesse Sheidlower, Helen Rogan, Alfred Gingold, Nina Roberts, David Greenberg, Nancy Butkus, Gene Stone, Nat Hentoff, Emily Yoffe, Karen Greenberg, David Livingston, Gil Roth, Lauren Thierry, Gary Rosen, Julia Vitullo-Martin, Kitty Barnes, Qanta Ahmed, and all the Templeton people, Dora Steinberg, Mark Steinberg, Mike Yogg, the Greenberg family, Tina Brown, Harry Evans, Larry Rosenblatt, Amy Gutman, Robert Vare, Sarah Alcorn, Jeffrey Goldberg, Garland Jeffreys, Lucian Truscott, Lisa Singh, Caroline Marshall, Alana Newhouse, John Roche, Deb Friedman, Rebecca Wright, Liz Hecht, Sarah Kernochan, Rich Molyneux, Lidia Jean Kott, Julia Kott, Xander Kott, Laura Frost, Megan Bowers, Christine Sarkissian, Julia Sheehan, Helen Whitney, Ross Wisdom, Charlie Finch, Rebecca Wright— and all my Facebook friends.

To name a few.

And finally, in the last edition of my Shakespeare book I thanked Tara McKelvey "for helping me to understand the meaning of love in the Sonnets." This remains true, but I neglected to add she's helped me understand so much more.

# ABOUT THE AUTHOR

Ron Rosenbaum was born in Manhattan, grew up in Bay Shore, Long Island. After graduating from Yale with a degree in English literature, he dropped out of Yale Graduate School to become a writer full time. His most recent books include *The Shakespeare Wars: Clashing Scholars, Public Fiascoes, Palace Coups; Explaining Hitler: The Search for the Origins of His Evil*; and *The Secret Parts of Fortune*, a collection of his essays and journalism from *The New York Times Magazine, Harper's, Esquire, The New York Observer, New York* magazine, and *The New Yorker*, among other periodicals. He edited an anthology on the subject of anti-Semitism, *Those Who Forget the Past*. He co-wrote an award-winning PBS *Frontline* documentary, *Faith and Doubt at Ground Zero*. He has taught writing seminars at Columbia, NYU, and the University of Chicago. He is currently a cultural columnist for *Slate*, and lives in New York City.